The
Most
Important
Year

The
Most
Important
Year

Pre-Kindergarten
and the Future of Our Children

Suzanne Bouffard

AVERY
an imprint of Penguin Random House
New York

AVERY

an imprint of Penguin Random House LLC
375 Hudson Street
New York, New York 10014

Most Avery books are available at special quantity discounts for bulk purchase
for sales promotions, premiums, fund-raising, and educational needs.
Special books or book excerpts also can be created to fit specific needs.
For details, write SpecialMarkets@penguinrandomhouse.com.

Library of Congress Cataloging-in-Publication Data

Names: Bouffard, Suzanne M., author.
Title: The most important year : pre-kindergarten and the future
of our children / Suzanne Bouffard.
Description: New York, New York : Avery, 2017. | Includes bibliographical
references and index.
Identifiers: LCCN 2017031130| ISBN 9780399184949 (hardback) |
ISBN 9780399184963 (epub)
Subjects: LCSH: Early childhood education—United States. | Early childhood
education—Social aspects—United States. | Education, Preschool—United
States. | Education, Preschool—Social aspects—United States. | Children
with social disabilities—Education (Preschool)—United States. | BISAC:
SOCIAL SCIENCE / Children's Studies. | EDUCATION / Preschool &
Kindergarten. | FAMILY & RELATIONSHIPS / Education.
Classification: LCC LB1139.25.B69 2017 | DDC 372.21—dc23
LC record available at https://lccn.loc.gov/2017031130

Printed in the United States of America
1   3   5   7   9   10   8   6   4   2

BOOK DESIGN BY NICOLE LAROCHE

While the author has made every effort to provide accurate telephone numbers,
Internet addresses, and other contact information at the time of publication,
neither the publisher nor the author assumes any responsibility for errors, or for
changes that occur after publication. Further, the publisher does not have any
control over and does not assume any responsibility for author or third-party
websites or their content.

For Theo and Ellis

Contents

The
Most
Important
Year

Prologue

Sixty parents clustered in the cafeteria of the Eliot K–8 Innovation School, some balancing toddlers on their hips, others finishing their morning coffee. "Welcome to the best public school in Boston!" Principal Traci Griffith greeted them, warmly and without the ego that one might imagine to accompany such a statement. It wasn't long into her overview, which she had been giving for months during similar school tours, before an anxious parent asked, "How many pre-K spots do you have for next year?" "We have thirty-two seats," Griffith replied smoothly, quickly adding, "But we have four kindergarten classrooms, so that means there are forty-four new seats in kindergarten every year." That provided little reassurance for the parents who would soon be entering their four-year-olds in the Boston Public Schools (BPS) lottery. Griffith didn't have to say what many already knew: all but three of the Eliot's current pre-K students had been virtually guaranteed a spot because they had a sibling already attending the school.

The odds were long for Luca Murthy, but he was blissfully unaware of the stress his parents and so many others were carrying. Luca was only three and was more concerned with Legos than lotteries. But he would turn four before the next school year, making him eligible for one of the nation's most successful public pre-kindergarten programs, or what the Boston Public Schools call K1. (The grade traditionally called kindergarten is known as K2.) Luca, his family's firstborn, wouldn't have the advantage of a sibling spot at the Eliot, and he wasn't guaranteed a K1 spot at all. The Boston program serves only about twenty-five hundred children, around half the city's four-year-olds.

Above the cafeteria, in Jodi Krous's classroom, it was easy to see why parents wanted to send their children to the Eliot for pre-K. Sixteen children were engrossed in activities set up at tiny natural-wood furniture and in woven baskets full of books, puzzles, and art supplies. They were energetic and talkative, but calm and focused. On the rug, some used large wooden blocks to experiment with ramps and how fast toy cars would go depending on the angle of the blocks. At the easel, Krous asked two girls what they were painting and wrote their responses on the bottom of the paper so that when she hung it up later, everyone could see their thought processes. A quiet, reluctant boy got a hug from Krous and a reminder that his mother would be coming home from a business trip that night. "Yesterday you made a great double-decker bus out of Play-Doh. Do you want to make another one?" Krous suggested. "Oh, look, your friend wants to know what a double-decker bus is!" She bent down, gently touching the boy's shoulders, encouraging him to look directly at the other child and share his expertise with her. Krous had told me that she chose to teach at the Eliot because "you feel a lot of joyfulness here," and the parents on the tour seemed to sense it, too.

Krous seemed to accomplish the impossible task of noticing everything happening in the room at once, providing just the right question or comment to nudge the children to think a little more deeply. When a child proudly approached her with a book he had made using familiar story characters, she shared his enthusiasm and then prodded him to write down the words the characters might say. Watching children mixing and painting with watercolors, she asked them, "What happens when you use different-sized paintbrushes?" When she used the word "water" while talking about painting, she noticed that a nonverbal child used sign language to say "drink," showing she heard Krous's words. Another boy came over to show her how he had pasted the letters of his name on cardstock. "Wow, you have eight letters in your name!" Krous exclaimed. "Do you have the longest name? Go find Olivia's name. Find the one that starts with an *O*. Now count how many. What about Matthew?" When she asked him how he got his correct answer of seven, he cheerfully replied, "I counted already!"

It was obvious that every moment of the school day was thoughtfully planned to facilitate children's learning, and that appealed to Luca's mother, Maria Fenwick. An educational consultant and former Boston Public Schools teacher, Fenwick had done her homework. She had long known about the Eliot and been drawn to the hands-on experiential learning that is a hallmark of the school. She had heard that Griffith and her staff were knowledgeable and dedicated, and that was clear in Room 105, from the rhyming songs Krous led during morning meeting to build vocabulary and language skills ("How are you, caribou? I'm fine, porcupine!") to the way she asked children to tell her stories that would be transcribed and later acted out by the class. Fenwick was particularly impressed with the way that evidence of the students' learning covered the walls. At children's eye level were detailed self-portraits they had drawn during a unit on color, birth certificates created for pretend infants during a unit on families, photographs of block architecture annotated with descriptions of how the children made them. Each child's contribution was unique and creative, no evidence of photocopied worksheets anywhere.

Almost any parent would walk into Krous's classroom and want to send her child there. But few get that opportunity. The thirty-two spots at the Eliot, a nearly hundred-year-old school located in the city's historic North End, are among the most coveted in the district. "When I call parents to tell them they have a spot at our school, I get to tell them, 'You have won the lottery—literally,'" says Traci Griffith. Less than ten years ago, however, the Eliot was undersubscribed, ranked near the very bottom of the city's schools, a site of hopelessness and apathy that had been abandoned by neighborhood families. Less than a block away from the Eliot are a statue of school alumnus Paul Revere in the spot where he began his famous midnight ride, and the Old North Church, where patriots hung lanterns to give the "one if by land, two if by sea" signal. The change that has taken place at the Eliot has been less fiery than the war fought by the American patriots, but no less transformational. The introduction of the K1 program was not solely responsible for the transformation, but it played an important role, drumming up parent interest in the school, building early and long-lasting relationships between children and staff, and laying the crucial foundation for school success that high-quality preschool can provide.

The Boston Public Schools' K1 program is part of a growing national movement for public pre-kindergarten, or pre-K. Every year, over one and a half million American children are enrolled in pre-K programs funded by public dollars, and thousands more attend private preschools, for a total of about 66 percent of the nation's four-year-olds. But for most of the remaining third of children, preschool is out of reach for financial or logistical reasons. Unlike most other industrialized countries, the United States has not made a serious commitment to early childhood education. We rank twenty-eighth out of thirty-eight countries in the percentage of four-year-olds enrolled in programs, in large part because we do not fund pre-K for everyone. In countries like the United Kingdom, research has convinced policymakers and the public that pre-K should be a universal right, with guaranteed funding just like kindergarten through twelfth grade.

But there is growing demand for pre-K in the United States. (Parents and educators use a variety of terms, including "pre-K," "preschool," and "nursery school," and there is no standard definition. For example, in the

Boston Public Schools, three-, four-, and five-year-olds can enroll in K0, K1, and K2, respectively, while in charter schools I visited in Washington, DC, three-year-olds were in classrooms called preschool, while four-year-old classrooms were called pre-K.) In recent surveys, around 90 percent of parents believe that the preschool years are a critical period of development, and policymakers are beginning to agree. Cities from Seattle to New York have allocated public funding for municipal and district pre-K programs, housed in elementary schools, early childhood centers, or a combination of settings. Most of these programs are limited in size or eligibility criteria, but a few offer a pre-K spot to any family who wants one, like New York City, which created slots for nearly seventy thousand four-year-olds, and Washington, DC, which is one of the only places that offers a free spot not only for every four-year-old, but every three-year-old as well. States are in the pre-K business, too: more than forty states fund some sort of pre-K program at a cost of over $6 billion. And the federal government has supported tens of thousands of new slots via grant programs.

Public investment in pre-K has surged because of research showing how critical the early years are for later success in school and life. The brain develops faster during early childhood than at any other time, especially when a child is engaged in enriching relationships and activities, like reading, singing, building, and pretend play. Studies show that when pre-K programs are well designed and run by knowledgeable staff, they provide those kinds of experiences and give children a solid start in school. Classrooms like Jodi Krous's are linked with a host of benefits: higher reading and math achievement, lower rates of grade retention and special education placement, and, in some cases, stronger social skills and self-control and even more positive parenting practices later in life. The first glimpses of this potential came from studies of model preschool programs created in the 1960s. Intensive programs designed by child development experts, like the Perry Preschool Project in Ypsilanti, Michigan, and the Chicago Child-Parent Centers, literally changed the course of many lives. Children who participated grew up less likely to be incarcerated and more likely to be earning incomes that could sustain a family. Today, the research base goes far beyond those studies of small, intensive programs, showing that high-quality programs run by cities and states can make a difference for children that lasts well into the school years.

In Boston, children who have been in classrooms at the Eliot and other public schools have entered kindergarten about a half year ahead of their peers in language and literacy, math, problem-solving, and self-control skills like paying attention and resisting the impulse to talk out of turn. Those kinds of behavior skills are even more important than knowing letters and numbers, according to a survey of kindergarten teachers, because when kids know how to wait their turn, deal with frustration, and get along with others, it's easier for teachers to teach and for children to learn. In New Jersey, which has another model program that has been running longer than Boston's, the positive results continue to roll in as children get older. The most recent study showed that fifth graders who had gone to pre-K were doing significantly better in school than their classmates. Similarly, children who attended state-funded pre-K in North Carolina are more competent in math and reading in fifth grade than their peers, and they are almost 50 percent less likely to be placed in special education. Graduates of Michigan's Great Start Readiness Program are more likely to pass state tests, take challenging math classes, and graduate from high school.

Maria Fenwick knew about the research on the benefits of pre-K and understood from her own experience in the classroom how important it is for children to be prepared for school. She knew Luca would learn his colors and letters whether he went to K1 or not, but she wanted him to learn how to be part of a class, be exposed to experiences he wouldn't get at home, and get excited about school and learning. Pre-K can set the tone for a child's entire educational career. Seeing schools as a fun, exciting, and caring place can lay the foundation for lifelong curiosity and learning. On the other side of the coin, students who have negative experiences with school early on can carry those feelings with them forever.

Although Fenwick was doing all she could to get Luca into K1, she recognized that pre-K is even more crucial for students like the ones she had taught, whose families have fewer resources than hers. In Boston and elsewhere, the benefits of pre-K are particularly striking for children from low-income families, who tend, on average, to be behind their peers even before they start kindergarten. Achievement gaps across income appear shockingly early—some studies have found they are present as early as nine months of age in behavior and cognitive skills—and they are well established by kindergarten, when children in the highest income groups significantly outperform children in the lowest income groups. Achievement gaps are also evident across racial and ethnic groups, with white and Asian American students outperforming African American and Hispanic students, although those gaps shrink considerably after income is taken into account. The good news is that achievement gaps are narrowing, in large part because of investments in early childhood education and care (defined broadly as daycare, preschool, and home-based services like having trained educators visit with and support parents). The bad news is that the gaps remain significant, and a child who starts off behind is likely to stay behind. School readiness gaps across income levels narrowed over the past twenty years "only about half as quickly as they opened in the 1970s and 1980s," according to *Education Week* coverage of research by Stanford professor Sean Reardon, who analyzes national data on achievement gaps. If that slow rate of progress continues, it could take another hundred years for the gap to close completely, the article pointed out.

Former president Barack Obama invoked early childhood education as a solution to that problem, calling it "one way to break the legacy of racism and poverty. If a three-year-old, four-year-old kid is in [a strong early childhood program], they can get to where a middle-class kid is pretty quickly." In 2013, Obama proposed an unprecedented investment of $75 billion over ten years to ensure that all four-year-olds have access to pre-K. That's an almost unimaginable number, and it hasn't been realized. But Obama did allocate about $250 million in the form of federal-state partnership grants to develop and expand pre-K programs for low- and moderate-income children, referring to them as "among the smartest investments that we can make."

That claim is based on studies showing that children's outcomes translate into financial benefits for society. In the long run, pre-K saves the government somewhere between $3 and $8 for every dollar invested, because people who went to pre-K are less likely to be on welfare or involved in the criminal justice system and more likely to be working and paying income taxes. Those findings are particularly striking given that they were produced by economists, who were interested in the bottom line rather than in a "moral argument" for pre-K, as one researcher put it. Several unlikely figures have become vocal pre-K advocates based on the financial argument, including Federal Reserve Chair Janet Yellen and Nobel Prize–winning economist James Heckman. Heckman points out that it is more efficient to invest when children are young than to remediate problems that arise later because of inadequate education, and that the success of later interventions depends on whether children have gotten a solid start. Fight Crime: Invest in Kids, a nonprofit of law enforcement leaders, puts it more bluntly: "I'm the Guy You Pay Later," they titled a report advocating for investments in pre-K.

The economic case hits closer to home for many parents, including Maria Fenwick. Luca was already enrolled at a private preschool just down the street from his family's apartment, which had a stellar reputation and a waiting list of its own. His mother was thrilled with the school and had become a board member in addition to the expected parent volunteer duties. But the tuition was almost $11,000 for only a few hours a week, ten months a year. Fenwick found the free tuition offered by BPS enticing, especially when she considered that Luca's little sister, Marin, would be starting preschool soon, too. Fenwick knew she was lucky to have good options in both the private school and the public system, but "we could be saving for a house instead of paying tuition," she dreamed.

At a time when wages are stagnating and income inequality is at its highest rate in nearly a hundred years, many Americans are finding it increasingly difficult, often impossible, to pay for childcare and early education. For parents like Fenwick, childcare eats up a huge portion of their income. In more than 60 percent of families with a married couple, both parents work outside the home, and most single parents do (70 percent of mothers and 80 percent of fathers). But early childhood care and education costs more than public university tuition in more than half of the United States, and even exceeds rent in many communities. For the average family making minimum wage, the costs constitute 64 percent of their salary, and in some states that percentage is considerably higher. Parents today know that public pre-K gives their children a solid start in school, but they also know it gives their families a life raft in an economic storm. In New York City, almost half of parents surveyed about their experiences with the pre-K program said they would have had to work fewer hours if free pre-K hadn't been available, and 12 percent said their children's participation enabled them to enter the workforce. Pre-K is about far more than childcare, but childcare is an undeniable part of the equation.

For Fenwick, as for many parents, there was an even more powerful factor than finances in the decision to enter her almost-four-year-old in the BPS lottery: getting a spot in a choice school for K1 would guarantee her children seats in a good school all the way through middle school. In many cities like Boston and Washington, DC, pre-K is the entry to the public school lottery system that determines where children will go to elementary school and sometimes even middle and high school. The competition for the best public schools can be fierce, and as districts have incorporated pre-K at ages four and even three into the public school system, the opportunities to throw one's hat in the ring have been pushed down to younger and younger ages. Fenwick, like many parents, felt she had to take "every shot we can get at a good BPS spot." She hadn't always felt that way, especially when she was teaching in some of the city's lowest-income neighborhoods. "Before I had kids, I said I wouldn't take a K1 spot from a disadvantaged kid," she recalls. "But now I feel like we have to do it, because we can't afford private school on the other end." Fenwick and her husband had moved to Boston's Charlestown neighborhood specifically because the area was zoned to have priority for the Eliot. For them, school quality was the most important factor in deciding where to live. But choosing the charming and rapidly gentrifying neighborhood of brick buildings and historic gas-lit streetlamps put some financial stress on the family, and it meant renting an apartment rather than saving up to buy one.

Fenwick and her husband also wanted Luca and Marin to be educated in a diverse environment, with children from different cultures and all points on the economic spectrum. Luca wasn't getting that yet. When one of his preschool classmates came over to play, he was shocked to discover that Luca's apartment didn't have a playroom. Fenwick and her husband didn't want their children to grow up in an environment where that kind of privilege was assumed or where most of the children look the same. Luca, whose father is Indian American and whose mother is white, was the sole dark-haired, dark-eyed child in his class's morning meeting circle when I went to visit.

For Luca's family, public school was a given. The only questions were when he would start and where. When it came time to enter the lottery, the Eliot would be a no-brainer first choice. But what about backup schools? Parents are able to enter up to ten school choices, but Fenwick and her husband didn't want their shy, quiet four-year-old who was used to a part-time program to have to take a school bus across the city twice a day, so they ended up choosing only two schools, both close to their apartment. They crossed their fingers and hoped for the Eliot. If Luca got a spot at their second choice, they would have a tough decision to make: take the spot or try for the Eliot a year later. If he didn't get a K1 spot at all, Fenwick would implement her backup plan of keeping Luca at the private preschool for another year. But that backup plan carried a hefty financial risk. Like most private preschools, Luca's required that parents put down a deposit for the following year before hearing back about the public school lottery. Some schools also apply withdrawal fees if a family signs up but then opts out when they get a public school spot. It is an understandable business practice for preschools nervous about filling their seats as they lose more and more families and revenue to public schools. (Spots become harder to fill as the summer approaches, as large numbers of families have already made their decisions.) But it puts families in a tough position, essentially forcing them to pay a high-priced insurance policy to make sure their children aren't left out of a formative year that many parents and educators are coming to see as the foundation of a child's formal education.

That kind of insurance policy wasn't an option for Ayannah Hilton. Hilton, a single mother struggling to make ends meet while finishing a community college degree, also hoped for a K1 spot for her son, Jeremiah. Jeremiah is a bright, outgoing child with a broad smile, and his mother wasn't worried about his ability to adjust to a new school. But she wanted to make sure he would get a solid start in pre-K, especially in developing his language skills. As a toddler, Jeremiah had been slow to talk, and he eventually began receiving speech services through an early intervention program. At age four, he was talking more, but his mother wanted to see him speak in more consistent sentences and expand his vocabulary. She hoped he would get those skills in a K1 classroom. When the lottery results were announced, she learned he had gotten a spot at a school down the street from their apartment in Boston's Dorchester neighborhood. But when Hilton looked into the school's schedule, she concluded that she couldn't get Jeremiah to and from school and be at her job and classes on time. "You have to make the schedule that works for you. It's hard because there's so many limitations," she lamented.

Hilton decided that a community center with childcare and preschool would be a better option, especially since Jeremiah and his two-year-old sister, London, could be in the same place. But that wasn't a straightforward choice either. Jeremiah and London had already tried three centers that Hilton found lacking in organization, cleanliness, and nutritious food. One had been shut down by the state a week after her children started attending. Around that time, Hilton was working out at her local YMCA when she noticed that it had an early childhood program. She was able to get spots for both children, along with substantial financial assistance. The hours and location were convenient, the facility had tight security, and the meals were more varied and nutritious. Jeremiah started in the preschool classroom, dubbed Young Achievers, during the summer he was four.

The Roxbury YMCA is about five miles and a world away from the Eliot, located in one of Boston's most violent and disadvantaged neighborhoods. It provides early childhood programs as well as fitness and health programs to families from surrounding communities. Most of the children who attend are from families that economists call insecure: they don't always know if they will have dinner or where they will sleep. Some children, like Hilton's, have a stable and loving parental figure, but others have seen more than a lifetime's worth of stress and trauma. Some children have lost parents and other family members to violence. A few mothers worried about getting their children to and from school, because they had to pass through gang and drug territories. Like the parents at the Eliot, the parents at the Roxbury Y wanted the best for their children. And like their peers at the Eliot, the children at the Y were in preschool to build relationships and skills to get ready for kindergarten. But they had far more pressing issues on their minds, like how to handle the fear and anger building up inside of them and all too frequently bubbling over in the classroom.

When I first visited the Roxbury Y's four-year-old classroom, children ran around the room shouting, biting, and hitting one another. They pounced from one corner of the room to another, strewing books and tossing Play-Doh at classmates. Feelings of anger and distrust were palpable, and everyone seemed to be resorting to their most base instincts for self-preservation. Making the situation more chaotic, the classroom environment was the virtual opposite of the Eliot's serene space. Classroom materials were sparse and old, signs on the walls arbitrary and difficult to comprehend, and the space disorganized and dingy. But over the following year, the Young Achievers classroom would undergo a transformation of its own. When Hilton inquired about spots for her children, the Roxbury Y's early childhood director told her that the four-year-old classroom would be partnering with the Boston Public Schools to offer the same curriculum children would be getting if they were attending K1 at an elementary school. That was good news for Hilton, who had wanted a K1 spot all along. Not only would Jeremiah be getting the skills he needed for kindergarten, he would be getting them free of tuition, just as if he were in a public school.

Unbeknownst to Hilton, BPS's early childhood team had long been grappling with how to handle the unmet demand from thousands of would-be K1 families who hadn't gotten spots in the lottery. The number of children served in the K1 program is tiny compared to New Jersey's forty thousand or New York City's seventy thousand. Many families who apply for K1 seats are turned away, in part because the school buildings in Boston's old and densely populated neighborhoods don't have space for more four-year-olds. District and city leaders had long aimed to close the gap, and they were now tapping into community centers to build capacity and quality.

In Boston, and across the country, the early childhood education landscape is a patchwork of diverse public and private options, including public schools, community-based organizations, for-profit childcare centers, Head Start programs (which use federal funds to serve low-income children), and home-based early care settings. That fractured landscape has a number of pitfalls, not the least of which is confusion for parents, but it has some upsides, too. Community-based organizations provide a set of services and strengths that public schools typically do not, like the ten-hour day so important to working parents like Hilton, proximity to families' homes and workplaces, comprehensive services that can include healthcare, and staff who share families' home languages and cultures. Many parents feel more comfortable sending their three- and four-year-olds to settings like the YMCA, the Boys and Girls Club, or the neighborhood childcare center than to public schools, and such centers often have more opportunity to engage parents in informal conversations at drop-off and pickup times. These factors were critical for Ayannah Hilton. She needed the extended hours offered by the Y, and she liked having the opportunity to talk to her children's teachers every day. On the other hand, school districts have some advantages, including the resources and infrastructure to put quality improvement plans and processes in place. For example, they already have systems set up for conducting assessments and evaluations, and for making hiring and promotion decisions in a standardized way. That may help to explain the consistency found in programs like Boston's K1, and in New Jersey's Abbott districts, where some programs are located in Head Start centers or community organizations but all are supported, coached, and assessed by the public schools. But critics argue that K–12 schools are already struggling to provide a consistently good education to elementary and secondary students, and they worry that schools will have similar problems with pre-K.

Leaders in Boston were trying to find a middle ground in which community centers remained independent but received guidance and support from the school district. With the help of a federal grant, BPS hired extra early childhood staff to help the Roxbury Y and other community centers implement the K1 model, tweaking, improving, and, in some cases, transforming the way teachers taught four-year-olds. The centers were chosen specifically because they serve high percentages of low-income, high-needs children—in other words, the children who stand to gain the most from pre-K. For many teachers and children, the program turned out to be a revelation. But BPS staff immediately bumped up against big infrastructure challenges that are endemic to early childhood education, especially in centers that serve low-income neighborhoods, where children need the most but often get the least. As everyone involved would learn, high-quality curricula and teacher training are essential, but not sufficient, to ensure that deeply entrenched, problematic practices improve, and so do children.

Early childhood education is at a crossroads in America. Pre-K has more research and political support than ever before. We know that children can and do benefit. We also know that many don't get that chance. Despite the large increase in public and philanthropic investments, the National Institute for Early Education Research (NIEER) estimates that if the current rate of growth in pre-K enrollment continues, it will take *fifty years* to serve all low-income children and even longer to serve everyone. In those fifty years, tens of thousands of children could fall behind—children who could otherwise have the potential to become the next president or the researcher who will cure cancer.

In the United States, there has always been some degree of wariness about early childhood education, a view that it amounts to government overreach during a period in development when children should be home with their mothers. That perspective is tied to long-standing ambivalence about women in the workforce. After the U.S. Congress passed legislation for public funding of childcare in 1971, President Richard Nixon vetoed it, arguing that it was a government intrusion, harmful to children, and even communist propaganda. Even some of America's most well-regarded pre-K programs were almost axed before children walked through their doors. They had to be funded on the sly, by savvy politicians and advocates who wrapped them into larger reform initiatives because they knew there would be too much resistance to public funding of early childhood education if they took a more transparent route. One of the country's first universal programs is in Oklahoma, one of the most conservative states in the country. To pass the legislation that funded it, lawmakers and business leaders behind the bill had to sneak it in as part of a larger education reform bill because their previous attempts had provoked claims of a "nanny state." Today, Oklahoma's program is one of the most popular in the country and three-quarters of four-year-olds are enrolled, but some other states continue to fight difficult political battles for pre-K.

Even among supporters of pre-K, there has been a heated debate about who should have access: all children or just those from low-income families. The latter approach—known as "targeted pre-K"—has some prominent advocates, including economist James Heckman and sociologist Bruce Fuller, who believes that New York City's universal program is helping middle-class families while not improving access enough in low-income neighborhoods. The targeted approach sounds logical, and it is used in a number of cities, including Seattle, which has been gradually and strategically building a public pre-K program since 2015. But it's not as simple a solution as it sounds. There is some evidence that kindergarteners make greater gains over the course of the year when a higher percentage of their classmates went to preschool, suggesting it should be a priority to ensure that all children have access to high-quality pre-K. And there is mounting evidence that children benefit from diverse classrooms. Low-income children do better in economically mixed pre-K programs, and preschoolers with low language skills progress further in classrooms with children who have strong language skills, which tend to be correlated with family income. In Boston and Tulsa, Oklahoma, which both have economically integrated programs, children from middle-class families like Luca Murthy's benefit from pre-K as well. The gains are highest among low-income children, but that is not necessarily problematic. After all, these children tend to start behind, and one of the goals of public pre-K programs is to narrow achievement gaps. That can only happen if low-income children and children of color gain more than their peers. There is another compelling argument about the benefits for middle-class children: many educators and parents like Luca's mother, Maria Fenwick, believe that their children learn valuable social lessons from going to school with children who come from different backgrounds.

Ensuring access to pre-K won't help children of any background unless their classrooms are high in quality—and not all preschoolers are currently enrolled in enriching classrooms like Jodi Krous's at the Eliot. In cities and towns all across the country, the quality of pre-K programs varies widely, and that should worry parents, regardless of their income or neighborhood. Overall, quality is disappointing, whether you look at public programs like Head Start or private programs like for-profit child-care chains. Researchers find that only a minority of programs are of truly poor quality, but excellent-quality programs are also rare. Most programs operate somewhere in the middle, with considerable room for improvement.

Quality matters. That might sound like common sense, but pre-K studies have often been framed as answering the question "Does pre-K work or not?" ignoring the essential questions of why, when, and for whom. Studies show that children benefit from pre-K only when the programs they attend are rated as good or great, especially in how well their teachers provide age-appropriate instruction. Children like those in Jodi Krous's classroom do better than those in classrooms without engaging teacher-child conversations. States with more comprehensive quality standards do better than those without. Even countries with stronger financial investments in pre-K and higher-quality scores outperform others.

Children from middle-class and affluent families are more likely to get high-quality early education than their peers from low-income families, but even for them it isn't consistent. In communities all around the United States, some children are in programs where they learn very little or, conversely, where they are expected to learn and perform well beyond what is appropriate for three-, four-, and five-year-olds. The anxiety of parents applying to the Eliot is understandable. Still, it is nothing compared to the stress of parents of lesser means, who often struggle to find or afford a spot at all.

Quality should not be a luxury, and it doesn't necessarily look luxurious. In fact, it doesn't look like what many parents assume. Parents want the best possible education for their children, but few are trained educators like Maria Fenwick, so most of us don't know which questions to ask or what to look for when considering pre-K classrooms. The things that are easiest to see aren't usually the things that matter most for kids. An alphabet sign on the wall doesn't mean kids are really engaging with reading and learning. A daily email with a photograph of your daughter is nice to have, but it doesn't tell you much about whether the teachers are talking to her in a supportive way or sparking her curiosity about science. And in their earnest desire to see children learning, parents sometimes forget that a pre-K classroom shouldn't look like a third-grade classroom. It should have play areas instead of desks, and for most of the day, an audible hum instead of silence. Some educators worry that the components that matter most are getting lost as pressure to meet the demands of achievement testing get pushed down to earlier and earlier ages. Locating pre-K in public schools may exacerbate the problem in some cases, because many school administrators aren't familiar with early childhood development and best practices.

The real question is not whether pre-K matters. The real question is: How can we make sure that Jeremiah, Luca, and all preschoolers get what they need to succeed in school and life? That is the question at the heart of this book. It takes a journey into model programs in Boston, New Jersey, and Washington, DC, looking at what effective pre-K teachers do and why. It delves into how young children learn reading, math, social skills, and the other building blocks of school and life success. Following children and parents who have—and have not—been lucky enough to find excellent programs, it examines where we are and where we need to be to give all children a solid start in school. If we have the curiosity, the money, and the will to follow the lessons of the nation's successful programs, it just might be possible to make high-quality pre-K a reality for every child.

One

The Art and Science of Teaching

"What are the most important things for children to learn in pre-K?" asked Abby Morales, program director and coach for the Boston Public Schools early childhood department. She looked out at the roomful of teachers in front of her. Some had been teaching for years, while others were brand-new. Some taught in low-income neighborhoods and others in more economically integrated schools. None had taught Boston Public Schools' K1 curriculum before.

"Social skills," one teacher called out. "How to express their emotions." "How to follow rules and be ready for kindergarten." After a few moments, Morales asked the teachers what they noticed about their peers' responses. "I noticed there was very little about actual academics, math, and reading," answered a teacher named Melanie. Morales nodded. She knew that many of the teachers and program directors were worried about bringing academics into their programs for the first time. "Those of us who have been in early childhood for a long time remember when there wasn't a curriculum, when it was all about play and following the interests of the child," said Morales, who had taught for twelve years and worked as a coach for almost ten more. "Yes, this curriculum is about literacy and math, but it's also about all of these social skills you have mentioned. It's all about building better people."

Morales knew that academic and social skills can't really be separated, especially in the earliest years of schooling. Decades of research show that children who have stronger social and emotional skills are more likely to succeed in school in early childhood and beyond. Children who can listen, pay attention, and inhibit impulses like talking without being called on are more able to take in information the teacher is presenting. Those who know how to make friends and navigate conflicts are more well-liked by their teachers and classmates, which ends up providing them more opportunities to learn and get positive feedback. And when all or most of the students in a class possess these skills, it's easier for teachers to teach and for the whole class to focus. But in a national survey, kindergarten teachers reported that many incoming kindergarteners hadn't developed those skills, and that managing behaviors was the biggest challenge teachers faced in the classroom.

Children don't develop social and emotional skills automatically; those skills have to be taught, and in every environment where children live, learn, and play, including school. Critics of social and emotional programs in schools often claim that such skills should be taught at home, that parents are the only ones who should be responsible for children's character. But anyone who has spent time with young children knows that even those with engaged families and decent social skills sometimes struggle with taking turns, waiting, or coping with being left out of a game. Children learn how to deal with those challenges in the places where they occur, and because their parents aren't present at school, they need their teachers to guide them.

Experts agree that teachers don't have to choose between academics and social-emotional skills, and they shouldn't. But some early childhood classrooms struggle to find the balance. Some choose to focus strictly on the social side, potentially putting children at an academic disadvantage in kindergarten. Others focus so much on reading, writing, and counting that they risk skipping over a set of fundamental skills for kindergarten and beyond.

"So why do we need a curriculum?" Morales continued, taking off her hip glasses and placing them in the pocket of her sundress. The teachers were quiet at first. Then they started to raise their hands and offer up suggestions. "To have consistency across classrooms from day to day." "To prepare the environment for the children." "Intentionality."

"Yes!" Morales cheered, lifting one fist in the air and doing a little dance move. "Intentionality" could be one of her favorite words, it's so apparent in her work with teachers, her interactions with children, even the stylish way she dresses. Intentionality would be one of the biggest themes in her training and coaching with this new group of teachers, some of whom would soon be teaching in Boston Public Schools and others who would be implementing the BPS K1 model in community-based preschools, like YMCAs and Head Start programs.

On that muggy August afternoon, Morales's goal for the day was to introduce the two curricula used in K1, one for math and one for language and literacy. But she emphasized that the point of the curricula was to help teachers facilitate learning in an organized and thoughtful way, not to march through a set of cookie-cutter activities. "Curriculum is a tool, not a rule," Morales stressed to the teachers, using a favorite mantra among BPS early childhood coaches. "It helps you focus and be explicit about certain skills, but it's the thoughtful implementation of the curriculum that really matters. The curriculum on its own isn't enough." Over the coming hours and months, Morales would describe and model the kind of thoughtfulness she was expecting of teachers, and the teachers would quickly come to love the curriculum and what their children were learning from it.

On that first day, though, the teachers' faces were a mixture of relief and anxiety. Most were comforted to have a structure to follow ("so I don't have to make up the math part on my own," as one of them put it), but they also seemed overwhelmed by its scope. "How are we going to fit all of this in?" some whispered to their colleagues as they began to flip through the two-inch stack of pages that coaches were handing out—a ream of paper that covered only Unit 1. BPS staff were in the process of revising the original literacy curriculum to better suit their purposes and students, and they were building the plane while flying it, to use an expression common among educators. "We apologize that there are no page numbers," one of the coaches offered, explaining that the do-it-yourself layout program he was using didn't allow for pagination. "We're doing this rewrite on a nickel and a dime and a hope and a prayer," Morales told the teachers. They didn't look surprised. The teachers of one of the most respected pre-K programs in the country had been asked to bring their own three-ring binders. There simply wasn't the funding to do everything.

One teacher put down her packet, raised her hand, and pointed out that the Head Start program in which she taught already had a long list of requirements (almost fourteen hundred of them), including how to structure mealtimes, ensure that all children are getting health and dental screenings, and schedule home visits with families. Since its creation in the 1960s as an educational and antipoverty program for low-income children and families, Head Start has had multiple goals. Although academics have come to be a larger focus since the mid-2000s, they were originally a side note to the program's other services, including health, nutrition, and employment for low-income parents. "How are we supposed to do it all?" asked the teacher, to the nervous nods of others in the room.

The multiple requirements the teacher brought up are one of many challenges for community-based programs. Community centers typically have to coordinate multiple funding streams and regulations that come from different entities, like departments of education and state childcare agencies. Staffing is another big challenge. For starters, directors need more staff, because they have to meet state-mandated adult–child ratios over the course of a ten-hour day, as compared to a school's typical six-hour day. And the fact that community programs rely on family tuition, state subsidies, or both means that teachers usually get paid significantly less—almost $14,000 a year less—than public school teachers. As a result, community-based preschool teachers tend to have less formal training and education in child development, and some studies find that they tend to turn over more frequently, as they look for better-paying jobs. The BPS-community partnership program aimed to address that problem by funding a sizable increase in teacher salaries. The salary difference wasn't publicized to parents like Ayannah Hilton, but it made a difference in the centers' ability to hire and keep qualified teachers to work with Jeremiah and his peers.

That additional funding was helpful to programs as well as individual teachers. Financial sustainability is a big issue in community preschools, especially now that public schools are offering pre-K. In early childhood centers serving children from infancy to school age, the four-year-olds essentially subsidize the younger children. Four-year-olds don't require quite as much individual attention as younger children (at least when it comes to meeting basic needs and ensuring safety), so their classrooms aren't required to have as many staff, and that means that the centers can use some of the tuition from the older children to pay the staff serving the younger children. But when large numbers of preschoolers leave private centers for the public school system, the programs become financially strapped. If all four-year-olds made that transition, the infrastructure of infant and toddler care would likely collapse. One community center director told me her organization is thinking of eliminating infant care because the center is losing tens of thousands of dollars a year. Those kinds of figures are why even the limited number of twenty-five hundred K1 spots had roiled the early childhood community in Boston, creating tension between the district and some of the community centers that simmers to this day.

Abby Morales was sympathetic to the Head Start teacher's concerns.

She had taught in a community preschool for more than ten years herself. She also knew what it was like to launch into a new way of doing things. She remembered the early days of the K1 program, when a few core staff members would meet on street corners under lampposts because they lacked adequate office space—a far cry from the sunny space the staff of twenty now occupies on the fourth floor of BPS's recently renovated office building.

"Picture a pickle jar," Morales told the room of teachers in front of her. "You have some big, fist-sized rocks, then some gravel, sand, and water. How can you make everything fit?" After a dramatic pause she answered her own question. "You have to put the big rocks in first, and then the other things can fit in around it. That's the way it is with the curriculum. You have to put in the big rocks first, like centers and small-group math. Then you can add other pieces, like Let's Find Out About It and storytelling." Spotting confused looks, Morales assured the teachers they would learn about those curriculum components later. "One of the other big rocks for you as teachers is this: don't lose sight of the joy in this. You should be as curious and surprised about teaching as the children are about learning. Focus on the things that engage them as learners, not on things that make you a classroom task manager." "Task manager" is not a phrase most preschool teachers would use to describe their jobs, and yet, in many preschool classrooms, that is very much what it looks like, with teachers giving constant orders about what to do and handing out consequences when children fail to follow rules.

Some of the teachers continued to look nervous. "Our job is to help you put the pieces in place," Morales continued. "We're going to be coming into your classrooms at least every two weeks to observe, talk with you, give you suggestions. We're there to support you, not to evaluate you." With a conspiratorial smile to accompany another of the coaches' favorite expressions, she added, "We are not the curriculum police."

Morales then dove into the curriculum, starting with the time when children and teachers gather for the morning meeting. "Morning meeting is active learning; it's different than circle time. We don't do the calendar. We don't do classroom jobs." Surprised twitters spread across the room. Circle time is a staple of preschool classrooms, during which children sit and listen while the teacher and one or two children dutifully go through a routine set of questions and answers: the day of the week, the date, the alphabet, the letter of the week. Morales was asking teachers to leave these components at the classroom door, because they are examples of what she calls passive learning, where kids receive information rather than constructing it. Morales saw the teachers exchange startled looks. "I can feel the resistance here," she said with a little smile. "I get it. We're all used to those routines. But we want instruction to start moving. Maybe the kids like doing the weather, but it's not pushing new learning. Once they learn it, they're not getting anything out of it. If you keep doing the same thing every time they come to the rug, chances are kids are going to wander off and say, 'Peace out, I know this already.' We will do songs, but we're going to keep changing them and augmenting them, because we want to keep the level of engagement high and not stop with things that are familiar."

Many parents might be surprised by the level of thoughtfulness that goes into these kinds of plans and training sessions. When our children come home and sing songs they learned at school, most of us find them charming and are glad our kids can sing along to "Row, Row, Row Your Boat" in the bathtub. But it may not occur to us that our children's brains develop more when they are constantly learning new songs and hearing new words in those songs. So much of what good early childhood teachers and programs do is easy for the average person to miss.

Morales then went on to explain how the centerpiece of the curriculum is hands-on learning centers, six to ten activities that change every day and that teach children concepts and skills through play: "We know that children learn in hands-on ways. Kids have to be active agents in their own learning. That means they need choices and engaging things to do." The concept of centers wasn't new to teachers, but the method was.

In many classrooms, centers amount to free-play activities, where teachers put out materials they think will interest the class and children choose whatever they want to focus on. But research finds that three- and four-year-olds don't make much progress in literacy, math, or other concepts when they are simply left to play with no structure. In the K1 curriculum, children still choose their activities and rotate from one area to another, but every center has an intentional learning goal and a link to an overarching unit theme and weekly focus. They are connected to themes like Families, Things That Grow, and the World of Color. At the core of each lesson is a book, carefully selected to illustrate certain concepts and serve as a springboard for center activities. When a class reads Ezra Jack Keats's *Peter's Chair*, which addresses sibling and parent relationships, children not only discuss what happens when a new sibling is born, they learn about Keats's artistic medium of collage and experiment with using it. When they read *The Little Red Hen Makes a Pizza*, which puts a twist on the traditional tale of the industrious farm animal to emphasize community, children talk about cooperation and friendship, write recipes, and make "number pizzas" with paper plates and plastic chips to explore the concepts of same and different amounts. Karen Katz's multicultural book *The Colors of Us* inspires a self-portrait activity; after noticing different skin colors, children mix paint to create their own skin color, use observational painting techniques to create detailed, realistic self-portraits, and write their names.

Another thing that sets K1 apart from other approaches is the level of thoughtfulness with which teachers are expected to explain and facilitate concepts. "You want to set up the environment in a way that invites the kids to explore and discover. And you are going to introduce one or two of the centers at morning meeting every day, to help kids delve into what they will learn there," Morales continued, explaining that when teachers walk around and facilitate centers, their job is to ask questions, provide suggestions, and provoke new ideas. That might sound easy, but it takes a very skilled and thoughtful teacher to do it well. As Morales explained,

"You don't want to tell them exactly what to do, like 'Here's how you make a penguin,' because then maybe they will just copy what you did. Instead you might want to show some videos of penguins and say things like, 'Here are some videos that might inspire you.' Then you ask them what they notice, or point out elements of their work from the day before." As a model, she showed a brief video of a veteran K1 teacher introducing centers during the World of Color unit. The teacher explained the materials that were at the paint center, showed examples of how some children had mixed colors the day before, and brought out a color fan she had borrowed from a paint store for inspiration. Studies show that when teachers have these kinds of discussions to orient the class to the activities they are about to do, children learn more about literacy and math, develop larger vocabularies, and are more skilled at regulating their own behavior. It's particularly important for teachers to explain the "what" and "why," as the veteran teacher did in the video. Morales also pointed out some of the teacher's other best practices: "She didn't tell them how they had to do it. She didn't tell them 'don't do this' and 'don't do that.' She said, 'Here are some of the things you *can* do.'" The teachers nodded quietly and took notes, as Morales went on to explain how they could use that approach in every aspect of their teaching.

When the teachers took a break, the teacher named Melanie shook her head and said, "I wish I had had this before we started last week. This is going to change everything we do tomorrow. I'm really excited, but it's a little bit like 'Whoa!' There's just so much." She had taught preschool before, but not like this. When she had been hired at the East Boston YMCA about a month before, she had learned about the program, but she said that she "had no idea what goes into it. Even when you try to be diligent and look through the materials, you can't know until you are here in the training what it really takes. I didn't really understand the part about the child driving it and being such an active part of it. That's really new, instead of us telling them what to do all the time."

Meg Hackett appeared to share the combination of excitement and trepidation. Thirty-year-old Hackett was the new lead teacher for Jeremiah and the other four-year-olds at the Roxbury YMCA. She wasn't just new to the Y, but new to teaching pre-K. Hackett had been a special education teacher for older children and had worked with toddlers in home-based early intervention services, but she had never taught a pre-K curriculum.

At the end of the first day of training, Hackett huddled to plan with Kamilah Washington (who everyone, even the adults, calls Ms. K). Washington was the Roxbury Y's "floater teacher"—a person who covers whatever classroom needs support, either because a teacher is absent or children need more adults in the room than usual. Washington had been an assistant teacher in the Young Achievers classroom the year before, but she had no formal background or degree in education or child development, and the grant funding the new program required that assistant teachers have at least an associate's degree in early childhood education. However, the Y had been unable to fill the assistant teacher spot, so they made arrangements with BPS for Ms. K to attend all the trainings (about one a month) and cover the classroom until another teacher was hired. Washington, who had just started taking courses in pursuit of her associate's degree, said, "I'm excited about this." Looking back on her first year, she mused, "I didn't know what I was doing. I felt bad for the kids, but I was doing my best. I've worked with kids for about five years in camps and stuff, but I was basing it on my childhood and the things I know." That's common among preschool teachers, almost half of whom do not have a college degree. Research is mixed on whether having a bachelor's degree leads to better teaching and more learning, but many state- and federally funded programs require one, because coursework theoretically provides at least a base level of knowledge and some opportunity to reflect on child development. Like most parents, Ayannah Hilton didn't ask about teachers' backgrounds when she was looking at preschool programs for her children, because she assumed the teachers were qualified if they had been hired. She was more concerned about looking at basic health and safety issues, and she figured the teachers were pretty much interchangeable anyway, because she was used to seeing the same pool of teachers, as they left one center and moved to another nearby. But she wanted her children to learn and get ready for kindergarten, and those goals are highly dependent on the quality of teaching a center provides. Teaching varies more than many parents realize.

As Hackett and Washington contemplated their daily schedule and talked about how they needed to clean out the classroom and "start fresh," they were energized but not entirely confident. Hackett asked how often they would get coaching, and Morales assured her, "As often as you need it. When I'm working with a new center, I am in there all the time." Morales knew that following the K1 model would be a big shift for the Y and many of the programs. She knew the teachers would need support, but she also knew she couldn't do the work for them. Just like when she facilitated children's learning as a teacher, she would need to gently guide teachers and centers. And there was no time to waste. Jeremiah and the other children had only one shot to have a successful year in pre-K, and it could turn out to be the most important year of their schooling.

Two

Getting Connected

When I first visited the Roxbury Y's preschool class, it was clear that Hackett and Washington were going to need the help Morales and her colleagues were offering. The children's vocabulary and knowledge were way behind those of the children at the Eliot and other preschools I had visited. I asked a sweet-faced, distracted little boy to count the number of hula hoops he was holding on the playground. As I pointed to each one he said, "One, three, seven, two." I discovered that he and several children knew the names of numbers but not how to count. When I asked children what letters their names started with, most of them shrugged. But there were far more fundamental issues to work on. As I looked around the playground, watching children push each other off the climbing structure and a few minutes later wail when they were hit or bitten, I knew that getting them to a place where they could learn math was going to take some serious effort to first build the children's social and emotional skills.

When Meg Hackett interviewed for the position of lead teacher in the Young Achievers classroom, she hadn't planned to teach pre-K, and she had never been to the Roxbury Y. The Y is located at one end of Martin Luther King Jr. Drive, across from fast-food joints, discount stores, and check-cashing places. The neighborhood is made up largely of public housing projects and low-rent apartments. There is no subway stop, but buses run from the neighborhood to nearby Dudley Square, a historic Roxbury neighborhood that is undergoing revitalization, including the renovated historic building that recently became home to the BPS central administration offices. But the neighborhood is also home to pervasive gang and drug activity. When Hackett moved to Boston, she had doggedly pursued the regional YMCA's hiring manager in an attempt to secure a program director position in one of Boston's quieter, leafier neighborhoods. But when she finally got an interview, the manager convinced Hackett that she could earn more money teaching preschool in Roxbury.

If it sounds surprising that the preschool teacher salary was an incentive, that's because it was unusually high, thanks to the federal Preschool Expansion Grant that funded the BPS-community partnership. Massachusetts was one of eighteen states funded by the Obama administration to open more pre-K classrooms, and Boston was using its share of the money to bring the K1 program to community centers. Along with the requirement that lead teachers have a bachelor's degree in early childhood education came a significant salary boost. The grant required that teachers be paid commensurate with starting public school pre-K teacher salaries, around $51,000. That was notably higher than the national median salary of $28,570. Nationally, wages are so low that a shocking half of the nation's early childhood educators are enrolled in some kind of public assistance program such as the Supplemental Nutrition Assistance Program (SNAP) or Medicaid, for a cost of over $2 billion a year in federal spending. Three-quarters of early childhood teachers worry about having enough money to pay their monthly bills and, appallingly, over 50 percent worry about their ability to feed their own children, never mind access the kind of high-quality care and education they are striving to provide in their classrooms. I talked to one early childhood teacher who couldn't afford to send her son to the university-affiliated center where she taught, because even with a large employee discount, it would have cost her $1,000 a month. It pained her to send her child to a succession of low-quality childcare centers, one of which was later shut down by the state because of neglect and safety violations. No doubt the teachers at those centers were being paid the low wages that are characteristic of the field, and it's likely that turnover was high, as it is every year in about half of the country's centers. Those trends are a problem for children as well as teachers. It's hard for children to trust their teachers when they don't know when they'll be leaving. And several studies show that early childhood teachers' wages are strong or even the strongest predictors of the quality of care they provide.

In Boston, the grant funding for higher teacher pay was meant to entice more educated teachers into preschool classrooms and keep them there, and to improve quality. The salary enhancement did indeed entice Hackett, who has a master's degree in early childhood special education. But she didn't realize that her paycheck would be coming from the three-year, time-limited grant, or even that the Roxbury Y had been chosen as one of the participating community-based organizations. That information was included in the official job posting, but Hackett doesn't remember ever seeing the posting, and she even had a hard time getting a copy of a job description. The first she heard of the collaboration with BPS was when she showed up on her first day of work to find camera crews and Boston's mayor in her classroom, holding a public announcement about the grant. Executives at the Y dispute this, but it appears that somehow some critical communication was missed. Less than two days later, Hackett was at the training where she met Abby Morales and the other coaches.

When I visited her classroom a few days after that training, she looked a little shell-shocked. Hackett is about five foot three but seems taller. Her appearance is neat but with a funky edge; she has a tasteful purple streak across the front of her short dark hair and the words "shine on" in tiny, elegant script tattooed down one forearm. As she surveyed her chaotic classroom, she had stress written all over her body. She looked frequently at the clock, clearly wondering how she would make it through the day. When I asked about the BPS curriculum, she shook her head and said, "At the end of the day, it's about getting their basic needs met and helping them develop positive behavior." Washington was more blunt: "Our priority," she told me, "is to get them home alive."

Hackett and Washington had already decided that they needed to overhaul the classroom, but it was a tall order. Children pulled dress-up clothes and books off shelves and ran around the space, crashing into each other, sometimes by accident and sometimes on purpose. An old, dingy rug was the only marker of the group meeting area (formerly known as circle time). The walls were covered in visual aids that were well-intentioned but completely inappropriate for four-year-olds. One wall held stars with each child's birthday written in a numerical format, like 2/16/09. Another held numbers and letters posted in random order, and an adjacent one boasted handwritten addition problems—for a roomful of children who struggled to count to ten. On one bulletin board were the words "No Bullying" and on another were "10 Goals for This Month." Even if the children had been able to read, these concepts were far too sophisticated for them.

Hackett wondered aloud when Morales or another coach would appear. It turned out that Morales had seen the classroom even before Hackett, and she was concerned, too. Before the press conference, she had thought about coming in to reorganize the classroom, but she knew the teachers needed to own the process and the classroom. So she waited, and shortly after Hackett started, Morales offered to come in on a weekend to help her rearrange the space. They spent hours together, taking down all the posters and bulletin board displays and replacing them with pictures of the students and their artwork, leaving space for others yet to come. Commercial materials that you buy from a catalog make life easier for teachers, but Morales implored Hackett and the other teachers not to use them, explaining that it's important for children to see that they and their teachers created their own materials: "At the beginning of the year, your walls should be relatively blank. The message to kids should be, 'Everything in this room is the product of a learning process we will create together.'" Indeed, that was what I had seen at the Eliot. As I looked around at the walls during my first visit in September, Jodi Krous noticed my surprise and assured me, "The walls are pretty empty right now because it's the beginning of the year, but a month from now you'll see they are filled with the children's work." She explained that posting student work and documenting their process with photographs and notes is helpful for communicating with parents and the many Eliot staff who are in and out of the room, and also for gathering data about what children are learning. Most important, she said, it helps her own process of thinking and reflecting on the children's learning: "The documentation on the walls helps me be really transparent about my process and explain it to other teachers, so I'm not just doing it in my head."

Morales and Hackett also organized the toys so that children could find and play with them more appropriately, set up an art center with an easel, and added a writing center against one wall so kids wouldn't get distracted there. They moved the tables and chairs so Hackett could put the center-time activities in places that would capture children's attention, direct the flow of foot traffic from one part of the room to another, and create smaller areas so that when children sat together during mealtime they could focus on their classmates and not get overwhelmed by having twenty people eating together—an experience that could cause sensory overload for many adults. Embodying Morales's focus on intentionality, nothing in the reorganized classroom was left to chance. But just attempting to rearrange the furniture and replace broken materials would turn out to illustrate the systemic challenges that Hackett, and many early childhood education teachers, were up against. Some of the furniture was bolted to the floor, following state safety regulations but limiting the teachers' flexibility. Even after Morales and Hackett moved other pieces, the cleaning crew kept rearranging it at night. And Hackett's supervisors also came in and put the furniture back to its original positioning, not realizing her plan for how it could facilitate learning and instead worrying about whether they were following state guidelines.

The physical environment was just one of the problems in the classroom, but it likely contributed to the stress level. When classrooms have too much decoration, it can be distracting for students and cause them to learn less, according to research conducted at Carnegie Mellon University. The researchers recruited a group of kindergarteners and taught them six science lessons, three in a heavily decorated classroom they created for the study and three in a classroom with blank walls. Children spent more time off task in the decorated classroom, and as a result learned less from the lessons. When tested on the material, they got 55 percent of answers correct in the sparse classroom compared to only 42 percent in the decorated classroom. Although the researchers don't recommend that classroom walls be entirely blank, they urge teachers to be thoughtful about the amount and type of materials they post. It's possible that classrooms saturated with colors, posters, and materials can make the environment feel chaotic or cause sensory overload, even for typically developing children who do not have sensory challenges.

Paring down and reorganizing the Young Achievers' classroom helped, because it reduced triggers for conflict, like not having enough materials or space for multiple children in a certain area. But the space alone couldn't transform the behavior of the class's fourteen boys and three girls.* The class was loud, conflict-ridden, and not accustomed to following teacher expectations, even though many of the children had attended other classrooms in the center in their younger years. Children disobeyed

---

* Centers with enough children to fill multiple classrooms can usually create a more equal gender balance, but those struggling to fill their spots have to leave classroom composition to chance.

teachers' requests and orders; one called Hackett an expletive. Even children like Jeremiah Hilton, who was usually mild-mannered and affectionate, sometimes acted aggressively when they saw their classmates doing the same. "He picked up a few bad habits," his mother reported. Ms. K frequently found herself separating children physically, sometimes carrying one into the hallway and sitting with the child until he or she calmed down. She wasn't unkind to the children, but her usual low-key manner would get rattled with frustration and her voice would raise in volume and sharpness.

Hackett worried that several of the children had undiagnosed developmental problems, like autism and conduct disorders. She was frustrated that she didn't have access to the special education services of the Boston Public Schools, because although her classroom was supported by BPS, it wasn't officially part of the district. In a public school, a student could be evaluated by a specialist right in the building during the course of a school day. Children in other settings were also entitled to evaluations, but they usually took much more time, often requiring multiple phone calls to schedule, coordinating time and transportation for the family to get the child to school, and navigating long wait times in the midst of high demand for services. Once diagnosed, children in the public schools could receive services either in mainstream classrooms or separate ones; some children were entitled to a one-on-one classroom aide. (In Jodi Krous's classroom at the Eliot, one severely disabled child had both a full-time aide and a full-time nurse.) That kind of support takes a huge amount of pressure off teachers and allows them to focus on the class as a whole while someone else provides the additional supports that make learning possible for children with special needs, and it allows schools like the Eliot to have inclusion classrooms where kids with special needs are incorporated into classrooms with typically developing children. But those kinds of supports are not available in community centers, even in classrooms like Hackett's, where many kids have experienced trauma and badly need services. Hackett's classroom didn't even have the planned-for third teacher, because the Y was still struggling to find someone qualified. Fortunately, Hackett and Ms. K had formed a tight bond, and their partnership was going well. But that wasn't enough to meet all of the kids' needs, especially since Ms. K wasn't trained to deal with severe emotional and behavioral issues.

Nonetheless, Hackett was able to make connections with many of the students, even those who had been particularly challenging for previous teachers. The key was her commitment to building positive, trusting relationships with the kids. Without that base, she knew, she wouldn't be able to help them develop their social and emotional skills, much less their ABCs and 123s. Strong and positive teacher-child relationships are the most important factor in classroom quality, regardless of whether the children are poor or wealthy and of what their home lives are like, because relationships lay the foundation for everything else. When children's relationships with teachers have a lot of affection, warmth, and positive communication, children do better in literacy, math, and later school achievement. One large study even found that children with a lot of conflict in their relationships with their preschool teachers are more likely to be referred for special education further down the road. This might be explained by motivation—children with positive teacher relationships tend to like school more and get more excited about going to school—and also by the fact that positive relationships provide more opportunities for learning to occur. The Center on the Developing Child at Harvard has summed up research on the importance of relationships by describing the need for "serve and return" interactions, which operate much like a tennis match: when a child initiates a conversation or interaction, the adult responds in a warm and engaged way, inviting the child to add more and keep the volley of conversation and engagement going. This research has focused on interactions between infants and parents, but it applies at later ages and with other adult caregivers, too. At an even more basic level, if your teacher enjoys being with you, she's more likely to sit down and ask you about your drawing, and if she shows you affection and empathy, you are more likely to open up to her with information about the drawing, questions about the world, and problems you are having.

The Y was lucky that Hackett had strong relationship skills and knew how to build emotional support for her students. From her graduate training, she knew that trust and relationships can be damaged by trauma and instability, and many of her students had experienced both. Hackett suspected the aggression she saw from many of her children came from a place of mistrust, fear, and anger. "A lot of these kids need attention so badly that they don't care if it's negative attention," Hackett told me during her second month on the job. (I later noticed that she had placed a reminder of that at her makeshift classroom workstation—a poster that read, "The kids who need the most love will ask for it in the most unloving of ways.") So she gave them the positive attention they were craving. She would scoop them into her lap, turn them upside down to shake out their grumpies, and hug them when they left for the day. She tried to keep perspective about how young they were and how much room there was to influence them. "I see them walking around trying to be tough and rapping, but then I think, 'You wet your pants this morning!'" she told me with equal parts humor and affection for the children. "These kids have seen a lot, heard a lot, curse a lot. But they are still four- and five-year-olds, and that's how I treat them and love them." For Jeremiah and some of his classmates, that was a welcome change. Many of the children had been to several different centers, and they were accustomed to teachers who yelled, cursed, and handled negative behavior by saying things like, "What's wrong with you, boy?" or ignored a child when she hit another.

The ability to connect with and support children isn't necessarily a quality that teachers inherently possess, but it can be built. Coaching from experienced mentors can improve teacher-student relationships and, in turn, children's learning. One popular method of coaching is based on decades of research on teacher-student relationships conducted by psychologist Robert Pianta. He encourages coaches to assess and facilitate three different kinds of teacher support for students: emotional support, classroom management, and instructional support. Despite what it sounds like, emotional support doesn't mean therapy; it means being encouraging, nurturing, and responsive to student needs, and it is linked to academic success for young children and adolescents alike. It is one of three skills assessed on a measure of classroom quality developed by Pianta and his colleagues, the Classroom Assessment Scoring System (CLASS), which is used by many preschool programs and required for Head Start programs to evaluate teacher effectiveness.

One of Hackett's strategies was to give the children positive reinforcement. This was particularly effective with a child I'll call Mara. "Mara was the child I was warned most about when I started," Hackett mused one day, "but within a few days, I learned that if you give her praise for good behavior once an hour or so, she's fine for the rest of the day. She keeps calling to us to show us the good things she's doing. Almost right away, I thought, 'Oh, I got this one!'" Experts support this approach to providing positive reinforcement. Psychologist Becky Bailey, who created an early childhood approach called Conscious Discipline, has found that it's more effective to tell children what *to do* instead of what *not to do*; for example, to say "Use your walking feet" instead of "Don't run" and "Keep your hands to yourself" instead of "Don't touch Sebastian." What you focus on, you get more of, she points out, so when you call attention to children's positive behaviors, they engage in more of them. That's why many pre-K teachers calm down their classes by saying things like, "I like the way Angel is sitting crisscross applesauce," instead of saying, "Manuel, for the third time, sit down!"

Jeremiah didn't act out much, but Hackett could tell he had other needs, especially in building self-confidence. At the beginning of the year, he was very shy and easily rattled, especially if he feared he had done something wrong. He was also clearly very bright. Hackett and Washington worked to make the classroom a space where it was cool to be smart and lavished praise on children who answered questions about books they had read or offered answers to simple counting problems. So when Jeremiah began to raise his hand and answer questions, Hackett could see he felt proud and excited, and she saw him start to come out of his shell. "He likes being a smart kid," she noticed, so she started creating special jobs for him to do to boost his confidence and give him more responsibility. "I need you to help me carry these papers to the photocopier, because I know you can do it," she would tell him, or "Can you help the other kids write this word?"

It was easy to see the trust children began to feel in Hackett, as they gave her hugs and opened up about their lives. Jeremiah talked about Ms. Meg "all the time" at home, according to his mother. He would report on the plans Ms. Meg had for the class, and he was visibly proud whenever he got a compliment from her. Hackett could tell the children felt safe; some cried when it was time to go home. But helping the kids feel trust with each other was a tougher task, especially because many of them were accustomed to using physical means to assert themselves. But Hackett patiently worked at it, giving children language to use instead of hitting, providing opportunities for partners or small groups to cooperate during class activities, and assuring children that everyone would get a chance to use new materials and do new activities. Fairness is very important to young children, as any parent knows, and it's particularly important to children who are not used to getting what they want or need, according to Judy Schickedanz, an early childhood expert who ran the Boston University laboratory preschool for decades. In her experience, children who are used to scarcity and competing for resources grow particularly anxious, and sometimes aggressive, if there aren't enough materials for everyone or if they don't know whether they will get a turn. She has developed a number of strategies to address that. For example, she has found that children and classrooms function more smoothly when an art center has three cups that each have the same two crayon colors rather than one cup of six different colors. Hackett was learning that little things can make a big difference.

On a mild November morning, I walked into the Young Achievers class-room to find that things were running more smoothly. When it was time for morning meeting, Hackett calked out, "OK, everybody, fried egg!" The children giggled and hurried to sit in a circle on the rug, like a fried egg with a yoke in the middle. Later, when it was time to read them a book from the curriculum, she said, "OK, scrambled eggs!" and the children clumped together so they were all facing front and could see the book. Hackett had learned the strategy from Morales at a training, and several others from her BPS coach. As the coaches explained, simple strategies like fried eggs/scrambled eggs work because they are easy for children to understand and relate to, are quick and efficient, and are a more fun alternative to commands like "Sit in a circle." When I saw Hackett use it, I was impressed by how much more quickly her children complied and focused. Transitions had been tough for them; when I first visited, Hackett tried valiantly to keep things under control, but strategies like threatening children that they wouldn't be allowed to go outside if they didn't fix their behavior didn't work. Transitions continued to be a challenge, but after Hackett started working with the coaches, she had a pocketful of new strategies that seemed to be working better. As children lined up to go outside, some of them had trouble waiting for others who were still struggling with their jackets. They began to needle and push each other, yell, and leave their spots in line. Hackett held her hands above her head and began singing "Open Shut Them," and the children in line calmed down and joined in, opening and closing their hands in the air in time with the lyrics. Once everyone was lined up, she helped them focus by standing soldier-straight and playfully saluting, to which the children chanted happily, "Aye, aye, Captain Meg!"

Strategies like these are the preschool teacher's tricks of the trade, but they are rarely taught in teacher training programs. Teacher preparation programs for future elementary and secondary school teachers almost always require their students to do "field experience placements" or "student teaching" in classrooms with veteran teachers, but those kinds of experiences are less likely to be required for future early childhood educators. Even when such opportunities are available, they tend to be more limited and offer fewer concrete strategies than those for future K-12 teachers. Teachers tend to learn about classroom management from one another, or through trial and error, since most teachers have little time or opportunity for collaboration with colleagues. Some lucky teachers like Hackett learn them from mentors or coaches.

One of Hackett's first projects with her coach was to establish a daily schedule that was predictable for the children and doable for Hackett. She created cards for each component of the day and hung them on a wall near the rug where children sat for morning meeting. Each morning, she would walk the children through the schedule, and then remind them each time they were to transition to a new activity. When a child would ask when they could go outside, she could return to the schedule and say, "Remember? We go outside after centers." Young children thrive on routines like these. In a world that feels huge and often overwhelming to their small selves, they need to know what to expect, and it's particularly helpful when they have cues they can recognize and relate to, like music and visual aids. Routine is especially beneficial for students like Hackett's, whose lives are anything but predictable. Knowing when they will get to eat, play outside, read books, and do other daily activities reassures children who might otherwise worry about whether they will get all of those needs met.

With a routine in place, Hackett could begin to implement activities from the curriculum. With coaches' encouragement, she started with centers, the activities that form the core of the curriculum. Starting with the Families unit, she put dolls and baby-care items in the dramatic play area, where her often-aggressive students began to clothe, feed, and nurture the babies. She invited students to draw family portraits and helped them write their names and label the people they drew; more than one portrait included Ms. Meg and Ms. K. She observed the students closely and tweaked things that weren't working. No one was going to the easel, so she moved it to a more central place in the classroom, and voilà, students flocked there to paint. On one day I visited, she noticed the centers like the writing table or the book corner that weren't getting any attention, so she sat down in each of them and began doing the activities herself. Students gradually came to sit by her side and found themselves engrossed in the activities. One of the secrets, Hackett discovered, was to vary the activities regularly, while maintaining the most popular ones several days in a row. Play-Doh was a big hit, but there weren't enough spots at the table and arguments broke out. So the next day, Hackett moved it to a bigger table and added more chairs and materials. She was learning that for children's behavior to improve, not only do the children have to adapt to the environment but the environment has to adapt to the children.

Although many of Hackett's children continued to struggle with emotional and behavioral issues throughout the year, they were lucky. In many early childhood classrooms in America, the kinds of behavioral challenges they faced are dealt with in ways that are far more punitive and far less constructive. Across the country, preschoolers and kindergarteners are suspended and even expelled at an alarming rate. In 2005, Walter Gilliam, the director of the Edward Zigler Center in Child Development and Social Policy at Yale University, reported that preschoolers were being expelled for behavior problems at a rate three times that of grades kindergarten to twelve. His analysis of almost four thousand preschool classrooms showed that more than 10 percent of teachers said they had expelled a student in the past year. Boys were more likely to be expelled, and particularly African American boys, like those in Hackett's classroom. Gilliam's study sparked an increase in awareness about preschool discipline, but according to a study by the U.S. Department of

Education's Office for Civil Rights, not much improved over the following decade. In a study during the 2013–2014 school year that included over one million preschoolers, African American preschoolers were over three and a half times more likely than white children to be suspended, and African American boys made up 45 percent of male suspensions despite making up only 19 percent of preschool enrollment. During the time that Hackett was helping her children adjust to being in a classroom together, a school just down the road from the Y, which also serves a predominantly African American population, was suspending one out of eleven elementary school students for a total of 325 suspensions, 68 of them in kindergarten. And they weren't alone: in 2014–2015, Massachusetts preschoolers and kindergarteners were suspended over six hundred times.

Young children don't learn anything while they are suspended, and they don't learn anything *from* being suspended. They need more direct connections between their actions and the consequences; they can't understand why they have been removed from class. Many of the infractions are minor, developmentally appropriate behaviors like talking out of turn, which children do not understand. Even the more serious ones, like aggression, can feel to children like appropriate responses to frustration. That's why the major problem with suspensions and expulsions is that they miss an opportunity to teach children why their behavior was inappropriate and what they can do differently next time. Because young children are hands-on learners, they can learn a better alternative only by trying it out in the classroom and by watching their classmates model it for them.

Expulsions and suspensions are not the only problem. Some early childhood teachers handle student behavior in ways that punish and shame children. I saw teachers call four-year-olds lazy. In classrooms serving both poor and affluent children, white kids and kids of color, I heard teachers say more "don'ts" than "dos" and issue a lot of threats— to take away recess, to call a student's parents, to send a child to the principal. I talked to coaches who had to inform teachers that it was un-acceptable to make off-task children sit on the floor in the middle of a circle of desks, with all of their classmates glaring down at them. These kinds of approaches do not teach children how to change their behavior. And young children learn very quickly to label themselves or their class-mates as "bad" kids who aren't as good or as deserving as others. Those labels stick, and they are powerful, eroding children's beliefs that they can do better and causing them to stop trying. This is particularly detrimental for young children of color, for whom the labels compound messages they receive elsewhere in society about their value.

Hackett's children, who anyone would identify as having serious be-havior challenges, often showed themselves to be curious and sweet and smart. But they were frequently misguided and acting out. Fortunately, they were young enough to be able to turn their behavior around, and they had a teacher who saw the good in them and helped them do that. Hackett and Washington were on the way to improving quality, although they weren't yet able to implement all the activities from the curriculum. But they had reason to be optimistic about their chances of turning things around quickly. For an example of how that change could happen, they needed to look only five miles away, at the Eliot.

Three

Beautiful Little Puzzles

When you walk into the Eliot School, it's hard to imagine it without early childhood classrooms. After you enter through the grate-covered metal door, the first thing you see is a bright "Welcome to Kindergarten!" sign. The K1 and K2 classrooms are just inside the entry, hugging the main office. The corridor is covered in young children's artwork and lined with cubbies adorned with the bright-eyed photographs of three-, four-, and five-year-olds. Learning spills out of the classrooms and into the hallways, where a robotics instructor plays a game with a small group of children or a teacher helps a child choose artwork to display in her portfolio. Teachers and administrators fluidly enter one another's classrooms and offices to ask questions, offer suggestions, or even check in on a student from last year's class. It's not uncommon to see Principal Traci Griffith walk into a classroom and scoop a four-year-old into her arms or tie a tiny shoe. The atmosphere is so engaging and welcoming that you barely notice the building's age or the funky smell from the basement bathrooms that Griffith has been trying to get rid of for years.

But none of this, except perhaps for the smell, was here ten years ago.

In the early 2000s, the Eliot was ranked near the bottom of Boston's schools. Test scores were low, and morale was even lower. Students, many of whom spoke English as a second or third language, struggled, and teachers and administrators believed they could do little to help them. Teachers and staff who worked at the school during that time have described the culture as one of low expectations for both children and adults, dominated by a belief that students couldn't achieve because of the challenges they brought to school—behavior challenges, learning issues, family traumas. Many families in the school's immediate neighborhood had abandoned it for private options, so students were bused to the Eliot from other parts of the city, making it hard for parents—many of them immigrants and in demanding low-wage jobs with little flexibility—to spend much time there. The school's driving goal was to raise .test scores, but that mission was undercut by the prevailing ethos of hopelessness. One former teacher says, "We lost sight of our main goal of helping students live up to their potential, because we spent so much time focusing on test results." Teachers felt they had little chance to change the culture, because the school was run with a top-down, punitive management style that provided few opportunities for teachers to make suggestions or collaborate with colleagues.

Then in 2007, the Eliot's principal left midway through the year, and the acting superintendent offered the job to Griffith. "I want to give you a dollhouse, but it's broken inside," he told her of the historic school, the oldest continually running one in the city, which had educated some of the country's founding fathers. Griffith, a longtime BPS teacher but a new principal, was ecstatic. "Great. Where's the Eliot?" she asked. Griffith is always up for a challenge, but she was unprepared for what she found on her first day at the school. She had no orientation from the previous principal, no assistant principal, not even any pencils. It was April Fool's Day, but the lack of support was no prank. The sense of hopelessness that had been festering was palpable. Students felt that the adults had given up on them, and the high rate of teacher turnover supported that belief. On her first day, a student told Griffith that he was on his fourth teacher since the start of the school year. "There was no sense of team, of being in this together," Griffith recalls, shaking her head.

So in the thirteen weeks she had left in the school year, she made it her number one priority to build community, both inside and outside the school. She recruited new teachers and new families, convincing them that she could turn things around. Griffith is both passionate and pragmatic; when she talks, she leans forward and makes eye contact in a way that is down to earth but transmits her lofty vision. As one parent she convinced to send a child to Eliot her first year affectionately puts it, "She could sell snow in Alaska." Griffith leveraged the district's support to bring in a committed assistant principal, craft a new mission and vision, restructure the school day, and utilize new literacy and math resources designed for struggling schools like hers. But there was something else she wanted from the district, and when the new superintendent visited and asked what she needed, Griffith didn't hesitate: "I need a K1 classroom," she said.

Griffith's request for a K1 program seems surprising, given that she is a former middle school teacher and has no background in early childhood education. But she had been watching the K1 program get off the ground at the schools where she did her principal training. There, she had observed one of BPS's early childhood coaches working with teachers. "I got to see what a good early childhood classroom should be," she remembers, and what it took to build one and integrate it with the older classrooms. She was struck by similarities between the preschoolers and the preadolescents. "I saw both groups of kids trying to find their voices, self-regulate, and get ready for a big educational transition, albeit in different ways," she reflects.

Griffith also saw K1 as a strategy to support the relationship-building with children and families that she believed to be central to the school's turnaround. "In my prior schools, I had seen the connection that comes from having ten years with children—the kind of attachment that comes from being able to go back to the teacher who taught you how to zipper your jacket and the kind of impact that long-lasting adult relationships have for children. With full-day pre-K, you could create this amazing opportunity for children to learn how to be part of a larger community." Ten years later, Griffith believes K1 has done that at the Eliot.

But it took time to build the high-quality program she has today. Boston's pre-K program got off to a rocky start. In 2005, Boston's mayor and outgoing superintendent announced that they wanted the public schools to add preschool classrooms, and they did just that. To lead the program, they hired Jason Sachs, a Harvard-educated researcher who had been running an effort to improve the quality of the state's childcare programs. He had been visiting community-based programs across the state, observing them and helping them get better. But unlike many early childhood leaders, Sachs had never taught preschool. He identified himself (and still does) as a researcher. So one of the first things he did in his new job with BPS was commission a study of classroom quality to inform what he did moving forward.

The results of the study, which came out in 2006, were eye-opening. The report found that 75 percent of classrooms didn't have enough classroom materials, 25 percent of classrooms did not have a teacher's aide, 95 percent of classrooms did not consistently follow handwashing and other health guidelines, and the outdoor play space used by 47 percent of the early childhood classrooms was rated very dangerous. Furthermore, only between 18 and 30 percent of teachers met the "good" benchmark for support of language, literacy, and social and emotional skills. Only about a third of teachers used language with rich vocabulary, and half the teachers failed to be sensitive enough to student needs to recognize when children needed help or to provide age-appropriate activities.

Sachs knew he had to revamp the program if children were going to learn anything from it. Presenting the report to the school committee, Sachs told its members, "Congratulations, you did a great thing by funding pre-K, but you're not going to get to outcomes without quality," he recalls now. He was ready to jump in and improve quality, but he was appalled when the school committee agreed to share the results of the report with the *Boston Globe*. The newspaper published a front-page story about the dangerous and low-quality pre-K classrooms. "I could have lost my job," says Sachs, who had seen his prior job eliminated when political battles led to his program budget being cut. But it ended up working out in his favor. The school committee was praised for its transparency. Transparency would become a hallmark of Sachs's as well, with his staff, with his bosses, and with me.

Almost everyone who talks about Sachs's role in BPS describes him as a visionary. He is thoughtful, strategic, and ever-focused on creating structures that improve quality. His staff describe him as inspiring. He describes himself as "mission-driven," and considers his biggest achievement the creation of systems and structures that will "stand on their own" and outlast him. Frequently dressed in a hoodie and sneakers, he is down to earth and seemingly allergic to pretense. One community leader who has worked with him extensively and considers him a friend says, "He's brilliant. He pisses people off along the way, but we wouldn't have this [high-quality pre-K program] if it wasn't for him." At first glance, it's hard to see how Sachs could piss people off. He has an unassuming manner and a quick, dry sense of humor that he sometimes turns on himself. He usually lets his staff members lead their meetings and gives them the credit for his department's success, saying, "I hire people smarter than me and I get out of their way." It's a genuine sentiment—Sachs is not trained as an early childhood educator, after all—but a vast oversimplification. His role is to stay focused on the big picture, to think about whether each and every decision will lead to better outcomes for children. When he sees something that isn't good for kids, he doesn't beat around the bush, and that's probably where the part about pissing people off comes in. When he visited a model preschool program in New Jersey and spotted a weak teacher, he stunned an administrator when he bluntly asked what was going to be done to help her improve. "I can be offensive sometimes, but I don't mean to be," he told me a little sheepishly. "I just ask the hard but important questions."

Some of the hardest and most important questions came after the 2006 report was completed and made public. Sachs made a series of decisions that would completely redesign the program. "I knew in 2006 that we needed a curriculum for pre-K to third grade," he told me. Curricula are the backbone of quality, because they create consistency within and across classrooms. They give teachers a structure to follow and leaders a basis for training. They ensure that teachers address what children need to learn and have cues for how to do it well. "Curricula eliminate the randomness" sometimes found in early childhood classrooms, according to coach Abby Morales. But Sachs wasn't familiar with pre-K curricula, so he started by examining the literacy and math curricula the district was already using and said, "If it's good enough, let's get it in place and we'll modify it later." That's exactly what he and his staff did, using the programs and ultimately revising them to incorporate additional elements that teachers and staff felt were missing. He was fortunate that the district, which had tried out a few different curricula and thrown out one teachers disliked, had chosen well.

The curriculum BPS uses today is based on one that was in place when Sachs started, called Opening the World of Learning, or OWL. It is designed to develop children's skills in a stepping-stone fashion, building on one skill to develop the next. This is surprisingly rare in preschool curricula, which Sachs says tend to be organized around topical themes rather than skills. Sachs believes this is done for marketability rather than educational rationale, because the themes are logical and orderly for district administrators who buy curricula but don't know much about early childhood. (And there is evidence that curricula are sometimes chosen based on political connections and influence rather than educational value.) Many early childhood experts agree with Sachs about the importance of curricula for creating structure and consistency—although many also agree with Sachs and Morales that curricula should be used flexibly as "a tool, not a rule." Yet few early childhood curricula, even those that are most popular, have been shown to be effective in research studies. That's not the case in Boston, where both the literacy and math programs have been shown to lead to high-quality teaching and student learning. They have been so successful, in fact, that Sachs and his staff have gone on to develop and test new curricula for kindergarten and first grade, and second- and third-grade curricula are also planned. It's rare for early childhood departments to have enough influence to extend their practices up to later grades. But Boston's early childhood program isn't typical. Sachs attributes that to the years he has spent in the district, building and then proving the value of pre-K. His department has gained an enormous amount of respect and influence since the early days, as evidenced by its prime location at BPS headquarters, right next to the math department. "Traditionally, math and literacy [departments] owned everything," Sachs explains of Boston, but now "I sit in an academic office almost like an academic subject area."

Curriculum wasn't the only important decision that Sachs made in the early years of the program. He knew that programs are only as good as the people who implement them, and he recognized that great teachers are the linchpin of great classrooms. He had high expectations for the K1 teachers, requiring them to have graduate degrees and solid training. But he also had high standards for supporting and compensating them. They had to be paid the same as other teachers in the district, which was not common practice in other districts. (Today, the average early childhood teacher salary in BPS is around $70,000, light-years higher than the national average for preschool teachers.) "Teachers getting paid thirteen dollars an hour can't do this," he says, alluding to the notoriously low pay of most early childhood teachers, which drives problems with recruiting and retaining committed, knowledgeable staff. "If you want teachers to be reflective and constantly fine-tuning their practice, you need committed and well-compensated staff." One of his first priorities was finding those staff.

"I interviewed so many more people than I usually do" for the first K1 position at the Eliot, recalls Principal Traci Griffith. She, like Sachs, understood the importance of hiring the right teacher to get her K1 class off the ground. "We were looking for that right person—someone vibrant, passionate, with a strong connection to kids. We met some good people, but they would come in and do a demo class and they didn't have the relationship with the kids that we wanted to see." But when a colleague introduced her to Jodi (Doyle) Krous, she knew she had found the person she was looking for.

Before I met Krous, I had heard her described by BPS early childhood staff as an extraordinary teacher. When I first talked with her at a training session, I was struck by her unassuming and almost reserved manner, how she talked about her students and her teaching in an almost nonchalant way. But when I began visiting her classroom, I realized those were manifestations of her natural ease with children and her calm but engaged way of interacting with them. She bends down to their level or sits on the floor to talk with them (even when six months pregnant) without ever raising her voice, asks them for their suggestions but reminds them when it is time to listen rather than talk, and notices which children need extra support, inviting them to sit next to her when they are having a tough day or using sign language with a nonverbal child. (Hers is an inclusion classroom that integrates children who have special needs with general education peers.) When the children need to be redirected, she is firm but warm, and as she leads them to the rug with a group song, all it takes is her calmly uttering a child's name to refocus a straying student. She adores and respects the children in a genuine way, as they do her.

They are as likely to hug her as to share an idea for a new classroom activity, knowing they will find a receptive audience for either.

One day near the beginning of the year, I watched how effortlessly Krous wove together literacy, numeracy, and social skills. During morning meeting, she asked the class, "What do you notice about our circle this morning? Leah, you raised your hand and noticed something." When Leah pointed out that many people were missing, Krous cocked her head and said, "Where is everyone today? Lauren, can you help us count how many friends are here today? Then we'll talk about where everyone else is. Everyone help her count!" Together the class began to count, and when they got to the spot in the circle where Jeremy would normally sit, she asked, "Who usually sits here? Juh, juh, juh . . . Jeremy. He's at a doctor's appointment." When they finished counting, she reiterated that the total was nine and pointed on the wall next to her, a number line on which each number was represented on a separate index card, with both the numeral and the corresponding number of dots so that children could connect the numeral with the quantity. Next she led the children in a guessing game, using words they had learned the day before while reading the book *Corduroy*. "This is a body part and the overalls go on top . . . the straps of the overalls . . ." The children cried out: "Shoulders!" "Right! Can you touch your shoulders? Let's see who knows where shoulders are. Henry knows. Olivia knows." Next she moved on to the word "palace." "Was there really a palace in the book? There wasn't, you're right. But Corduroy thought something looked like a palace. Yes, Jessie, that's right, upstairs in the store."

All the activities I saw Krous lead went smoothly, but she laughingly told me that's not always the case. Krous is what Abby Morales would call a "relentless researcher of her classroom," constantly trying new things and then reflecting on what worked and what didn't, why some children responded to new strategies while others didn't, and what could help each child and the class as a whole. Teachers who approach children this way, as beautiful little puzzles to be solved, find ways to engage, challenge, and reach all children, even when those children need different things.

One of the things that sets Krous apart is how she encourages her students to be relentless researchers, too. During a curriculum component called Let's Find Out About It, I watched how she helped children come to their own understandings rather than telling them facts. "Yesterday we talked about materials you can make signs with. Today we're going to talk about . . . ," and she held up a book with traffic signs on the cover. "I noticed that yesterday the signs you made only had words. Some signs also have pictures. Sometimes you see the sign and you know right away what it means." She held up a stop sign picture and the children called out, "Stop!" Krous nodded. "I bet if you go to another country, I bet you would know a stop sign." She held up pictures of Chinese and French stop signs and asked the children what they meant. "How did you know? Right, the color. It's a hexagon, Cassie says. Let's count the sides of the stop sign . . . Oh, so it's not a hexagon. It's an octagon. Cassie, thanks for making us check. Let's look at some more signs." She showed "no bikes" and "no cows" signs and helped the children figure out how to decipher the meaning of a sign with a slash through it. Then she asked them to brainstorm traffic signs they could make for the block center.

"They are good thinkers," Krous told me, but it was clear from watching her that she had had a hand in that. She created the time and space and encouragement for the children to be reflective about what they were learning. It was striking to see how the environment she created for the children was similar to the one Sachs created for his staff. He models what he expects the coaches to do, who in turn model that for teachers, who then do it with kids. This kind of consistency across the levels of a school system is very beneficial, but that's not always recognized, in part because parents don't have the chance to see how teachers take what they learn in meetings and trainings and apply it in the classroom.

In December, I sat in the hallway outside Krous's classroom as she brought one child at a time out to create a portfolio of their work from the past three months. "This is a special box," she told each child, pulling out a clean pizza box, one of twenty donated by a pizzeria down the street that was the perfect size for storing art. "It's going to be like your treasure box, and we're going to keep all of your best, favorite work in it. You get to pick out the work you want to put in it. Let's lay out your work." As she laid out art pieces and writing, Krous asked thought-provoking questions like, "OK, why this one?" and "Do you remember what you learned from that?" and "Do you remember some parts that were hard, and some that were easy?" For each chosen piece, Krous transcribed the child's thoughts and paper-clipped the note to the corresponding work. At the end of the semester, she would sit down with each child's parents and show them the work in the box, explaining what the child had learned from it and how it reflected his or her development, from writing skills to creativity to independence.

This kind of thing would surprise many parents and even many teachers. Many people assume children can't do this kind of reflective thinking, or it simply doesn't occur to them that it might matter. But as I watched Krous go through the process with a little boy I'll call Henry, it was clear that the activity was both possible and valuable. Henry started by choosing a painting he had created during a center activity from the K1 curriculum called Painting to Music, during which children listen to music and paint what the music makes them think of. Henry pointed to a brightly colored painting with thoughtfully composed dots and lines, an arresting piece of art for a four-year-old. Krous asked him how he did it, going step by step. "So it sounds like it's kind of important that you did the flare pens first because otherwise you wouldn't have been able to paint this picture. How did you decide to do this picture? Do you remember?" "I was inspired by the Miró painting," he told her, referencing a unit they had been doing looking at art by famous painters. Henry's comment made his artwork seem even more impressive. It was clearly influenced by the famous painter but also clearly original. It was obvious he had gotten something from the painting, because he wasn't regurgitating it; he was reinterpreting it. And he was only four.

Krous planned to go through the portfolio process with each child, including those with learning disabilities. She resolved to take more pictures of one little girl's processes in the classroom, because she produced very little in the way of concrete products. Another teacher might have skipped over these children, figuring they simply couldn't do the portfolio exercise. But the relentless researcher found ways to include them and challenge them.

BPS staff told me that Krous has always been a gifted teacher, but that she has worked hard to get where she is today. From the beginning, she took extra courses and signed up for voluntary trainings. Even now, seven years into her teaching career and a mentor to others, she seeks professional development well beyond what is required by the school and the district. And she attributes much of her success to a key part of the BPS model: the support of an expert early childhood coach.

People sometimes make the mistake of thinking that good teachers are born, not made. In fact, even naturally talented teachers need time, experience, and continuing professional development to be great. Just as architects and doctors continue to train and improve throughout their careers, so should teachers. Although Jason Sachs placed a high priority on finding good teachers, he knew that even the best teachers need ongoing training and support. He also knew that typical teacher training, in the form of onetime workshops, doesn't work very well. A far more effective approach is pairing teachers with veteran educators (usually called coaches or master teachers) who regularly observe the teachers in their classrooms and provide advice about what they can do better.

Sachs's commitment to coaching comes from personal experience as well as from reading the research on its benefits. When he's not at work, he and his wife run a fencing school, where they coach young people in the skills and strategies of the sport. When he suits up, Sachs provides the same combination of high expectations and focused support that he does with the BPS staff. One night, I watched him give a first lesson to a young woman who had been regularly hanging around the school waiting for her brother. Sachs knew her well and had been trying to persuade her to try fencing. "She's an athlete. I know she could be great," he told me, but she had taken some convincing. As he walked her through some basic moves, he gently chided her for being timid and encouraged her to be bolder in aiming for his chest plate. They worked and worked, and he didn't let her off the hook until she got it right. At the end of the lesson, he shook her hand. "At our fencing club, we have our strongest people working with our weakest people, to get them up to speed. I watch them and I scaffold them," he had told me the first time I met him, "and we do the same in BPS."

Sachs is adamant about the value of the early childhood coaching, even for teachers who have been on the job for a while. "I have thirty-one years of experience teaching fencing, and my mentor still laughs at how I do it. That's OK. It takes time to get it right," he explained. That's why he has made coaching available to all K1 teachers, although not all at the same time. All new teachers get frequent coaching, and veteran teachers get coaching occasionally, when requested, or when they are going through an intensive process of getting accredited by a national early childhood education organization. Since 2006, Sachs has hired veteran early childhood educators who are great with teaching kids *and* adults. They need to know preschoolers in and out, but they also need to know how to work with teachers in ways that are helpful and positive. Relationships are the most important part of their jobs, because they are there to help teachers, not evaluate them.

Sachs remembers the first time he met Marina Boni, who is now a BPS coach for Jodi Krous, her Eliot colleagues, and a small group of other BPS teachers. (Coaches typically work with twelve to twenty teachers.) She was pretending to be a wolf, prowling among the preschoolers in the classroom where she taught in Cambridge for more than twenty years. The image is easy to picture: Boni being serious yet playful, fully committed to a vision shared by the children around her. Her engagement with her work is total and visceral, whether she's vigorously shaking her curly auburn head when she disagrees with Sachs or acknowledging a child's comment during morning meeting by pointing a thumb to her chest and a pinky to the child in a hand symbol that means "making a connection." The first thing you notice when you meet Boni is her energy. She speaks quickly and passionately, with her eyes fixed intently on you and her hands gesturing in the exuberant manner of her Italian heritage. She sits and stands with an erect but expectant posture, calling to mind a spring that is ready to uncoil. "Marina is a force of nature," sums up Griffith, one of many educators in Boston whom Sachs jokingly calls "Marina's disciples."

The next thing you notice about Boni is her deep respect for children. When she visits a classroom, she will crouch down to child height to ask a student, "What are you building?" And when he tells her it's a ramp, she will nod her head and with a serious voice that suggests this is the most fascinating thing she has ever heard, say, "A ramp. I see. What do you think will happen if you put a car on it?" When the child says, "It will go fast," Boni furrows her brow in concentration and reflects back—"It will go fast"—and then asks him a critical question that is at the root of many of her conversations with children and teachers alike: "How do you know?" That question gets students and teachers to stop and reflect, to think deeper and more critically. It conveys the importance of being intentional about what children are learning.

Boni grew up in Tuscany, which is adjacent to Italy's Emilia-Romagna region, home to the city of Reggio Emilia and the network of outstanding early childhood centers for which it is famous. But she wouldn't learn about the Reggio Emilia centers or their world-renowned approach to early childhood education until long after she had moved to the United

States and begun working as a preschool teacher. Boni came to the United States as a teenager, to attend an elite girls' boarding school in Virginia that had educated generations of her family since before her grandmother, the daughter of a historical New England family, married an Italian count. The boarding school was an immediate culture shock. "I had been a radical who occupied my school's administrative office and participated in protests. When I got to Virginia and saw these girls riding their horses, I thought, 'These people are really out to lunch,'" she recollects. She never came to fit the prep school mold. "I spent a lot of time outside the Safeway grocery store with petitions for social justice," she laughingly recalls. She continued her commitment to social justice at New York University, but she wasn't sure what she wanted to do after college. When a friend pointed out that she loved children and might want to try teaching, she began subbing at preschools in Cambridge, one of which became her second home. Boni had only been teaching a little more than a year when she heard about an exhibit that was coming to Boston called *The Hundred Languages of Children*, which documented the Reggio Emilia approach to early childhood education. When a colleague told her it was about an Italian approach to educating preschoolers, she was intrigued. And when she saw it, her teaching—and her students—were transformed forever.

Reggio Emilia, a small city in northern Italy, is an unlikely place for a revolution in early childhood education. In fact, it didn't start out as a revolution, but as a modest grassroots effort to help local children and parents. At the end of World War II, a group of parents and community members literally built the centers from the ground up, using the proceeds from the sale of a tank, some trucks, and some horses that the German army had left behind. The community's efforts were led by Loris Malaguzzi, a frustrated middle school teacher who had heard about a nearby village building a school for young children. Malaguzzi and the group of citizens worked at night and on weekends to build the school, using land donated by a farmer and construction materials from bombed-out houses. Eight schools were built, mostly in poor sections of town, the first of which was named "the school of the tank" in Italian.

As the centers grew, they became informed by developmental psychologists and education experts, who were increasingly focusing on the role the child plays in constructing his own learning. Those ideas found a receptive ear in Malaguzzi, who had left the state-run middle school where he taught, frustrated by what he later described as the school's emphasis on following orders, "prepackaged knowledge," and "stupid and intolerable indifference toward children." After spending some time in Rome to study psychology, Malaguzzi found that "a simple, liberating thought came to our aid, namely that things about children and for children are only learned from children." With this guiding principle, the schools came to focus on children as active learners, not simply the empty vessels waiting to be filled with knowledge that teachers had traditionally thought them to be. Malaguzzi and the Reggio teachers became intent on listening to children, paying attention to their interests and needs, and fostering their curiosity. They became guides and facilitators whose role was to help children become reflective, creative problem-solvers and thinkers.

Visitors to Reggio Emilia usually remark on the schools' beautiful, light-filled atmosphere and the freedom with which children move in and out of the classrooms and outdoor spaces. Reggio teachers put an extraordinary amount of thought into how they prepare the classrooms every day, organizing the materials, suggestions, and learning prompts—what they call "provocations"—in a way that invites children to explore, collaborate, and reflect. Children choose their activities and construct their learning, but teachers set the stage in a way that guides them to interesting pursuits. Although children do artistic and creative work throughout the centers, each center also has an atelier—a studio that provides a dedicated space for using artistic materials and being messy and creative—and an atelierista—a master educator who works with both students and teachers on artistic pursuits. That doesn't mean children are daydreaming and drawing hearts and flowers all day; the centers use the arts as a vehicle for critical thinking, reflection, discussion, and learning skills like literacy and science.

The most crucial role teachers play is in the questions they ask and the dialogue they facilitate with children about what they are learning, how, and why. They are constantly challenging children to look at things from new angles, try original ways of doing things, and reflect on why, with questions like Boni's "How do you know?" In those conversations, they use rich vocabulary and complex concepts about geometry, physics, art, and other topics. Children are never drilled on the alphabet or numbers; instead, they explore those concepts as they come up through rich, meaningful explorations. Malaguzzi explained that he was "convinced that it is not an imposition on children . . . to work with numbers, quantity, classification, dimensions, forms, measurement, transformation, orientation, conservation and change, or speed and space, because these explorations belong spontaneously to the everyday experiences of living, playing, negotiating, thinking, and speaking."

Reggio classrooms are also known for their extensive documentation of children's work. Teachers are continually collecting and displaying artifacts that illuminate children's thinking and learning processes. They might take photos of the stages of a project—say, children using blocks to build a city—and put them up on the wall, along with children's evolving sketches or plans of what the city will look like. They will typically include a brief written description of the children's process, including quotes and children's challenges and strategies. These are not finished products hung on the walls as decoration but raw works in progress intended to show the process of thinking and learning and to facilitate communication with parents, so that families understand not just what children are doing but why and what they are learning from it.

The kind of thoughtfulness and respect for children that are embedded in the Reggio Emilia approach resonated deeply with Boni when she saw the *Hundred Languages of Children* exhibit, which was named for a poem written by Malaguzzi. The poem describes the depths of children's thoughts and creativity as "a hundred languages" and "a hundred hundred hundred more," and then goes on to lament the way that schools and society force children to use only one "language" and learn without using their hands, hearts, imaginations, or joy. "And thus they tell the child / that the hundred is not there. / The child says: / No way. The hundred is there," the poem concludes.

Marina Boni had always known the hundred was there, always believed that "children can do anything," as she puts it. But she hadn't ever been able to articulate it as clearly as what she saw in the exhibit. The Reggio Emilia approach, born so close to her own place of birth, was a revelation. She was particularly struck by photographs of a project in which an atelierista had invited children to explore what they could do with many different kinds of paper. The project had unleashed extraordinary creativity, and Boni couldn't wait to try it in her own classroom. As soon as she got back to her school, she placed huge sheets of white paper on the floor and let children roll, jump, and walk on them. Then she led them to discuss how the paper felt and how different kinds of paper reacted to movement. She asked her children and their families to bring in any kinds of paper they could find and then they used it to create new projects every day. They wrapped everything in the room with toilet paper, made cardboard houses and tinfoil costumes, and built a huge indoor climbing structure. "From the paper, kids got a sense of freedom and opportunity," she remembers now. "A material they had only considered for drawing or painting could become a crown, or a shoe, or a house, or anything." The children were completely engaged. When asked how she managed the project, Boni laughed and said, "I have an extraordinarily high tolerance for chaos." But beneath the laughter lies a very serious intention: Boni didn't want her children to be orderly little robots; she wanted them to become fascinated with materials and media, to discover how to explore and create, and learn how to talk about their observations and experiments. In short, she wanted them to become learners.

For the next ten years, Boni experimented with Reggio-inspired projects in her classroom. Then in 2000, a friend and former school principal invited her to participate in a project called Making Learning Visible. The project, whose name was inspired by a common phrase among educators in Reggio Emilia—"by making learning visible, you make learning possible"—was a collaboration with leaders from Reggio Emilia and the Harvard Graduate School of Education. Through it, Boni and the other teachers received professional development and in-classroom coaching from the Harvard and Italian experts. One of the mentors asked Boni "a lot of questions about 'What are the students learning?' and 'Why are you doing it this way?'" She remembers that "I hadn't really been challenged to articulate my teaching in the way she was pushing me, except maybe in graduate school." One of the outcomes of those challenges was that Boni grew much more intentional about what and how she taught. Another was that she began to pass on that demand for articulation to her young students.

In the fall of 2001, Boni decided to deepen her understanding of the Reggio approach by "attaching herself" to one of the famous study tours that Reggio leaders organize for educators from around the world to learn about the approach. (She would later take Krous and a few other BPS teachers back to Reggio Emilia with her.) On the visit, she was particularly struck by a classroom in which small groups of children were doing observational paintings of cauliflowers. The table was arrayed with real heads of cauliflower in different positions, and the paper and paints were set up to encourage children to paint from specific perspectives. The teachers would ask the children to paint what they saw and then ask them to reflect on what they had painted, with questions like "How will someone looking at your painting know this is the stem?" and "How can you show this part of the cauliflower head?" The resulting paintings have stayed vivid in Boni's mind. "They were spectacular—like a professional artist." Boni also remembers watching three- and four-year-olds involved in studying the movement of the human body. On a long paper on the floor, children were drawing people in various states of movement. When one boy said his figure was jumping, the teacher asked him, "How will people know your figure is jumping?" He thought for a moment and responded, "Well, the knees bend when he jumps." The teacher kept going: "How will people know his knees bend?" At that point, the little boy crouched down with an eraser, and redrew the figure with knees at an angle from its feet. The teacher didn't lecture at him or judge his art; she engaged him in a conversation that expanded his thinking about the task—and about the nature of representation and even thought itself.

"In this country we don't think about questions and how we ask questions. How are people going to know? How are they going to understand what you are writing, what stories you are telling?" Boni muses, pointing out how helpful the questions can be for getting kids to explain their thinking—and in the process understand the process of thinking better themselves. "It's such a different way of thinking about children. In the U.S., I often hear teachers say, 'My kids can't do that.' You would never hear a teacher in Reggio say that. They believe kids can do anything." Then she added, "There is so much work we need to do to get people to really listen to what kids are saying."

One day, I observed Boni visiting with a teacher in East Boston who was new to the K1 program but not entirely new to teaching. Boni walked into the classroom like she had been part of it from day one—and, in fact, she had. In every one of the classrooms she visits, she knows the children's names, personalities, family situations, strengths, and challenges. She is quick to point out skills a child possesses that a teacher may have missed, and she is supportive and nonjudgmental when offering suggestions of how to help each one. On this day, she moved fluidly from helping children to consulting with the teacher to folding herself into a child-sized chair in order to take notes on her laptop. After morning meeting and centers, she sat with the teacher for a one-on-one while the children went outside for recess. She began with positive feedback and the teacher's progress on the goal they had set at their last meeting. Then she brought up the theme for the rest of the session: "How do you ask just enough that they use their cognition and develop careful thinking skills?" She pointed out times during centers when the teacher had tried to get children engaged by asking them questions but limited their thinking and conversation by asking yes or no questions. "How can you play your role so that you do less of the talking and they do more?" she asked. When the teacher introduced an activity of using eyedroppers to experiment with watercolor paints on tissue, the teacher had asked the children, "Do we need to soak the whole paper?" and the children had chorused "Nooooo." Instead, Boni suggested, "You could ask, 'I wonder what will happen if we put lots of paint on the paper?'" That kind of question, she explained, makes children think more and makes them more curious. It also makes them practice making predictions.

These shifts in language may seem subtle, but they are important. Research shows that the kinds of conversations adults have with young children make a big impact. Starting in the late 1980s, David Dickinson, Patton Tabors, and Catherine Snow conducted the Home-School Study of Language and Literacy Development to find out how teachers' and parents' interactions with young children influence language and literacy skills all the way through high school. They found that children develop more advanced literacy skills when the adults in their lives do three things: expose them to a broad and varied vocabulary, provide lots of stimulation in the form of books and conversation, and engage them in extended discourse—conversation that uses explanations, narratives, or pretend play to help children understand things outside of the immediate moment. When a teacher asks a question like Boni's "I wonder what will happen if . . . ," it invites children to engage in a dialogue and use more vocabulary. The Home-School Study suggests that these kinds of conversations are especially important for children who do not get much linguistic stimulation at home. Although parent-child talk is also critically important, children in the study who had little language support at home but lots at preschool did better than the group average, whereas children with the reverse combination did less well than their peers.

When you watch Boni working with teachers, it's easy to see the impact of good coaching—how it helps teachers step back and think about what they are doing and how they could do it better, how it energizes and inspires them. School districts are sometimes criticized by the public for spending money "outside the classroom," on infrastructure like coaching and support staff, probably because we don't have the chance to see their value at work. In many places, the kind of coaching used in Boston is seen as an impractical luxury, but it is actually the backbone of everything else.

Marina Boni is one of the reasons Traci Griffith decided her school needed a K1 program. Griffith had watched Boni work with teachers at the school where she did her principal training, and it had opened her eyes to the power of early childhood. After she had secured a K1 classroom, she specifically requested Boni to be the coach for Krous and, later, the school's other K1 teacher. She believes it has paid off. Griffith is one of many school leaders in Boston who thinks the K1 program has been key to building a learning-focused community and preparing children for kindergarten and beyond. After Griffith took the helm, the culture at the Eliot was transformed into one of curiosity, exploration, and joy. Achievement scores shot up, and students found themselves much more prepared for middle and high school.

But the rapid improvement at the Eliot came with a price. The school's success began attracting more middle- and upper-class families, which was a double-edged sword. On the one hand, it brought the neighborhood's support back to the school and increased the energy among the parent community. On the other, it quickly and radically changed the student body. The population Griffith and Krous had initially set out to serve began disappearing from the school. In 2007, the Eliot, which was underenrolled, served kids from diverse neighborhoods across the city, including some with the highest concentrations of poor and non-English-speaking families. But as the school's performance and reputation improved, more middle- and upper-class families from the school's neighborhood zone began to choose it, rather than opting for private schools or moving to the suburbs when their children reached school age. Griffith believes that those choices were reinforced by the economic downturn of 2008, with families concerned about their finances drawn by the savings of free pre-K and the opportunity to get in "on the ground floor" of a promising public school for the next ten years. And she admits that her own efforts have unintentionally played a role, as she recruited local families and community support in her first few years to bolster the school's enrollment.

As a result of all these factors, it has become virtually impossible to get a spot at the Eliot if you don't live in the geographic priority zone, and unlikely even if you do. Eliot's zone includes not just the North End and Maria Fenwick's neighborhood of Charlestown but some of the wealthiest parts of the city, including Beacon Hill, a charming neighborhood just behind the state house that is home to former Secretary of State John Kerry. At a recent Eliot tour, prospective parents were almost universally white, well-educated, well-dressed, and savvy about their educational options. The majority I talked to said they were also applying to private schools in case they didn't get into the Eliot. Jodi Krous told me stories of prospective parents attending tours and asking about their odds of getting in so that they could decide whether to put their condos on the market and begin looking for houses in the suburbs. She laughed, recalling how hard it was to fill her class when it first started. "My first year a lot of middle-class, educated parents were really nervous about four-year-olds in a public school, and in the Eliot in particular," she recalls.

The gentrification of high-performing urban schools is an uncomfortable reality for educators like Griffith and Krous, who are grateful for and even solicitous of neighborhood support but who also believe in equity. It can also be a conundrum for parents like Maria Fenwick, as they select schools for their children. And parents are having to face those decisions earlier and earlier, sometimes even before their children are out of diapers. Getting all children off on the right foot is an often-stated goal of pre-K, but in many ways, creating equity is as big a challenge as building quality. Some school districts intentionally try to build equity by cultivating socioeconomic diversity through lotteries or magnet schools, but they are rare. And a small minority of community-based programs manage to serve children from a broad range of backgrounds by accepting tuition-paying families while also reserving spots for children with government subsidies. But since those kinds of diverse settings are few and far between, a lot more schools will need to undergo an Eliot-like transformation for all children to get an excellent education.

Four

Doing the Math

"Write down your thoughts and feelings about math. The first things that come to mind," began Carolyn Christopher as she kicked off a training on using the Building Blocks math curriculum. Several of the Boston teachers in attendance groaned. "I hate math," they said, or "I always liked math, but I was never good at it." One teacher shared, "I was always the one crying in math class," while another quipped, "We're not good at math—that's why we became preschool teachers!" It was a joke, but one that contained more than a grain of truth. Research has found that many teachers feel uncomfortable with math, and the lack of confidence is most pronounced among teachers of the youngest students. While some people shrug this off, thinking that middle and high school math are the real concern, early math is foundational. Long-term math achievement is affected by the positive or negative messages children, especially girls, receive when they are very young. And in pre-K, children don't have separate teachers for math and other subjects, so their teachers have to be competent and confident if children are going to learn math well.

"It's so important for children to learn early that they can understand math," explained Connie Henry, BPS's elementary math program director, who was leading the training with Christopher. "I grew up thinking math was something you either got or you didn't, and now I know that isn't the case." Christopher nodded, sympathetic to the nervous teachers in front of her. Christopher, who has an unassuming manner and a sweet, youthful face that belies her years of teaching experience, had never dreamed she'd be standing here leading a math training. Then, ten years ago, she had attended a training very much like this one that was led by Doug Clements, one of the creators of the Building Blocks preschool math curriculum.

"When I first heard about Building Blocks, I wondered 'What *is* a math curriculum for four-year-olds?'" she recounted. "I thought, 'What are we going to do all year long?'" In the nearly ten years she had been teaching, her math instruction had been pretty much limited to basic counting and simple shapes. But when she began attending the Building Blocks trainings, she quickly realized there was far more math she could be doing with her preschoolers. In one early session, she and her colleagues spent a half hour discussing the definitions of shapes. Clements started the discussion by showing the teachers a handful of items and asking if they were triangles, including half a sandwich and a slice of pizza. The teachers thought the pizza slice was a no-brainer; in fact, Christopher and others had been teaching their children to recognize it as a triangle for years. They were shocked when Clements told them it wasn't, pointing out the rounded edge at the top of the slice that defied the rule of a triangle being a closed shape with three straight-lined sides and three angles. Christopher and her coteacher felt chastened by that conversation, realizing many of the things they had been teaching for years were incorrect. "We thought, 'OK, we have to go back to our classroom and do this the right way,'" she recalls.

Now she was helping other teachers do it the right way. Christopher replicated the triangle demonstration with a Building Blocks game called

"Is It or Is It Not?," which used flat plastic shapes of different types and dimensions. "Is this a triangle?" she asked, as she held up an archetypal triangle, with a point at the top. Teachers nodded confidently. Then she turned it ninety degrees and asked, "Is it still a triangle?" They nodded again. "Of course it is. Why?" "Because it has three sides," several teachers called out. Christopher said, "When I did this with my kids, they thought it was a triangle only when the point was facing up. That's because we typically teach them about shapes by just showing them and saying the name. It's good to know the name, but it's more important to know *why* a shape is what it is, to know 'Does this shape fit a certain set of attributes?'" Christopher held up one more three-sided object: an ice-cream-cone shape with a concave curve where the ice-cream scoop would go and asked if it was a triangle. Several teachers shook their heads. "A lot of kids have a really difficult time with this one. They insist it is a triangle, because they see three sides. But a triangle is a closed shape with three *straight* sides and three angles."

One teacher gestured at an octagon Christopher had in her hand and said, "My kids would probably insist that is a circle. Do you have kids who argue with you?" "Oh, yeah!" Christopher laughed. "In fact, I think this is the point—to get them to have a disagreement and a discussion." The goal, she implied, was that teachers shouldn't be drilling kids on facts but teaching them to understand why. "I've also had parents argue with me," Christopher went on. "They sometimes come in and say, 'Why did you teach my daughter that a square is a rectangle?' and I have to explain that it *is* a special type of rectangle," because they were taught in school that a rectangle looks like a shirt box and a square looks like a Saltine cracker.

"The language we use is really important," Christopher added, and she began to sing. "Twinkle, twinkle little star, how I wonder what you are." Then the familiar ditty took an unexpected twist: "Up above the world so high, like a rhombus in the sky," she sang. The teachers giggled and Christopher laughed along with them, explaining, "There's really no such shape as a diamond. I always made my students sing it with rhombus. My own kids at home do, too, even my three-year-old. It's important to teach them the correct words for things, so that they won't start off with any misconceptions."

It turns out that children harbor all kinds of misconceptions about math, and so do adults, largely because we were taught them incorrectly, or left to puzzle them out for ourselves in incomplete ways. But why does it matter if young children know why a rhombus is not a diamond and why a square is a special kind of rectangle? Research shows that children who have a strong foundation of math skills in the earliest years do better in math and even reading all the way throughout school: they feel more confident and excited about math, they take more challenging courses, and they have higher math ability. And children's math skills at kindergarten entry predict their math achievement through elementary and middle school. Boosting young children's math knowledge could have a big impact on their educational trajectories and on our society: on an international test that compares achievement of students all around the world (the Program for International Student Assessment, or PISA), the United States ranks an embarrassing fortieth out of seventy-two countries in math (among thirty-five industrialized countries, its rank is a dismal thirty-first). And scholars have been pointing out that we don't have enough college graduates in science, technology, engineering, and math (STEM) fields to fill all the job openings in related industries with domestic employees. With those long-term patterns in mind, it makes sense to start improving math education as early as possible.

Before you can teach young children math, you have to know how they learn it and make sense of it. Researchers like Doug Clements and his partner Julie Sarama have made big strides in understanding those processes. Traditional wisdom from child psychology was that young children weren't capable of developing math knowledge. Jean Piaget, one of the founders of child cognitive psychology, thought that children couldn't understand math until age six or seven, when they entered a stage he called concrete operations that is characterized by the development of logical reasoning. But although Piaget's contributions helped create useful frameworks for understanding cognitive development, it turns out that he vastly underestimated young children's capabilities. More recent research has found that preschoolers are capable of understanding counting and even more advanced concepts like addition and subtraction—if you ask the questions the right way. One study found that when experimenters showed three-, four-, and five-year-olds a puppet counting either correctly or incorrectly, the children were able to answer successfully when told, "It is your job to tell [the puppet] if it was OK to count the way he did or not." Children who saw the puppet skip an item, double count, or make another mistake were highly accurate at correcting him. Other studies have shown that, even before they know how to add and subtract, preschoolers can grasp the statistical probability of an event occurring based on watching previous trials. They can't necessarily articulate it the way an educated adult would, but they can place an object in the correct place depending on what they have seen the experimenter do. Even babies understand some mathematical concepts and physical properties well enough to be surprised if shown a video that defies the rules of gravity, number constancy, or addition. Researchers have used novel methods for measuring how very young children understand the world, for example by varying the way they ask questions about number sense (e.g., giving children choices rather than asking open-ended questions) and timing how long babies look at videos or objects (because they look longer at things that are surprising). Perhaps Piaget's limitations are not surprising, given that his primary research method was observing his own children, an approach that would never fly in today's scientific climate.

Unlike Piaget, Clements and Sarama have studied how large groups of children learn math. Using their results and others', they have mapped out what they call learning trajectories, the paths through which children learn specific mathematical concepts. A learning trajectory breaks down the steps children need to go through in order to master a concept like counting. Counting might seem like a simple activity, but Clements and Sarama have documented the many stages children go through to become proficient counters, from saying the numbers in order to attaining "one-to-one correspondence" or the ability to count one number for one object, to understanding cardinality, the fact that the last number in a series is the total number of the set. Cardinality is important; without it, children struggle with addition because they don't understand the concept of starting out with, say, six and adding four more. Instead, they always have to start counting at one. BPS staff have found that cardinality is a concept many children are missing, even in first grade.

The curriculum is made up of activities matched to each stage in the trajectories, so that teachers can help children build their skills and get to successively higher levels of thinking, ultimately mastering concepts like creating patterns and using data to solve problems. The activities are fun and engaging, mostly in the form of games, and connected to the real world. Parents and older students often lament the fact that their math instruction has been disconnected from everyday life. But the goal of Building Blocks is "finding the mathematics in, and developing mathematics from, children's activity." Clements talks about how teachers can "mathematize" their daily experiences in order to pique children's curiosity and answer questions in ways that are understandable. For example, when a teacher wants to demonstrate a math concept like giving each child two napkins, she might bring out a puppet named Mr. Mix-Up, who gets constantly confused and needs the children to correct him. When he gives a child four napkins, the children gleefully tell him that he has given them too many. The puppet capitalizes on children's love of silliness, and it also gives them an opportunity to demonstrate their competence and feel confident.

"OK, we're going to play a game called Snapshots," Christopher told the teachers. She took out a pretend camera made out of a manila folder with a plastic cup lid in the middle to look like a lens and a tab at the top to look like a flash. After she explained, "I'm going to take a snapshot with my camera," she quickly flipped the folder's cover down to reveal a paper with black dots on it and then closed the folder shut. The dots had been visible for just under a second. "How many dots did you see?" she asked. "Four!" several teachers called out. Then she switched the paper inside and repeated the activity, to which teachers shouted out, "Five!" "How do you know?" Christopher asked them. "I saw three on the top and two on the bottom," said one teacher. "I saw a compressed pentagon," explained another. The next snapshot was harder. Several teachers guessed twenty-one, while one thought twenty-seven. "How did you get your answer?" Christopher asked again. This time, the answers were all over the map. "I saw three groups of six and then added three at the end." "I saw it in twos: $2 + 2 + 2 + 1$ was 7 and I did that three times." "I thought I saw four sets of six plus three, but now I realize it was three sets," said the teacher who guessed twenty-seven.

"This is great," encouraged Henry. "You all saw it different ways. This is what we should do with children. We should have number talk and let different answers arrive, because you want kids to talk about their thinking—not just the answer they got, but how they got it."

Christopher nodded and then explained the purpose of the activity. "What you just did is called subitizing," she said. Subitizing is the ability to quickly recognize a number of objects or symbols without counting them. (The terminology comes from the Latin word for "suddenly.") Most of us subitize when we toss a pair of dice; you don't have to count the four dots that come up on each one, you just instantly recognize the fours, and you know that four and four is eight. Subitizing is a fundamental skill that allows us to manipulate numbers without counting them by hand. Without the ability to subitize, we wouldn't understand the meaning of the number "4," so we wouldn't be able to add it to the number "6" without going back and counting from 0. But subitizing is rarely taught explicitly, especially in preschool classrooms. In fact, Henry pointed out, textbooks often present math problems in ways that discourage subitizing, because they use pictures that are poorly configured or objects that are so complex they distract from the real learning task at hand. Simple black dots are better, she says. The Snapshot game allows children to practice subitizing and talking about their thinking. It also provides a much-appreciated opportunity for giggling.

The teachers at the training did their share of laughing, too, and they appeared to see the Snapshots as a fun and useful challenge. Roxbury Y teacher Meg Hackett was sold. "I'm going to try to do this during transitions," she said, as transition times were a big focus for her at the time. She thought she could use Snapshots to help kids focus when they came to the rug, for example. Those kinds of strategies had worked for Jodi Krous at the Eliot, who told me that children love the Snapshots and get good at them quickly.

As the training went on, Hackett and the other teachers learned about other fun activities to engage their children's mathematical thinking, including Number Pizzas, which had been popular in Krous's classroom on one of the days I went to visit. I had watched Krous explain the game ("I'm a chef and I'm making a pizza") and then tell the children she would ask each of them to take a break during center time to come play with her. With the first child, she set up a paper plate with a few red plastic chips and asked, "How many pepperonis do I have?" The child thought about it for a moment and answered correctly, "Three." When Krous followed up with "How do you know?" the little girl told her, "I counted three across, like this: one, two, three," touching each pepperoni with a finger. When Krous repeated the exercise with two pepperonis, the girl told her she didn't need to count with her finger because she "just knew." "Right, sometimes we just know. Because you see two things a lot, so you recognize it. When we play again, I want you to think about whether you need to touch the pepperonis or whether you can just see the number."

After this subitizing exercise, Krous went on to the next step and asked, "Can you make your pizza have the same number of pepperonis as mine? Can you make it match?" It's harder for children to produce a set of the correct number than to count an existing set of objects. When the little girl struggled, Krous created a pizza for her, with three pepperonis. But this time, the three red chips were configured differently, with one on top and two underneath. "Do they have the *same* number of pepperonis?" Krous asked, working on the concepts of same and different. The little girl shook her head no. Krous didn't tell her whether she was right or wrong; instead, she said, "Let's count," and as she touched each pepperoni she and the little girl counted, "One, two, three." The student looked surprised. "Yes, they are the same! They match. Sometimes, we can have the *same* number even if they are organized in a *different* way," Krous explained.

Games like this one provide openings for conversation about concepts that are often missed in early math instruction. For example, Building Blocks always uses zero in its number lines and activities, even in the Snapshots, because children often struggle with the concept of zero. "The kids *love* it when you do a Snapshot with zero dots inside," Christopher advised the teachers she was training.

A few of the teachers at the training had tried out some of the Building Blocks activities in their classrooms. They and veteran BPS teachers always told me that they really like the curriculum. But they had realized that teaching math requires more than just following a book of activities; it requires a lot of reflection and tweaking. "I have found that my kids can subitize, but they can't recognize the number when it's written down," a teacher at the training said. "So when we did the pizza plates, we also had children put clothespins with the numbers written on them on the finished pizza, so we could reinforce what the number looks like." Other teachers pointed out how the skills could be built even outside of the math games. "I hear my kids using the [mathematical] language in centers," one teacher said. "At the salon in dramatic play, they have started saying things like 'I have *more* rollers than you' or 'That costs *less* money.'" Christopher nodded and said, "Keep that in mind. Even if you are in dramatic play and you see an opportunity—like picking out patterns in dress-up clothes or practicing one-to-one correspondence in counting out plates." A lightbulb seemed to go on for several of the teachers. One staff member from the Roxbury Y cocked her head and said, "So we don't have to say, 'OK, now we're going to sit down and do math.' We can incorporate it into the day." That was exactly the kind of thinking Christopher and Henry were aiming for.

This is not the way math is traditionally taught in pre-K classrooms. It is not uncommon for pre-K classrooms to limit math concepts to a daily counting routine and having number posters around the room or numbered spots on the floor where children line up. But although those activities may teach children to recognize which numeral is which, they do little to teach them how to use math or to convince them that math is interesting and fun. When you see young children coloring in shapes on a worksheet or reciting addition tables, it's easy to see why so many children tune out math so early. On the other hand, when you see children learning math the way Christopher and her colleagues teach it, it's hard to see how any child could *not* find math to be fun. Teaching math in this intentional and integrated way doesn't necessarily come naturally, Christopher warns. For her, it was a process that took time. Now, she says, "I can't *not* talk about math every day, even at home with my own kids. Sometimes my husband rolls his eyes and suggests I lay off a little, but I can't! Besides, it's fun." And that kind of fun is not an extra benefit, it's actually the key to learning.

By January, the Roxbury Y's Young Achievers classroom was stable enough that Meg Hackett was incorporating some of the Building Blocks activities she had learned during the trainings. Ayannah Hilton's son, Jeremiah, and one of his friends ran over to a desk near the classroom entrance, eager to see what was in a glass jar. Together, they counted five colorful plastic toys and then grabbed two Post-it notes Hackett had left out for them to represent the number they saw, either by writing the numeral or drawing the corresponding number of dots. Jeremiah made a convincing "5," while his classmate drew more of a squiggle. But they were both engaging with the number activity. "It took a little while for them to get it," Hackett told me, but the children's enjoyment and accuracy were striking, given where they had been just a few months before.

Jason Sachs believes that the curriculum has been key to the children's engagement—and the parents'. When he first started working with the community-based programs, he and his staff noticed that parents would drop children off whenever it was convenient for them in the morning, making it hard for teachers to create continuity or engage children in activities. But once they saw that teachers were following a routine and that their children were learning from the activities, parents began making an effort to get their kids there during the suggested drop-off window. That meant more children were present for morning meeting and understood the expectations for what to do there.

One day during morning meeting, Hackett pointed to a flipchart with the lyrics for a song the class had been learning that incorporated counting and subtraction. The children knew the song and they loudly sang out the numbers as Hackett pointed to them: "Five little birdies, watching others soar. One flew away, then there were four. Four little birdies sitting in a tree. One flew away, now there were three." They subtracted one bird at a time until the last line said, "One flew away, then there were none." The song simultaneously taught children vocabulary—Ayannah Hilton's primary goal for her son—and counting, which Hilton hadn't gotten to yet at home.

Math also played a big role at centers. At one of the centers, Washington was sitting with two children who were sorting small plastic monkeys that could link their arms together to make a chain. One child was sorting them into piles by color (categorizing is an important early math skill), while another created a repeating pattern, and cried, "Look, Ms. K! I made a pattern—yellow-yellow-green; yellow-yellow-green!" At another center, a little boy matched plastic shapes onto a board with a complicated mosaic pattern and named them: "Triangle, hexagon, trapezoid."

Washington challenged him to think further: "When you put a trapezoid and a triangle together, what does that make?" He arranged the pieces and then cried, "A bigger triangle!"

What was most striking was how involved the children were in what they were doing. Hackett knew that whole-group instruction wouldn't engage her young students (they could barely sit through a story) and wasn't the best way for them to learn, anyway. Because she was still struggling with classroom management, she was finding it difficult to do the small group activities suggested in the Building Blocks curriculum, so she started incorporating them into centers. The strategy seemed to be working. Hackett's children were happily and busily, if noisily, doing their center activities, even though they continued to act out during other times like recess and transitions to and from morning meeting.

But the classroom social climate wasn't fully transformed. Hackett couldn't be available for every child or every conflict every minute, especially because there weren't as many teachers in the classroom as she, her supervisors, and coaches had hoped. Since the summer, the Y had been planning to hire an assistant teacher for the Young Achievers classroom. Washington was frequently called away from the classroom to cover other classes when those teachers were absent. And she came in late a couple of days per week, because she had an early-morning college class to attend. Staffing got even tougher when Hackett had to miss work for a number of emergencies, including a minor car accident, a critically ill pet, and a health issue. By Christmastime, the Y still had not been able to hire the third teacher they were looking for. That meant the daily schedule for teachers was unrelenting. Hackett and Washington had few breaks during their workdays. Hackett not only skipped most of her lunch hours, but she didn't even have time for planning, which was supposed to occur during naptime but rarely did, because the teachers were busy helping children fall asleep or stay occupied and quiet when they didn't. That isn't uncommon, especially in classrooms like those at the Y that are understaffed.

Marcy Whitebook is the director of the Center for the Study of Child Care Employment and has spent decades researching the early childcare workforce. When she began looking at working conditions in early childhood programs, she found that programs with the lowest teacher salaries also had the worst working environments—a double whammy for teachers. Unlike in public schools, where teachers are usually unionized, most community-based early childhood teachers have no planning or professional development time and no paid vacation or sick time. (When Hackett met public school K1 teachers, who are unionized, she was envious that they had lunch and an hour of planning time, and their day still ended at 2:30, while she was regularly working ten-hour days and was expected to do her planning after those long days and on the weekends.) Whitebook concluded that early childhood education suffers from "a sort of vicious circle": to give teachers release time, programs need more staff, but to attract staff, they need to provide better benefits, compensation, and working conditions.

Given the working conditions, it's not surprising that recruiting teachers is a major challenge for early childhood programs, especially to serve high-needs children. And several directors told me it has become much harder to hire staff since the growth of school-based pre-K, where teachers are paid more and have more support. In order to comply with state-mandated staff–student ratios (usually 1:10 or 1:11), teachers often float from one classroom to another depending on how many kids are there each day. In some centers, administrators move children around instead of teachers. In one center I visited repeatedly, it was common for half a dozen children from an adjacent classroom to come into the K1 partnership classroom halfway during morning meeting, because they had arrived late to their classroom and pushed it over the required teacher–student ratio. Both scenarios create inconsistency and confusion for children and for teachers trying to do a curriculum, or even create predictable relationships and routines.

Hackett's supervisors finally found an assistant teacher in January, but in the meantime, Hackett and Washington felt limited in what they could do. They often lacked the staffing to break students into the small groups suggested in the curriculum. On many days, they couldn't devote the one-on-one attention students needed to bolster their social and emotional skills. "I love the curriculum, but in reality, I could implement maybe 40 percent of it on a good day," Hackett reported, because of a lack of both planning time and providing extra support for the children's emotional needs. Even though she was coming in on weekends and working sixty-hour weeks, Hackett felt she wasn't able to do enough for the children. It was particularly unfair for kids like Jeremiah, who were ready and eager to learn more, she felt. "He deserves a classroom where teachers have time to plan. He's the one these [curriculum] programs are built for. He has that special spark and he wants to do it. But if he's not given what he needs to thrive, he could fall through the cracks." She thought about what Jeremiah was learning versus what her boyfriend's son was learning in K1 at a BPS school using the very same curriculum. She would ask her stepson-to-be what books he was reading and activities he was doing at school, and she saw that his teacher was far ahead of where she was with her students.

Hackett also felt that administrative policies and regulations got in the way of doing what she felt was best for children. The children often came to school hungry or with unhealthy but convenient foods that their stressed parents were able to procure cheaply and quickly, and they complained constantly of hunger. Hackett began providing extra snacks, on her own dime, because "I can't teach them if they're hungry." But she got repeated warnings from her supervisors to stop because she was going against state regulations that children should not eat more frequently than every three hours. (She continued doing it anyway.) In another situation, after months of trying to build relationships with busy and untrusting parents, a child's guardian asked Hackett to accompany her on a developmental evaluation for the child, who she and Hackett suspected had ADHD. Hackett believed the meeting had the potential to launch a breakthrough and was happy to oblige, delighted that she could provide moral support to the family and insight about the child to the clinician. But without the ability to cover the classroom in her absence, supervisors repeatedly turned down Hackett's request, even when she requested to use her own vacation time to do it. They rationalized that the classroom now had a half-time family liaison. But the liaison was new to the classroom and the child's family didn't invite her, because they didn't have the trust or history with her that they did with Hackett. Administrators were trying to keep the center running smoothly, and they pointed out that although this child needed support, the other sixteen children needed her at the same time. It's a conundrum many parents have experienced when their children have competing needs in the same moment, but on a magnified scale. Marcy Whitebook told me, "Directors have the most caught-between-a-rock-and-a-hard-place job in the world. You have all these financial and legal obligations. They don't have the time to be the pedagogical leaders they should be."

Hackett, who adored her students and was working as hard as she could for them, felt demoralized. Her relationships with her supervisors became increasingly tense. Her superiors began to worry that Hackett's lack of classroom experience had made her a poor fit for such a high-needs classroom. She felt that they weren't backing her up. She texted photos of her successful classroom projects to her BPS coaches but didn't reach out to Y staff. She was starting to feel burned out. Having fallen in love with the children, she was taking their stresses home with her and adding them to her own. She started taking anxiety medication because she couldn't sleep at night.

Levels of stress and depression are high among early childhood educators; for example, in a 2012 study, almost a quarter of Head Start teachers surveyed reported depression significant enough to warrant a clinical diagnosis. Teachers' jobs are undeniably taxing, but it's impossible to know if their mental health issues are related to their jobs or to other life circumstances. Many teachers in programs that serve low-income children come from backgrounds and communities like the ones they serve. That is a positive thing in many respects. For one, it allows teachers, children, and parents to relate to one another. But it also means that many of the teachers suffer from the same kind of trauma, chronic financial stress, and health issues as the families they serve. These stresses and mental health problems not only burden the teachers themselves, but they also impact students. Studies have shown that depressed early childhood teachers tend to have less warm and sensitive interactions with children, mirroring decades of studies on the impact of mothers' depression on young children. Of course, many teachers are energized by their work and, in all kinds of settings and communities, many find their work incredibly rewarding. But spending one's days with fifteen or twenty preschoolers is draining even under the best of circumstances. Those who think of preschool teachers as "just babysitters" might be disabused of that notion after spending one day with a roomful of energetic, curious, and complicated three- and four-year-olds.

Despite her stress, Hackett was making a difference. One day in January, I saw two boys who had pushed and hit each other earlier in the year curled up next to each other in "the cube," a comfy spot inside a large wooden cubby they could use to calm down or simply hang out. I also heard a child go from yelling and grabbing art supplies to telling a classmate, "I'm not done with that. Give it back, please. You can have a turn when I'm done."

Ayannah Hilton was pleased with what Jeremiah was learning. "He's not reading yet," she told me with an apologetic wince, but "he loves books and he tries. He'll ask me what a word says. And he tells me stories about what he reads, like, 'My friend and I were hanging out and we read a story about dinosaurs.'" That was a big difference from the way Jeremiah had talked before he started school. Hackett saw the difference, too. Jeremiah was gobbling up all the information she shared, and she was finding it hard to keep up with him, so she would send him home with extra projects. She would rip pages out of her curriculum book and give them to him because she didn't have time to make copies. She would write down a ten-word story and ask him to draw a picture of it so she could see if he was understanding some of the words, or request that he write down a question about a book they were reading. "He's able to explain stuff more, and he uses more details," his mother reported. "He's picked up a lot from being there." She also said that he had become "more aware of stuff," pointing things out on signs and in the neighborhood. "I'm like, 'How do you know that?'" She laughed. Another parent told me her son was "absolutely learning more. He's using vocabulary skills that are enhanced tremendously. He has learned to write his name and is learning how to put words in sentences. We had been doing some of that stuff at home, but he's really on it now." She also told me that Hackett had "added a lot of value . . . I feel like she does more with the kids, like taking them to the grocery store and stuff that will help them function in society. She hangs a lot of their work on the walls. It wasn't like that before."

It seemed like a different classroom than it had been in October. And Hackett seemed like a different teacher, more confident and competent, but also more tired and frustrated.

Five

The Luck of the Draw

Across Boston, early childhood centers were embarking on the same quest for quality improvement, but the journey started in different places for each of them. Overseeing the effort, Jason Sachs was aiming for consistency, because his goal was to expand access to the district's proven program, especially for families like the Hiltons, who needed a ten-hour school day. But consistently high quality would take time to build, because the centers started with different degrees of experience, resources, and knowledge. As a result, the pace of change varied. Some centers like the Roxbury Y saw slow but steady improvement, while others made rapid transformations. Initially, administrators weren't sure which programs were going to make the swiftest progress, and parents certainly weren't either. In most cases, parents weren't aware of the BPS partnership until after the school year started, if at all. That meant the chances of their children getting a great pre-K experience were largely up to an unreliable ally: luck.

Luck was something Folashade Coker knew about. She had won a visa lottery in her native Nigeria and immigrated to the United States when she was seven months pregnant with twins. When she arrived in Boston, she needed to find childcare for her older son, who was then a toddler. A neighbor recommended Nurtury, an early childhood agency with half a dozen centers that was started in Boston more than a century ago. (Before changing its name in 2014, Nurtury was known as Associated Early Care and Education.) She was fortunate to get a spot at a Nurtury center near her apartment and felt satisfied with the care her son received. But when the twins were six months old and Coker needed to start a new job, the center didn't have two infant spots available. (This is a common problem among families with twins, especially in infancy, because centers are required to have smaller staff–child ratios for babies, so there are fewer spots to begin with.) The only place she could find spots for both of them was at Nurtury's Tremont Street location. Tremont Street is located at the crossroads of several neighborhoods, including Chinatown and Roxbury as well as the affluent South End and Back Bay, but it is seven miles away from Coker's neighborhood of Hyde Park—a drive that in Boston traffic is a half hour in the best-case scenario. For years, Coker dropped off her children at two different centers before going to her job in the transport department at a Boston hospital. For a single mother with a nearly full-time job but no benefits, it was a big effort.

That made Coker even more disappointed to find that the quality of her children's classroom experiences varied markedly, not just across the two centers but even within the same one. When the twins, Roqeeb and Roqeeba, were three, they were randomly placed in different classrooms at Tremont Street, and their experiences were like night and day. "Roqeeb was playing with sand or toys, and Roqeeba would be reading, writing, doing circle," Coker told me. "And at home, I saw that she was really interested in reading or drawing . . . With Roqeeb, I had to show him everything, letters and everything." She complained repeatedly to the director, telling her that she was afraid Roqeeb wasn't learning enough and wouldn't be ready for school. Her older son had started attending a highly rated suburban elementary school through METCO, a grant-funded busing program that gives families school options outside of the city. The program requires an application and interview, and Coker was already thinking ahead to the twins' interviews. Getting in would require both strong applications and luck, because there is a lot of competition for spots. Some families put their children on the waiting list when they are newborns, even before they have left the hospital.

But as luck would have it, shortly before the twins' fourth year, the center they were attending was selected to implement the BPS K1 partnership in one classroom, led by teacher Herminia Santiago. Roqeeb and Roqeeba were both placed in Santiago's class. (Coker thinks her frequent requests and advocacy with the director may have been a factor.) "I was so happy when they told me [both kids] would be in the K1 classroom," Coker remembered. Santiago had been Roqeeba's teacher the year before, so Coker was hopeful that it would be a good year for both kids. Within a few months, she was delighted to discover that the classroom exceeded all her expectations. "It is so different this year," she told me. Roqeeb came home and talked about how his class went on frequent field trips and wrote about what they saw, planted things in the classroom and used scientific vocabulary to describe them, and read all the time. Even Roqeeba seemed more excited to go to school and came home with new stories and knowledge every day.

When I met Santiago at the first K1 training, she seemed a little reluctant about the program; she had previously been trained on OWL, the curriculum on which the BPS curriculum is based, so she didn't expect the program to add much to her teaching. But when I saw her again in the spring, surrounded by her students and their vibrant classroom, she had become a big advocate of the BPS program. The revised curriculum and especially the coaching had completely changed her teaching, she felt. "There is so much more to it than I realized," she said. She was getting through to the kids better, and they were doing thoughtful, creative work that she had never realized they were capable of. Most notable was how much more she looked forward to coming to work. "I absolutely love teaching this way," she told me, explaining that it was more interesting for her, as well as the children, than what she had been doing before. Santiago's joy was obvious. I could see it when she giggled while helping the children chop vegetables to make soup, when a boy told her about his lost tooth and she exclaimed, "No, sir!" and suggested they write a book about it, and when she read to the children, quietly but intently pointing out details and asking questions.

Santiago and her colleagues constantly encouraged the kids to be thoughtful and reflective. One morning I observed the class doing a part of the K1 curriculum called Thinking and Feedback, a process designed to help children notice and critique their own and others' work. Cliff Kwong, an assistant teacher, facilitated a discussion about one of Roqeeba's drawings. "OK, all you great listeners. Raise your hands to tell me: what is the first step of Thinking and Feedback?" he started, and then proceeded to have the children remind him of all the steps in the process. When it was time for the first step—"noticing"—the class of nearly twenty boisterous children went silent and stared with respectful wonder at Roqeeba's picture of an outdoor scene. Kwong coached Roqeeba in how to call on three quiet classmates to share what they observed in her work. "I noticed she made a tree, and her name, and, um, a blue tent?" a child offered. "Right, that's my brother's tent." Roqeeba nodded. During the "listening" step, the children remained quiet as Roqeeba described her process: "I made my tent and Roqeeb's tent and my big brother's tent. And I made when it is nighttime. And I made a tree and I put the light on in my tent. And I put my name. And I did these black zippers." Kwong followed up: "Those are zippers? Very detailed. I like that. OK, what's the next step? Wondering! Wondering is when you have a question. Who has a question about Roqeeba's image?" As classmates offered questions, Roqeeba was glad to share her technique. "I just did a line and colored in with black to show it is night." In the final step—"inspiring"—Roqeeba took suggestions from her peers of what she could do next. "But what could I *add*?" she asked, hungry for more feedback. At the end of the five-minute discussion, the children clapped and genuinely told her "That was a great job!" and "Thanks for sharing."

Coach Marina Boni had a big hand in creating the Thinking and Feedback process. "When I came to BPS, some teachers were saying, 'These kids aren't ready for this kind of thinking,'" she says, referring to the low-income children of color who make up the majority of the BPS population (and Nurtury classrooms). "And I said, 'Wait a minute, you're telling me our kids can't learn how to think and be reflective?' I didn't buy it." Kwong and Santiago clearly didn't buy it either. In their classroom and others across the city, it was obvious that children can be creative thinkers and astute learners.

Folashade Coker immediately noticed the difference in the classroom and in her children from the year before, and she was thrilled. Roqeeb and Roqeeba both knew how to write their names and hers, and when I visited, they recognized words like "pond" and "duck" that they had discussed on a recent field trip to the Boston Public Garden and that Santiago had placed on the wall with photos from the garden. They were also working on drawing and writing stories. But most striking was the creativity and curiosity they were showing. One day during centers, Roqeeba approached me with a tower of Unifix cubes (half-inch colorful blocks that stack). "Look, two rainbows!" She smiled. I looked down to see the colors of the rainbow stacked in the correct order from bottom to top, with another rainbow spectrum on top of it. "How many cubes are there?" I asked her. She began to sing a song with the colors of the rainbow, counting off on her fingers as she said each color, and then sang it through again. "It's twelve," she told me correctly. "Oh! And how many are in each rainbow?" I asked. Kwong helped her break the tower into two separate stacks and together they counted each one. Then he asked her, "OK, and now what is six plus six?" and she happily told him it was twelve. "I'm going to ask you that again at the end of the day!" he playfully warned her.

It was the very model of a teachable moment, and it seemed to come naturally to Kwong. But he had no background in teaching or early childhood before starting work at Nurtury in August. He had attended the center as a child—one who initially spoke little English—and applied for the job because he wanted to give back to his community and to an institution that had helped shape him. Over the course of the year, the BPS training had an enormous influence on the way he interacted with and taught the children. It also gave him and the other teachers a base to create a consistent, seamless approach, regardless of who was working with the children at any given moment. Watching the three teachers work together, it was clear that they saw themselves as a team and trusted each other. Like a well-choreographed dance trio, each teacher knew when to step in and where, each with his or her own personality but all using the same calm, engaged approach. One of the reasons the teachers at Tremont Street can do that is the consistency of their staffing. Santiago and her two coteachers (one of whom comes in early and the other of whom stays late, in order to cover the ten-hour day) were a steady presence in the classroom. "When they asked me to do this [K1 curriculum]," Santiago explained to me, "I told them I had to have two things: consistency and stability [of staff]. Those are the magic words, consistency and stability."

Before Roqeeba skipped away, she put her tower back together and looked through it as if it were a telescope, turning to me and saying, "Look, you can see a rainbow." When I bent down and asked her how, she instructed me to close one eye and look through the bottom of the tower with the other eye. It was like peering into a vibrant rainbow-colored tunnel, and it almost took my breath away. "How did you know that?" I asked her, to which she smiled and replied, "I just looked in and figured it out. It's like a slide. Like a rainbow slide." It was an apt metaphor. Roqeeba's day was full of play and joy and learning. Her mother was hopeful that would make Roqeeba and her brother ready for kindergarten, but getting there was the next step. For now, she felt grateful, and lucky.

When it came to selecting a pre-K program, Maria Fenwick had more choices than Coker, as do many middle-class two-parent families, but she would still need some good luck to get her son, Luca, the spot she wanted. Before entering Luca in the lottery for a seat in a BPS school, she visited several schools and saw definite differences. The Eliot had been just the first stop on her school tours. Needing backup choices, she visited her neighborhood's two other elementary schools, equipped with a list of questions like how much outside time students would get, how flexible teachers were about following children's interests, and how much opportunity there was for teachers to help administrators make decisions (a sign of a collaborative and progressive school). First, she visited a school that had a good reputation among families in her neighborhood, expecting to be impressed. But she was disappointed by the school's lack of creativity. "On the walls, I saw the same holiday crafts I did as a child, and every child had done them the exact same way," she reported. She was hoping that Luca's school would push him to explore new things and create projects neither she nor he had yet imagined. As she talked to teachers, she got the impression that the school "rested on its laurels" and missed opportunities to push its students to be curious and learn in meaningful ways. And she was concerned that most of the students she saw looked like her: middle-class and white.

The second school was more diverse, serving mostly children of color and low-income children, including many from a nearby housing project. The school's test scores were lower, and so was its popularity among middle-class parents. Some neighborhood parents told me they were concerned about the "lack of parental involvement" there, which is often code for fears about students and families being culturally different or less affluent, whether the parents are conscious of that bias or not. Fenwick could see through the bias and had an open mind when she went to visit. Unlike her neighbors, she wasn't very concerned about the test scores or even the imposing look of the fortress-like brick building.

When Fenwick showed up for her scheduled tour, the secretary was surprised to see her. The appointment had fallen off the school's radar, because so few families came to visit. But the principal greeted Fenwick warmly, and during their one-on-one tour, his dedication to the school and the students was obvious. He greeted each child he saw by name and answered every one of Fenwick's questions, talking in detail about the school's curriculum and instruction. As she toured the classrooms, Fenwick loved the diversity of the student body (the school's children are 84 percent low income and only 9 percent white, with fairly equal proportions of African American, Hispanic, and Asian students) and liked the way teachers were working with students. By the time she left, she thought the school might be poised for a significant transformation. "In a few years, this could be the next Eliot," she told me hopefully. Cautiously optimistic about the school, she decided to rank it second. The previous school didn't make it onto her list. From K1 to the later grades, the school just didn't have the kind of energy and engagement she was looking for.

Fenwick's judgments about the two schools were tapping into a distinction that researchers make between the "structural quality" and "process quality" of early childhood classrooms. Structural features, like staff–child ratio, physical environment, and nutrition are the easiest characteristics of quality to observe and measure, but they are actually not very good at predicting children's outcomes. More important are the interactions or processes in a classroom, like whether adults talk to children in supportive, nurturing ways; provide high-quality instruction; and keep the classroom running smoothly. Structural quality can help set the stage for process quality, but it doesn't guarantee it. That distinction isn't on the radar for many parents, and Fenwick believed many of her friends and neighbors were failing to grasp what matters most about schools. Several acquaintances came to her for advice, but few made the same school choices she did. When other parents kept reacting with surprise to her choices, she started to second-guess herself. And she found herself constantly wondering about a key question: What elements of a pre-K program really matter? What if Luca felt intimidated by the huge, dark building? Would he miss the kinds of projects he did at his private preschool, like visiting the beautifully appointed art studio and making mud houses for tiger slugs in the school's "outdoor classroom"?

It was inevitable that she would compare the public schools to the private program Luca was currently attending. Charlestown Nursery School (CNS) is well-known in Boston, and when you walk in, it's easy to see why. The space is gorgeous, the materials are first-rate, and the children are happily engaged in activities that made me want to relinquish all the privileges of adulthood and go back to preschool. CNS follows a Reggio Emilia approach. There are no alphabet rugs or wall calendars; instead there are mirrors, canopies made of rice paper, and photographs of children and their work, all annotated with teacher notes about the children's learning processes, typed and printed in the same gray sans serif font that CNS's director had selected, based on research showing which font is easiest on the eyes and the mind. CNS takes intentionality to a level that might surprise even BPS's Abby Morales.

That kind of intentionality was what had appealed to Fenwick when she stumbled on an open house when she was taking a walk with then three-month-old Luca. Fenwick, who had spent time living in Italy and studying Reggio Emilia preschools while in college, saw the beautiful classrooms, adoring staff, and photographs of sophisticated projects that teachers created based on children's interests, and she raced home to tell her husband, "We have to go there!" She placed Luca on a waiting list almost a year in advance of his eligibility age. When he turned two, he began attending part-time in accordance with the school's model: two half days per week at age two and three half days at age three. (CNS is an educational program; it is not a childcare option. Most of its students have either a stay-at-home parent or a nanny.)

At CNS, children get a lot of individual attention, and Fenwick knew that might not be the case in public school. She loved all the experiences Luca was having, but she was struggling to figure out how much attention and what kind of projects he really needed. She was also becoming acutely aware of the differences among pre-K options, and of the inequity in what was available to her family and to those with fewer resources.

On one morning that I visited CNS, Luca and his classmates entered to find half a dozen beautifully arranged center activities waiting for them. "Where would you like to start today?" the teachers asked each child as he or she entered. At one table, fresh flowers and leaves formed a rectangular border, leaving the middle open for children to create and experiment. A small round table was artfully dusted with sand that glowed with a gentle blue from a light underneath the table; paintbrushes were laid out for children to explore the movement of the sand. Across the room sat a small table with an antique map of Boston with small, colorful blocks to make buildings, and a water table filled with blue-tinted water and droppers and containers of different colors so that children could see how the color of the water changed their appearance.

When Luca and two other boys began to build "electrical towers" with magnetic tiles, teacher Carly Reagan offered them real wire to connect the pieces, sat down on the rug to ask thought-provoking questions about their designs, and took notes and photographs on an iPad. The next day, the boys entered to find that Reagan had set out a plastic picture frame holding a photo of two utility towers with electrical wires to give them added inspiration. As the boys ran to the picture and began revising their constructions from the day before, Luca watched intently. He is a quiet, observant child, and he said little until Reagan, sitting cross-legged on the rug, asked the trio of boys, "Are there wires like this outside?" Luca piped up then and said, "Sometimes they're on the ground in Charlestown." "Where?" Reagan encouraged him. "Sometimes they fall down. Right next to my house I see some of them go all twisty and to the ground," he replied, picking up the picture to study it. "Curious," Reagan mused. CNS teachers try to encourage children to come to conclusions on their own, rather than providing information. "Maybe we could go on a wire walk someday to see all the different wires and see what you notice." That night, Fenwick and the other parents received an email newsletter that included a brief description of the building project and the teachers' plans to take the children on a walk to look at electrical wires.

Fenwick was delighted with the way teachers encouraged Luca to think about and try new things. And she valued the thick "journey book" Luca took home at the end of each year, documenting his growth and progress over the course of the year, in photographs and detailed notes. Teachers are able to do those kinds of things because the level of support and compensation they receive is far beyond those found in the kind of community centers where Meg Hackett was teaching in Roxbury. At CNS, teachers are paid $55,000 a year for a three-day workweek. They have an hour and a half of planning time every day and get paid professional development. The school has funded several of them to travel to Italy to visit the Reggio Emilia schools. A board member and an educator herself, Fenwick appreciated that level of support for the teachers, and it made the school's high price tag worth it for her.

Fenwick had always felt fortunate to be able to send Luca to CNS, but as she visited public schools, she became increasingly aware that some of what Luca was getting there was nice to have but not essential. The tiny collections of mirrors on classroom walls were lovely but had been expensive. Snacks were served on porcelain white plates and children poured their own water into real glasses. And the commitment required from families was significant. Parents took turns bringing in fruits and vegetables, which teachers arranged into plates worthy of a catered event. Families of the younger children were given instructions on what kinds of diapers and wipes they were allowed to bring, and children were required to have two pairs of shoes at all times—one for inside and one for outside. And Fenwick, as a board member, was asked to make monetary donations in addition to Luca's tuition.

If the cost and commitment were a stretch for her family, Fenwick knew they put CNS entirely out of reach for many, especially children like those she had taught in some of the city's struggling neighborhoods. She was seeing firsthand how those children had access to fewer opportunities from a very early age. CNS's director had also taught in BPS, and she was very committed to partnering with local schools and community-based organizations to share her ideas and best practices so that more children could benefit from them. She had even welcomed a group of teachers from a center in a low-income neighborhood to observe class-rooms and then helped them figure out how to take the practices back to their own classrooms. But Fenwick knew that wasn't the same as giving the children access to the kind of program that Luca attended. She felt fortunate, no matter what happened in the BPS lottery. But she knew there was no guarantee of quality pre-K for anyone, so she worried, and she hoped for a little more good luck.

Six

Serious Play

In Washington, DC, every three- and four-year-old is guaranteed a pre-K spot in a DC public school. The district is rare in having a truly universal program, and rarer still in having spots for all three-year-olds. (Public pre-K programs tend to focus on four-year-olds.) But DC is a unique place, especially when it comes to educational reform. After decades of declining school performance and egregious administrative problems like letting new textbooks sit in storage facilities while students used outdated materials, the district began a set of ambitious reforms in the early 2000s. Even as the district overhauled teacher evaluation systems and opened dozens of new charter schools, the system was hemorrhaging students as middle-class families left the public schools in droves. To fully fund and staff schools, the district needed to attract more families. And with the increasing popularity of city living and the rising costs of childcare, one strategy to recruit families was to offer them free pre-K. DC has a long history of publicly funded preschool, especially for low-income families, and many long-standing pre-K advocates. But the school reform movement and the desire to boost school enrollment helped tip the political scales in favor of universal pre-K legislation in 2008.

The DC Public Schools (DCPS) pre-K program has some obvious differences from Boston's small and increasingly mixed system of both schools and community centers, but it also has some important similarities. One of those is a recognition that young children learn through play. Whether in social skills, planning, writing, or simple addition, preschoolers learn best through doing and by having fun, like solving puzzles, playing games, and pretending to do the things they see grown-ups do, like cooking and going to the doctor.

In Jason Harris's classroom at Powell Bilingual Elementary School, I watched three- and four-year-olds immersed in play about grocery stores and food. On one wall was a handmade "Safeway" sign that Harris and the children had constructed after a walking field trip to one of the supermarket chain's nearby locations in the mixed-income neighborhood of Petworth. Children had used their imaginations and hands to re-create the store in their classroom, bringing in empty cereal boxes and yogurt containers from home and finding the right place to line them up on a set of classroom shelves. They wrote labels for the shelves and other parts of the store (spelled imperfectly, as one would expect from preschoolers). They made pretend ice-cream pops out of paper, and Harris guided them to create price tags on sticky notes.

"What else do we need for our grocery store? What else did we see at Safeway?" Harris asked the children. "A cash register," one child suggested. "A cart and a basket," said another. Harris had these items stored away in a closet, ready to bring out at this moment. But then several children suggested something he didn't have in the closet that had made a big impression on the class: a bakery. "Ooh, yes, a bakery!" Harris responded. "How can we build it?" Together, they decided to use Play-Doh to make cookies and paper for chef's hats. The next day, Harris had the materials ready for the children to use, along with a picture book about how to make and sell cookies, which he read during story time to inspire them.

For decades, educators and policymakers debated the relative merits of play and learning in preschool, but there is now a clear consensus that the choice is a false one. Young children learn *through* play. Psychologist Kathy Hirsh-Pasek, an expert in how young children learn, explains: "Children do much better in inquiry-based learning than when they are just told something. When we are just told, we remember it for a very small amount of time." When they play, children actually use what they are learning, and that makes it easier for them to understand and remember later. They also are more engaged in what they are learning, because they are in "a meaningful social context, not in a boring or dissociated one," according to Hirsh-Pasek. Studies show that children develop social and language skills through play, especially pretend play.

Through play, children also develop an important set of skills called executive functioning. Executive functioning skills help us get things done and achieve goals, allowing us to pay attention, stay focused, resist temptations and distractions, do what is expected of us in the moment, and resist impulses that are inappropriate for a given situation. Researchers sometimes refer to executive functioning as being like air traffic control for the brain. Just as an airport needs to manage multiple planes flying in and out to keep everyone safe, on time, and moving in the right direction, people need to manage multiple streams of information constantly coming at us, to filter out unnecessary information, and to stay focused on the task at hand. Perhaps neuropsychologist Stephanie Carlson has put it best by saying that executive functioning is "most conspicuous in its absence." While we might not remark on when we and our children are engaging their executive functioning skills, when you walk into a classroom of children with poorly developed executive functioning skills, it's very noticeable.

Executive functioning is crucial for school success—perhaps even more important than knowing letters and numbers. Executive functions allow children to listen, follow instructions, and resist the temptation to shout out answers instead of raising their hands, which psychologists call inhibitory control. Children with strong self-regulation skills are more successful in school because they are more focused and well behaved and have better relationships with both teachers and peers. On the other hand, children with self-regulation problems can be very disruptive to the classroom. That can lead teachers, especially those who lack sufficient training, to be frustrated and label those children as beyond hope. Even for very skilled and empathic teachers, self-regulation problems can pose enormous challenges to classroom management and instruction. Psychologist Cybele Raver has conducted extensive research on self-regulation and executive functioning in preschool, and she has developed interventions that train teachers how to build children's self-regulation skills as well as management of their own emotions and thoughts. In Chicago Head Start centers and New Jersey pre-K settings, children whose teachers participated improved not only on measures of self-control and executive functioning but on math and literacy, even though the intervention didn't directly target academic skills. Raver's results suggest that executive functions enable academic success, rather than the reverse.

Children find all kinds of opportunities to develop executive functioning when they play, especially in pretend play, or what researchers call dramatic play. Stephanie Carlson has conducted numerous studies in her lab showing that pretending to be Batman or another fictional character helps young children control their impulses. At the beginning of one experiment, she asked children to select a character such as Batman, Bob the Builder, or Rapunzel and wear a prop representing that character. She then asked them to perform a tricky task in which they had to decide where to place cards of different colors. When she asked the children "Where should Batman [or their chosen character] put it?" they were significantly more accurate than when she asked them "Where should [the child's name] put it?" and both groups did better than those asked "Where should *you* put it?" In similar studies, she has shown that the character play helps children be more persistent, less distracted, and less frustrated with difficult tasks—even when offered the alternative of playing with an iPad, which parents know to be a nearly impossible temptation to resist. Carlson believes the pretend-play strategy works because it distances children from the situation. "When you are viewing the problem through the lens of someone else, you are able to see your options for responding more clearly," she explains. Indeed, lots of studies show that distancing is a helpful strategy for building executive functioning. In his classic "marshmallow studies" testing children's willpower to wait for a treat, Walter Mischel showed that children were able to wait longer when they turned to face away from the treat or when they envisioned it in a picture frame.

Other kinds of play can also promote executive functioning. When children play games and share blocks, they have to learn to wait and control impulses to grab toys or knock over someone else's structure. When they have engaging activities to choose from, they can learn to make decisions and have reason to stay attentive and focused. When they climb on the playground, they have to plan for how they are going to get from one level of the play structure to the next and reflect on whether the strategy they used last time worked.

But as a result of ever-increasing pressure to meet academic standards even in the early years, some preschoolers are getting a lot of instruction that requires them to sit, listen, and repeat, or to complete reams of boring worksheets that don't provide any kind of engaging or meaningful learning. Over the past five years, child development experts have been crying out for a return to play in pre-K and kindergarten classrooms, in books, articles, and media appearances, and through organizations with names like Defending the Early Years and the Alliance for Childhood that would have once seemed preposterously unnecessary. They have noticed the shrinking of recess time in kindergartens (although this tends to be less of an issue in pre-K).

Although play is clearly paramount for preschoolers, Hirsh-Pasek and other experts point out that not all play is created equal when it comes to teaching and learning. Studies show that children learn more from guided play than totally unstructured free play. In guided play, the child takes the initiative and constructs the learning, but the adult pushes the child's thinking by asking open-ended questions and coaching her to think more deeply. In one study on the merits of different kinds of play, Hirsh-Pasek created three groups of parent-child pairs and gave each pair a set of blocks. One group was asked to use the blocks to create a heliport, the second was given a preassembled heliport, and the third was told to use the blocks however they wished. Parents in the guided-play group used richer spatial and logical vocabulary with their children during the activity than the other groups. It wasn't because those families were special in some way; when all the families were then asked to use the blocks to make a garage, they all used descriptive, spatial language, suggesting that having some structure but not too much gives adults the opportunity to provide a rich learning experience.

"It's not that free play is unimportant," Hirsh-Pasek is quick to point out, and she believes all kids need time for that, too. "But if you want to learn something, you have to have some sort of learning goal in mind." A study of state-funded pre-K programs by researchers at the University of Virginia found that children learned less in literacy and math from free play than from all other types of instruction, including both direct instruction and guided play. (The study did not look at more complex skills like comprehension or problem-solving.)

In a classroom, teachers facilitate intentional play by asking questions or playing along with the students. "When my kids are in centers, I'm in there with them," Jason Harris told me. "How else am I going to facilitate their learning?" he wondered aloud, as he looked around at his students engrossed in their activities. Facilitating play to enhance children's learning isn't as easy as it sounds. It requires setting up the right kinds of activities and materials for children, and also knowing how to help without being overinvolved. There is a fine balance between effective facilitation and too much teacher talk, according to literacy expert David Dickinson. In a longitudinal study, he and his colleagues found that children did better on measures of language and literacy when they talked more and their teachers talked less during play. But that doesn't mean teachers were uninvolved; rather, they were listening and talking in limited but helpful ways.

Before Harris had sent children off to play at the grocery centers spread across the room, he and his assistant teacher had modeled how the children might play at the centers, using some of the vocabulary related to the unit. As he acted out a grocery store scenario, Harris used specific words like "bakery," "cashier," and "customer." After each, he would pause to ask the children to repeat them. Repetition is a common way to build vocabulary in early childhood classrooms, but often it is done in an empty way, devoid of any context. In Harris's classroom, it is integrated into the day's topic and the children's play, and it clearly works. As they went to centers, one little girl said, "I want to be the shopper, and you be the cashier." Her obliging classmate rang up the groceries after the girl walked through the "aisles" saying, "I need some cereal and some granola bars."

Harris also used the grocery centers to build children's math skills. He joined the checkout center, tossing an apron over his head and saying, "I'm going to be the bagger." He turned to the cashier and asked how much the customer's groceries cost. "Five dollars," the cashier responded, and the customer handed over some pretend bills. "Did you give her five?" Harris asked. The customer quietly counted the bills and shook her head. "Let's try again," Harris said, and helped the child count out the correct amount. Then he reinforced another important preschool skill, asking the customer, "What do we say when the cashier gives us our change and receipt?" "Thank you!" she chimed happily. Just as they finished, a child on the other side of the room called to Harris on a pretend phone. He picked up and said, "I'm at work right now, Dalia. I'll get back to you later." After he hung up, he told the cashier he was going on break and deftly exited the checkout line to help Dalia and a classmate solve a dispute over a pretend tortilla. The children at the checkout remained engrossed in their play.

Part of the reason the children delve into their roles and use such rich vocabulary and math skills is that Harris models how to do that for the class before he sends children to centers. This level of scaffolding might sound controlling, but it doesn't feel that way at all. The teachers don't tell the kids what to do; they just give them some ideas and encourage certain vocabulary and skills. The kids delighted in Harris's involvement, and they clearly used what they learned from it. When a visitor went to the bakery corner and ordered a cookie, the baker asked what kind of cookie she wanted and what shape, pointing to a poster behind him. "What's that last shape called?" the customer asked, and after he responded correctly that it was a star, he found a star-shaped cookie cutter and plunged it into the Play-Doh. He handed the finished product to her with a smile and "a bonus cupcake," and asked the cashier to write a receipt. In this one brief interaction, the students had used geometry, math, money sense, vocabulary, and social skills.

In many classrooms, center time basically amounts to unstructured free play, because activities are laid out with no learning goals in mind and no teacher facilitation. One district early childhood director told me that as a young teacher, she had been trained in a popular and nationally recognized model that was "laissez-faire, a philosophy that teachers are facilitators who put out materials for kids and see what they create, not instructors who guide lessons or activities." But over time she realized that her students weren't building skills and weren't prepared for kindergarten. And in some classrooms I visited, centers were basically a free-play background activity that teachers used to occupy children while they worked with others in small groups on recognizing words or reciting number facts.

At Powell, play is connected to everything else. The grocery unit also

included books, discussions, and field trips. The day after the students
played at their fictional Safeway, Harris took the students on a visit to a
nearby Hispanic market. As he led children through the aisles, he built
and reinforced their vocabulary. Vocabulary development is a big goal
during the preschool years, especially in a bilingual classroom like Harris's. About half the students at Powell are native Spanish speakers,
mostly from low-income immigrant families, and the other half are
English speakers, primarily from white, middle-class families. It's a rare
mix that creates both rich learning opportunities and occasional tensions
over expectations and goals for parent groups. But the goal of learning
two languages is common among the school's parents. Spanish-speaking
parents told me one of their main goals for their children's pre-K years
was to become fluent in English, while English speakers told me they
had chosen Powell in part because of the opportunity for their children
to learn another language. By the middle of the fall, the children were
impressively competent in both Spanish and English, regardless of their
native tongue. In Powell's pre-K classrooms, children hear both languages throughout the day. Typically, the lead teacher speaks English
and the assistant teacher speaks Spanish. Each leads a small group every
afternoon and the groups switch after two weeks so that all children con-
verse and receive instruction in both languages. Harris's classroom is
slightly different, because he is fluent in Spanish, so he speaks both languages with the children (and their parents).

As he walked the aisles of the market, Harris was tuned in to the
unique needs of each child, including a three-year-old native Spanish
speaker with little vocabulary in either language. "Joaquin, look!" Harris
pointed out enthusiastically as he strolled down a snack aisle. "You have
these crackers for lunch. *Cr*, crackers. You have crackers." In the next
aisle he pointed again and asked, "What is that, Joaquin? Rice! What
else?" "Frijoles," Joaquin responded quietly. "Right, frijoles! Beans!"
Harris reinforced.

Back in the classroom, Harris also encouraged children's ability to organize and plan, using a strategy called play planning. "What are you going to do first today, Jesly?" he asked a bubbly four-year-old before center time. On a small paper affixed to a clipboard, she drew a picture of herself baking cookies and told Harris, "I am going to make the cookies." "OK, your message is that you are going to make the cookies," Harris repeated. Jesly drew six lines at the bottom of the paper. Harris leaned over, counted the lines, and pointed out that she had missed one. Next he gently guided her finger across each of the lines as they said each word of the message: "I—am—going—to—make—the . . ." When they got to the end, Jesly realized she didn't have enough lines for all the words and she added another. "'Cookies' is a long word," Harris pointed out, "so how should we make that line?" She extended the final line to show it as a longer word.

After she finished her message, Jesly skipped off to the bakery and hung her clipboard on a dedicated peg to remind her of her plan. The entire exercise had taken only a few minutes, but it taught many things simultaneously: how to think ahead, make a decision, follow through, and represent the plan in writing. Each child begins with making the kind of lines Jesly made, which show that sentences are composed of words and that some words are longer than others. When they are ready, children begin to add punctuation at the end, write the first letter of certain words, or even write entire words. (Correct spelling doesn't matter.) At the top of the page are tiny symbols that Harris uses to code what the child was able to do independently and what she was able to do with help. That allows him, and the child's parents, to track progress over time. The process is known as scaffolded writing, because it gives children just enough support to move through the stages of learning to write so that they can become independent.

Jesly's mother, Sonia Cruz, says she has seen that progress in the play plans Jesly brings home at the end of each week and in notes her daughter writes, telling her mother how much she loves her. Cruz, who immigrated to the United States from El Salvador about five years before Jesly was born and speaks only Spanish, has been amazed by how quickly Jesly has learned English at school, and she's glad Harris teaches through play. "I have always believed that children can learn through play," she told me, but she wasn't sure how to help with that at home. She regularly read to Jesly and her older siblings, but through Harris, she has also learned how to play educational games. "At every parent meeting, he gives us a game to take home," she explained in Spanish. "At the first meeting, he gave us a game with dice and numbers and you have to count. I had never played that kind of game before. My children love it and they ask to play it all the time now."

Although many parents say they want their children to have more time for play, some parents are surprised by Harris's emphasis on play. I attended one of Harris's parent meetings, which take the place of traditional parent-teacher conferences and use a model called Academic Parent Teacher Teams. In these meetings, Harris sits with a group of parents to talk about something their children are learning. He explains a concept, demonstrates it, and answers questions. Then he gives each parent a piece of paper that describes how their child is doing in that area. On the day I attended, early in the school year, the focus was on the importance of parents supporting play at home. As Cruz and other parents entered the room, they found a kidney-bean-shaped table with child-sized chairs and a gift bag at each place. Inside the bags were colorful pipe cleaners, construction paper, and other art supplies. As Harris welcomed each of them, some in English and some in Spanish, he encouraged the parents to play with the items in their bags and make something their child would like to play with. Some parents dove right in, creating pipe-cleaner sculptures and pretend-play props, while others cautiously peered in their bags and chatted quietly with their neighbors. One parent became engrossed in creating a "Ghostbusters machine" for her three-year-old son, who she reported was obsessed with the movie (or at least the idea of it, since he hadn't actually seen it). When Harris gathered everyone back together, the mother was covered in paint and a broad smile.

Harris then talked about why play is important for learning, how he helps children play in meaningful ways, and how it could help their children if the parents could find a few minutes to play with them at home.

During the next part of the meeting, Harris explained how and why he takes notes on the children's progress and uses a measurement tool to quantify it. "We use a tool called GOLD," he explained, introducing an assessment that is popular in early childhood classrooms. "We take notes or pictures while children are playing, and then later we can use GOLD to record what they are showing us they have learned." He handed each parent a piece of paper. On one side were photographs of their child playing and notes about him or her, including anecdotes and quotes from their play that made some of the parents laugh affectionately. Also on the page was a number, a rating from one item on GOLD. Harris didn't want to overwhelm the parents with technical information, so he shared just one item about how well children are able to express themselves and be creative during "sociodramatic play."

Harris knew how much information he could get about children's thinking and learning from watching them play, but he also knew that it can be hard for parents to wrap their heads around that and to interpret data. So on the opposite side of the paper, he included a spectrum that showed the possible ratings children could have received on the item and explanations of what they meant. After he walked parents through each possible rating, he made the assessment tool come alive by doing what he would do with his students: he acted it out. Harris jumped up from his chair and danced around the room, singing the Disney mega-hit "Let It Go" with which nearly every child and parent in his school, including the Spanish-speaking ones, were familiar. Then he asked the parents how they would rate his play on the scale he had described. "Four." "Six," they called out. Next Harris grabbed a cape and sword and acted out another scenario in Spanish. He and the parents discussed how they would rate it, with Harris switching seamlessly between the two languages and all parents sharing their ideas in whatever language they could. "I would rate this one a four and the previous one a two, because in the first one I didn't use any props," he explained. Then he and his assistant teacher did the exercise again, this time starting with a conversation about who was going to play what role. Harris decided to be a dragon and pretended to make fire come out of his mouth by using red blocks. When they finished, the parents laughed and clapped, and one said, "That was definitely an eight because you negotiated your roles with each other."

Harris could see that the parents were beginning to understand how children can learn through play, but he still wanted to clarify. "Does that make sense, what we're looking for? That's where we eventually want students to be. Now we're going to think about, how do we get students from a three to a five? If you're playing with your student at home, what do you think is important to be doing with him or her?" One parent seemed to have already considered this. "It depends on your child. My child wants to tell me what to do. 'No, don't make an air hole in that tent, because water will come in.' My instinct is to just let him do that." Harris gave her an enthusiastic thumbs-up. Another parent said, "Also asking questions." "What kind of questions?" Harris probed. "Open-ended," she answered. "Right! For example, 'Why do we need an air hole?' That gets them to expand their thinking." As the conversation went on, a parent asked about how to encourage children to negotiate and compromise. Harris seized the opportunity to talk about building children's social skills, encouraging parents to model conflict resolution instead of just telling children what to do. "Maybe tell them, 'I don't feel like being a dragon today. What if I want to be the princess?' You could say, 'Can you be the princess first and then we'll switch?' You could also try doing something a dragon doesn't normally do and see how your child handles it." The meeting hadn't been framed as a parenting class, but the parents were getting tips on everything from how to build their children's vocabulary to how to help them cope with disappointment.

As he wrapped up the conversation, Harris told the parents, "Now it's your turn to play!" and he sent them off to do pretend play with each other. He knew this wouldn't be comfortable for some of them and that's exactly why he wanted to give them a safe opportunity to do it, so that they might feel more comfortable to do it with their children at home. The mother who made the Ghostbusters machine gestured to her friend and headed to the back of the room, where the two jumped around and pretended to zap each other. Two others found a dollhouse and began to act out the roles of mom and child, while a few more sat at the table drawing and collaging. At the end of the meeting, parents shared what they learned about how to help their children. One said she planned to ask her daughter more questions. Another said, "It stuck out to me that I need to be more present. I need to not have my phone with me all the time." One asked if telling stories to her child counted as play. Harris said yes and suggested that she could have her daughter act out some of the stories, as the children sometimes did in the classroom. As the parents gathered up the play props they had made for their children, the mother with the Ghostbusters machine said, "I'm really excited to take this home to him."

The emphasis on play, and the strategies like play plans and the scaffolded writing approach, are part of a curriculum that Harris and his colleagues use called Tools of the Mind. It is a research-based early childhood program whose creators see dramatic play as the conduit to literacy, numeracy, social skills, and executive functioning. Tools of the Mind, which is used in about 70 percent of DC Public Schools' preschool classrooms, is an unusual choice for a large urban district. "It was something of a risk, because the district had been focusing narrowly on literacy and numeracy skills," recalls Miriam Calderon, who introduced the program when she was director of early childhood for DCPS. But she knew there was a need for stronger executive functioning skills if children were going to be ready to succeed in school.

"As I visited [pre-K] classrooms, I heard a lot of yelling and challenging behaviors, and when I spent time with children, they were very
stressed," Calderon remembers. Many children had experienced or wit-
nessed trauma in their homes or neighborhoods, and Calderon, who had
once worked as a mental health provider in Head Start, knew that chaotic
and punitive classroom environments could remind children of their
traumas and exacerbate them. Yet those kinds of environments pervaded
the schools, in her view. She saw play disappearing amid a push for stronger academic skills, and teachers who were underprepared and overwhelmed struggling to help children develop self-control. "It would
become a cycle of misbehavior, in which adults thought children needed
to be disciplined, but that harsh discipline was actually making things
worse," Calderon recently recalled, sadness filling her voice. "The kids
were staying in the 'fight or flight' part of their brains in these classrooms
because there was stress and screaming."

The "fight or flight" part of the brain she referred to is a neurological
response to stress. When we experience stress, our bodies release certain hormones like adrenaline and cortisol. Cortisol prompts the fight-
or-flight response that allows us to cope with threatening situations,
and a moderate amount of it can be helpful, increasing focus and concentration. Scientists think this is an evolutionary adaptation that allowed
early humans to protect themselves from dangers like wild animals.
But when cortisol is too high for too long, it has the opposite effect, de-
creasing our ability to concentrate and use other executive functions. In
essence, persistently high levels of cortisol and other stress hormones
make the body think it is under constant threat, as if we were perpetually
running away from bears, and this keeps the fight-or-flight response on
at all times. That's distracting and exhausting, and it actually makes us
even more sensitive to potential stressors. The amygdala, a part of the
brain involved in emotional regulation, becomes hypersensitive to fear
and threat, so it triggers the release of cortisol even when the threat is a

small one. At the same time, stress leads neurons to atrophy in the hippocampus, which is involved in memory, and the prefrontal cortex, the brain area associated with the executive functions that would normally help us cope with stress.

In children who experience chronic stress, especially the ongoing problems of poverty and violence, cortisol levels tend to be either persistently elevated or persistently low. The latter pattern creates a kind of desensitized effect where the brain stops responding to stress altogether. Children who have either of these atypical patterns tend to have lower levels of emotional regulation, impulse control, attention, and other executive functions. They may be more likely to react defensively or aggressively to even small perceived insults or provocations from peers or adults. This can potentially benefit them in the moment, or so they believe, but it puts them at risk in the long run, especially when it comes to following the expectations of a classroom and focusing on schoolwork. New York University professor Clancy Blair and his colleagues have found that children who experience trauma and chronic stress tend to be rated by their teachers as having poorer self-control than their peers and to have lower levels of reading, writing, and math skills in kindergarten. This may be because the stress response can "result in some children appearing to be both more reactive to even mildly adverse experiences and less capable of effectively coping with future stress," according to Jack Shonkoff of the Center on the Developing Child at Harvard. In other words, in a cruel psychological irony, the children who experience the most stress also tend to have the least developed systems for coping with it.

Psychologist Becky Bailey has tried to simplify the neuroscience of this cycle into what she calls the Brain State Model. The children Calderon was seeing were in what Bailey calls the "survival state," the most basic state in which people are focused on the question "Am I safe?" Calderon wanted to get them to the more advanced "executive state," where they could focus on the question "What can I learn from this?" One of Calderon's immediate goals was to adopt a curriculum that would build teachers' knowledge about child development and provide strategies that simultaneously built academic skills and the foundational executive functioning skills to help children be more planful, attentive, and self-regulated—to get them out of that fight-or-flight part of the brain.

But Calderon was convinced that if she told district administrators and teachers they needed to focus on children's executive functioning and social-emotional skills, they would say that such approaches don't work for "these kids." She had heard educators insist that disadvantaged children, who on average start kindergarten behind their peers in literacy and numeracy, need a strict focus on academic instruction and drilling. She was worried about a backlash from teachers and parents who wanted to make sure their kids were learning to read and not simply "playing all day." (Indeed, a Powell teacher told me that she recently met another DCPS pre-K teacher, who said, "I remember when we did real teaching, not this play stuff.") The key step, she decided, was to implement Tools of the Mind at two enthusiastic pilot schools, so she could show others in the district that it could work, using a solid focus on literacy and math integrated with the emphasis on play, social-emotional development, and self-regulation. Her plan worked. Implementation went smoothly and students did well at both schools. One of them was Powell.

Today there is widespread consensus among child development experts that you really can't separate social, emotional, and academic skills, but that wasn't always the case. In the 1960s, a program like Tools of the Mind would never have been created, because the field was dominated by the philosophy of behaviorism, which held that behavior is learned primarily through imitation, coupled with rewards and punishments. Pavlov, who famously trained his dog to salivate at the sound of a bell by repeatedly pairing the bell with food, contributed significantly to behaviorism. So did B. F. Skinner, who invented the Skinner Box, which allows researchers to reinforce or extinguish behaviors in animals by adding or taking away food when the animal presses on a bar. Known as operant conditioning, this use of rewards and punishments was extended to humans as a way to modify undesirable behaviors.

But by the 1980s, behaviorism had begun to lose its grip on the field of psychology. The shift was influenced by the rise of cognitive science, which focuses on mental processes and how people make meaning of the world. Russian psychologist Lev Vygotsky was a big part of that shift. Unlike the behaviorists, Vygotsky believed that children are not passive vessels for learning but active participants in constructing knowledge. This is now widely accepted, but it was a revolutionary notion at the time. He proposed that children were most likely to learn in a particular state and time: when they are just on the edge of a new skill, in a state he called the zone of proximal development (ZPD). The ZPD is the space between what children can do independently and what they can do with the help of an adult or skilled peer.

In the ZPD, adults can best teach children by scaffolding them, or giving them just enough help so that they can achieve the task and gradually become independent at it. Scaffolding is how toddlers learn to walk: parents and loved ones hold their waists, then their hands, then one finger, and eventually we let go. Vygotsky believed it is how children learn to do more complex tasks, too, like paying attention and doing math. The idea that skills like focusing or controlling aggressive impulses could develop in stages with support from adults was a very different approach than the behaviorists' philosophy that you simply motivate people to turn habits on or off. Rather than relying on rewards and punishments, Vygotsky advised educators to build complex skills by providing children with mental strategies and then removing or replacing the strategies as the children mastered one skill and moved on to the next one. Simple strategies like tying a string on a finger to remember something or counting to ten to diffuse anger help children (and adults) think clearly, pay attention, and remember. Those skills support the ability to think abstractly, which becomes increasingly important for learning math and other complex subjects as children get older. They also allow children to take control of their own behavior and become "masters" of their environments rather than "slaves" to them, as Vygotsky put it. Vygotsky called these strategies tools of the mind, because they can extend thinking the way that tools like levers and wrenches extend our physical abilities.

Vygotsky's ideas captured the attention of many young researchers in the 1970s and '80s. Among them was Deborah Leong, a psychologist who eventually helped create Tools of the Mind. While teaching at Metropolitan State University in Denver, Leong heard that a group of Russian psychologists were interested in coming to the United States to study, teach, and spread Vygotsky's ideas. "This was in 1992, shortly after the [Berlin] Wall had fallen down and Russia was opening to the West," she recalls. A colleague introduced her, via the internet, to one of Vygotsky's students who had been applying his ideas to classrooms and teaching. Leong persuaded the college's president and her psychology department colleagues to offer a new endowed chair position—the college's first—to that scholar, Elena Bodrova.

Leong and Bodrova became fast friends and collaborators, and within the first week of working together, Bodrova taught Leong a powerful lesson about building executive functioning, not in a classroom full of children but while visiting Leong's home. Leong's six-year-old son, Jeremy, was a math whiz. "He was one of these kids who adds up all the numbers on a license plate when looking out the car window," she recalls. (He would later get a PhD in neuroscience and become a research fellow at Stanford.) But in all his math work, he made a common mistake: he wrote the number six backward. Leong didn't see it as a big deal, but her son's teacher was frustrated by it. The teacher would require the boy to write the number over and over again on sheets of paper, but the practice didn't help. She would tell him that he was lazy and not paying attention, but he was perplexed. "But I *am* paying attention!" he would insist to both his teacher and his parents.

One Friday, while Bodrova was visiting, Jeremy came home and, showing the previous day's homework to his parents, asked, "Is this wrong because this doesn't equal six or because I wrote the six backward?" Leong's husband, a geophysicist whose work requires a deep well of math knowledge, looked at the paper and "exploded," as Leong recalls, when he realized that his son's answer was substantively correct but marked wrong by the teacher for the superficial reason. As he turned to Leong and began to debate how to handle the situation with the teacher, Bodrova unexpectedly stepped in and said, "I can fix that." Leong's first thought was sarcastic, so she kept it to herself: "Oh, really? Go ahead and try." But not only did Bodrova try, she—and Leong's son—succeeded.

Bodrova suggested to Jeremy that he do his next math assignment in pencil, but that every time he came to a six, he put down his pencil and use a red pen. Before writing the six, he was to look up at a correctly written six hanging over his desk on a small piece of paper. He gave it a try, and by Monday morning, he was making all his sixes correctly, even without stopping and looking at the paper. Leong was stunned. Bodrova had found the answer to the boy's problem: she told Leong that Jeremy's problem wasn't with sixes per se but with executive functioning. He had many strong executive functioning skills—like attention, as he had insisted to his teacher—but he, like nearly all young children, needed support to build some of the other skills. "He didn't have the inhibitory control to stop the habitual action of making the six backwards," Leong learned from Bodrova. Somehow he had formed an incorrect habit and he didn't have the ability to stop himself from using it. He needed a strategy (changing pencils) to help him pause, break his usual thinking habits, and consciously remember to change the way he wrote the number. The most important thing, as Leong saw it, was that Bodrova taught him in a way that didn't make him feel ashamed and that maintained his motivation to learn—something his teacher's more punitive method didn't do.

On Monday night, Jeremy's teacher called Leong and gushed, "My

God, he's getting them all right! What did you do over the weekend?" When Leong passed on what she had learned from Bodrova, the teacher was intrigued. She and a few other teachers at the school volunteered to work with Leong and Bodrova to test other strategies to build students' executive functioning. When the pair began to visit classrooms and meet with teachers, they saw that teachers had identified a host of problems they didn't know how to address. "We realized that teachers sometimes don't take the child's perspective or understand what the children need," Leong says. So the researchers brought the children's reasons for their behaviors to light, and they tested different strategies to help them. When a teacher got frustrated that her students didn't seem to want to clean up, Leong and Bodrova observed and realized that children weren't un-motivated, they were distracted. So they created a song with multiple verses, so that children would know when it was getting closer to cleanup time. "You see them clean up faster and faster as the song goes on," Leong explains. "They have no real sense of time, so the song helps. They can understand as it gets closer to the end that they don't have much time left." When teachers complained that their students didn't write their names on the tops of their papers, the researchers realized kids were focused on other parts of the task, so they placed a paperclip over the name line and required kids to take the paperclips off before working on the paper, calling their attention to the name line, until the children got so used to signing their names that they didn't need the paperclips any-more. The paperclip was a kind of mental tool that Vygotsky called a mediator, a sign or symbol that represents a behavior and reminds chil-dren who aren't yet able to do the behavior independently. "We just solved problems one at a time," Leong says. Many of the strategies they tried didn't work, but the ones that did would eventually become Tools of the Mind.

Neuroscientist Adele Diamond has tested the results of Tools of the Mind, and she has also conducted dozens of studies in the lab about how executive functioning works and how to build it. One of her studies supported Bodrova's suggestion that stopping before acting can help in-hibit unhelpful automatic responses. Diamond and her colleagues devel-oped a test called the Day-Night Task, in which an experimenter shows a child pictures of night scenes and day scenes. Children are supposed to say the opposite of what they see—"day" when they see a dark sky with a moon and "night" when they see a light background with a shining sun. It sounds simple, but even adults get tripped up by similar tasks in lab tests, and the researchers found that four-year-olds typically got only about half the cards right; in other words, they performed no better than chance. But their accuracy jumped to almost 90 percent when the exper-imenter would show the card and tell the child not to respond until after the experimenter sang a three-second ditty with the words: "Think about the answer / Don't tell me." In a video of one of Diamond's young participants, the results are charmingly apparent. In the first condition, the boy makes several mistakes, but it's clearly an impulse problem, be-cause as soon as he answers incorrectly he sheepishly corrects himself. But in the second condition, he emits a brief "mmmm . . ." before each answer and then gets every single one right.

It might seem that strategies like mediators and pretend play indulge or coddle children. But in fact it's just the opposite. Mediators don't just com-pensate for a lack of executive functioning, they actually build it. Three-, four-, and five-year-olds naturally have immature executive functioning skills. It would have been useless to ask participants in the Day-Night Task study simply to wait three seconds before responding. As most parents can attest, young children often literally cannot wait without some sort of sup-port. (Many parents "reward" or bribe their children into such behaviors by promising treats, but that strategy just gets kids and parents through the immediate moment; it does nothing to build their long-term self-regulation.) Mediators, in this case the song, enable children to do the desired behav-iors on their own. In a classroom setting, mediators allow children to work and play more independently, with less adult intervention. Once children are able to regulate the targeted behavior, adults remove the mediators and children do an impressive job of controlling themselves. Diamond often cites a Tools of the Mind activity called Buddy Reading, in which children pair up and take turns "reading" a book by describing the story they see in the pictures to their partner. Most children love being the reader, and that means most have trouble being the listener. To help them wait and inhibit their desire to talk, teachers give the listeners a card with a picture of an ear. Diamond has seen it work with impressive consistency. And it usually takes only a couple of months until children are able to perform the activity without the card. Then they are able to move on to a new skill. "Executive functions need to be continually challenged, not just practiced," Diamond says. That might be because executive functioning is multifaceted and its development continues into adulthood, or it might be because people become disengaged when they are not challenged, which leads to the opposite of executive functioning. It may be because people need to be in Vygotsky's zone of proximal development in order to build executive functioning.

Tools of the Mind is built on this idea of the need for both practice and continual challenge. Activities like Buddy Reading's ear card are embedded throughout the day, because executive functioning skills have to be developed in an ongoing way and can't be built during a specific "executive function lesson." Play planning is an example of an activity that creates continual challenge and ongoing scaffolding by adults. At the beginning of the year, adults have to provide a lot of support for constructing and writing the play plans, but their support changes over the course of the year. As children learn more about planning their time and about writing lines for words, adults encourage them to do those pieces on their own. At the same time, they add in more scaffolding for new skills like writing letters. That ongoing and simultaneous focus on executive functioning, academic skills, and social and emotional skills is a hallmark of Tools of the Mind.

————

Making all those pieces mesh is hard work, and Jason Harris spends a lot of time thinking about where his students are and what they need. Every afternoon, when he sets up his classroom for the next day, he does far more than simply following an instruction book or pulling out the materials he has used in the past. When teachers implement the curriculum, they have a lot of flexibility to use the activities and mediators that meet the needs of their classrooms (although they also follow thematic units and daily lessons), and they are encouraged to "toolsify" other activities that they or their supervisors might want to include. That requires teachers to do the kind of thoughtful detective work about their students' needs that Bodrova and Leong did in the first pilot classrooms they worked with in Colorado. For Harris, that can mean thinking about why his students struggled to calm down during morning meeting, finding a new song that cues them to get quiet, or using a timer to help two students address a turn-taking dispute. "Our goal is not to have people *do* Tools but *think* Tools," Leong explained to me.

Therein lies both the promise and the challenge of the program. To "think Tools," teachers need extensive training in both the curriculum and child development, the time and systems to document and reflect on children's progress, and, perhaps most difficult to ensure, an inclination to view children's challenges as puzzles to be worked out. Teachers like Harris, who have that plus all the other supports they need, flourish with Tools, and so do their students. But everyone agrees that Tools is a constant work in progress, and that takes planning and resources. Powell's pre-K teachers talk frequently about how to implement the curriculum, support their students, and address challenges. They have daily common planning time, and they also regularly pop in and out of each other's classrooms to ask a question or share an idea. They not only receive training from the Tools of the Mind organization and regular visits from a DCPS coach trained in the curriculum, they also have an in-house coach, a veteran Powell pre-K teacher who now splits her time between working as an extra teacher in classrooms with special-needs students and coaching teachers and assistant teachers.

These kinds of investments in planning and working through implementation challenges are crucial for a program like Tools of the Mind, which requires teachers to be reflective. But many pre-K teachers, like the Roxbury YMCA's Meg Hackett, and especially their assistant teachers, lack the time and infrastructure to do that well. Another issue is that preschool teachers who have little formal background in child development are sometimes not in the habit of being reflective about their teaching and their students' learning, according to Monica Yudron, a professor of early childhood education at the University of Massachusetts–Boston. In both research studies and classes she leads for future early childhood educators, she has found that developing the habit of reflection can be one of the most challenging aspects of teaching. "Kids are constantly giving teachers clues about what they're learning and what they need next," she explains, but "teachers need to know how to integrate all of that information, because it isn't explicit, and teachers don't always recognize it for what it is." One behavior can mean several different things, and the teacher needs to figure out which one she's dealing with in each situation and with each child. For example, "a young student who is speaking out of turn, forgetting to raise her hand, and wiggling around on the rug might look disruptive—or she might be eager and excited to learn." Yudron says that teachers are more likely to see the positive interpretation when they have a little distance from the situation and the time to reflect on it. But, she points out, "there are often barriers that prevent preschool and pre-kindergarten teachers from regularly having this reflective release time during the workday, including staffing and scheduling issues"— exactly the kinds of barriers that Hackett was experiencing in Roxbury and that many community-based preschool teachers face as a result of funding and staffing challenges.

Those kinds of challenges may help explain why the results of Tools

of the Mind evaluations have been mixed. The first study of preschoolers, conducted by Diamond and published in the prestigious journal *Science*, found impressive gains in children's executive functioning, and a
recent study of kindergarteners by another research group found improvements in academic skills as well as executive functioning. But in
between those two reports were several randomized controlled studies
that found children in Tools classrooms did no better than other children. Leong believes those findings were related to implementation
problems in Tools classrooms, and to an overzealous effort to conduct
too many studies too quickly, without ensuring fidelity to the program
and quality elements like reflection time. She says learning from those
mistakes allowed her and her collaborators to build the high-quality
classrooms reported in the kindergarten study, leading to better results
for children. It is also worth noting that the measures of reading and executive functioning used in the pre-K studies are of questionable utility
in the real world. For example, one test measures attention and inhibitory control by asking children to tap their pencil once when the experimenter taps twice and vice versa. Researchers debate whether these
kinds of tests really predict how well students can focus and control
themselves in a classroom.

But teachers and administrators at Powell and other DCPS schools are
happy with what children are learning from the program. Harris and his
colleagues, including former principal Janeece Docal, who won the 2014
DCPS Principal of the Year Award, are big advocates of Tools of the
Mind. They see it building skills in vocabulary, writing, numeracy, and a
host of self-regulation and social-emotional domains, all embedded in activities that are engaging for children. But they also emphasize the importance of implementing the program well, and how much work that takes.
Docal was very strategic about building capacity among the early childhood team. In the first year of the program, she attended all the teacher
trainings and talked frequently with Leong and other Tools of the Mind
coaches, so that she knew how to support and evaluate the teachers. She

also increased the role of the assistant teachers. "Since they were doing the Spanish part, they couldn't be just cutting stuff out. They had to be teachers in training," she explained. And she created opportunities for teachers to work together across classrooms and grade levels, so that everyone would be on the same page. "I intentionally made pre-K and kindergarten have collaborative time together," she told me. "The play plans became a link between pre-K and kindergarten, so that kindergarten teachers would know where kids were with writing, oral language, and other skills. The pre-K teachers were able to say, 'Here's what the kids are able to do. Let's not lose ground when they start kindergarten.' It was a very positive model, because rather than pushing down expectations from kindergarten, we were pushing up, keeping the momentum going." In the transition from pre-K to kindergarten, momentum benefits everyone.

Seven

Ready to Read?

Although experts agree that children learn best through play-based approaches, some pre-K programs are teaching in exactly the opposite way, through direct instruction, where a teacher talks at children and asks them to repeat back what she says. Even more alarming is the rise of something that wasn't seen in pre-K until recently: pressure.

When Harris's colleague Lisa Gross started her teaching career, she found herself in an environment very different from Powell. Gross began teaching through an alternative certification program (as had Harris); she had majored in art in college, but after discovering a love of working with young children in an arts program, she decided she wanted to be a teacher. Her post-baccalaureate certification program, run by a national nonprofit designed to recruit liberal arts grads into teaching, required her to find a teaching position on her own before she could enroll. It is notoriously difficult to get a position in a DC public school, especially with the two strikes Gross had against her—no teaching certificate and no personal connections. But she was committed to staying within the public system rather than applying to charter schools. "I'm a product of public schools, and I believe in public schools. That's where I wanted to make my career," she explains. That commitment left her with few options, so she jumped at the first offer she received, figuring she had little opportunity to ask questions about the school culture or be choosy about her principal.

But even before her students arrived, Gross knew there was a problem in her school's pre-K classrooms. The supply closet in her classroom was nearly empty, missing the hands-on materials like blocks, puzzles, and art supplies that are the staples of early childhood classrooms. Despite repeated requests to school administrators, Gross never received new materials. She borrowed some pretend food for her dramatic play area from another teacher and took to visiting a public library near her parents' home every weekend to bring in books for her students. Her lack of support went far beyond the materials. Unlike the veteran pre-K teachers at her school, she did not have an assistant teacher. She began the year with a substitute, but that teacher was let go after only a few weeks for using racial slurs about students and was never replaced. Gross, a twenty-one-year-old first-year teacher, was left mostly on her own with seventeen high-needs preschoolers, many of them angry and aggressive victims or witnesses of family and neighborhood violence. Mentors and teachers from her certification program were of little help because none of them had experience with preschool. An early childhood coach from DCPS became a critical emotional support but could do little to address the systemic problems in the school.

The most troubling issues for Gross were in how she was told to teach reading. The school's principal made it clear that the number one priority for the pre-K classrooms was teaching sight words—words that children should know just by looking at them, without having to sound them out. The principal set specific growth goals that children were expected to meet every two weeks. According to Gross's records, every two weeks, three-year-olds were expected to know five more sight words than the previous period, or a total of 92 words, while four-year-olds were to know a total of 176. (There were specific targets for counting numbers as well.) Every two weeks, the principal would go over each teacher's progress toward those targets in data meetings, publicly shaming the teachers who did not meet them. "We were testing them all the time" to provide the data, Gross recalls, and that created stress for everyone. After her students performed near the bottom among the pre-K classrooms in one testing period, Gross was told by the teacher chairing the school's early childhood department to drill her struggling three- and four-year-olds with flashcards at recess and write the words on their lunch trays. "I'm ashamed to say I did this more than once, because I didn't want to be humiliated," Gross says. Holding up the flashcards, she felt helpless as students cried in frustration and fear when they didn't know the words. In staff meetings, the principal would say of teachers not meeting the benchmarks that "she's not with us; she's not on the team." And the results were even more broadly public: "We had to hang up the data with children's names in the classroom or the hallway so that parents would be shamed into drilling the skills at home, and teachers were competing with one another so that we wouldn't be called out in meetings as having the lowest scores," Gross recalls with a shudder.

Living in a culture of humiliation for both children and teachers, Gross cried every day in her classroom closet. She stuck out the year only because she desperately wanted to build a teaching career and knew that leaving a position halfway through the year would be a black mark on her résumé that could make it very difficult for her to secure a job in the future. Gross says her students' parents, many of whom hadn't finished high school, weren't concerned "because they didn't know that this wasn't just what high expectations look like." Like all parents, they wanted their children to be successful, and if the school said success meant knowing two hundred sight words, they wanted their children to meet that goal. Gross believes that many of the parents had had negative experiences with school themselves growing up and hadn't had the opportunity to know what a positive and nurturing classroom environment looks like, or how it can make students feel engaged, motivated, and safe to learn. But there is no evidence to back up the approach pushed by Gross's former principal. While it is true that knowing some high-frequency words like "the" and "she" by sight is helpful for early reading, the quantity targets that the principal set appear to be arbitrary.

There has been a seismic shift in expectations for literacy in young children in the past several decades, spurred in part by achievement gaps among children of different backgrounds and between children from the United States and other countries, and in part by brain research showing how important early language and literacy are to later learning. Most of us didn't learn to read when we were four or five because our teachers and parents didn't know that it was possible. Today, pretty much all experts and teachers agree that it is important for three- and four-year-olds to develop some of the foundations of reading, but not to be reading fluently (or even haltingly, for that matter). It *is* important for them to hear a rich vocabulary, engage in conversation with peers and adults, and be read to frequently. There is also largely agreement about the importance of teaching preschoolers to identify letters and build some of the precursors to reading, like rhyming. Studies show that children who know at least ten letters in pre-K are usually on course to reading well in second grade (although those who do best in second grade know more in pre-K: about eighteen uppercase and fifteen lowercase letters). Another strong predictor of elementary reading is whether preschoolers know the sounds that letters make. But there is no consensus that preschoolers should be learning to read words and texts.

The teaching of reading has been surprisingly contentious for generations, most notably during the "reading wars" of the 1980s and '90s. Classrooms became the battleground for a philosophical and political debate about whether children should learn to read by being immersed in interesting books or by learning the mechanics of how to sound out words. On the "whole language" side, proponents argued that it was more important for children to engage with and understand the overall meaning of a text than to get each and every word correct. On the "phonics" side, supporters emphasized the importance of "decoding" skills like knowing the sounds that certain letters and combinations of letters make, and how to blend them together. After years of vehement debate, and of the educational pendulum swinging back and forth, the phonics approach won out when the infamous No Child Left Behind Act of 2001 made it a central focus and promoted it through the Reading First initiative. States received billions of dollars to implement phonics-focused programs approved under Reading First grants. But in 2006, researchers found the impact of Reading First to be largely nil. (Investigators also discovered blatant corruption in the program; administrators at the U.S. Department of Education awarded grants only to states planning to use textbooks produced by companies from which the officials profited, despite the fact that the effectiveness of the texts was unproven.) Today, it is widely agreed that children need to know how to decode words and sentences, but they also need to understand the meaning of what they read, so teachers should provide a "balanced approach" to literacy that incorporates both of the above methods. Even education historian and critic Diane Ravitch, who was once a vociferous proponent of the phonics approach, now recognizes the need for a balanced approach, as she outlined in a 2014 commentary called "Why I Don't Care About the 'Reading Wars' Anymore."

Perhaps one of the reasons the teaching of reading has been so contentious is that the process of learning to read is highly complex. Becoming a reader is particularly tricky in English, because many letters make multiple sounds, and exceptions abound in spelling, pronunciation, and grammar. In some other languages like German and Spanish, each letter makes only one sound, so there is a direct and clear correspondence between each letter and its sound. (Media reports have recently touted the fact that children in the highly successful Finnish education system don't begin formal schooling until age seven, but they rarely point out that Finnish is a far simpler language than English, and that the typical Finnish child is able to master reading in a matter of months. In addition, the vast majority of Finnish children attend state-funded pre-K from ages three to six.) In order to read successfully in English, children have to achieve a wide range of skills, from sounding out words to recognizing words that don't follow the typical sound rules to understanding the meanings of words, sentences, and passages, to name just a few.

Preschoolers need to begin laying the foundation for some of those skills, experts agree, but there is no research showing that all preschoolers can or should be reading at age four. In fact, a national research study showed that only about 2 percent of incoming kindergartners can recognize sight words, and even fewer can read words in context. Even later in kindergarten, reading is relatively rare; another study showed that only about 7 percent of children can identify twenty or more sight words at the beginning of kindergarten. Yet in some schools like the one where Gross taught, racking up sight words is the goal. How did this come to be? Research shows that third grade is a critical marker for reading skill, when children have to be solid enough readers that they can make a transition that educators often describe as moving "from learning to read to reading to learn." But in order to prepare children to meet that milestone, many schools have pushed reading instruction and assessments earlier and earlier. Some of that pressure comes from administrators and some of it comes from other teachers. Tracy Crosby, the director of early childhood for the Elizabeth, New Jersey, public schools, frequently fields phone calls from pre-K teachers complaining that kindergarten teachers blame them for their former students' inability to read. When Crosby looked into the issue, she found that the kindergarten teachers were passing on pressure they were getting from the first-grade teachers, and so on and so on all the way up to third grade.

Fred Morrison, a reading researcher at the University of Michigan, believes the focus on sight words started because "the research has been saying that if we want to understand the variability in children's skills, we need to start earlier. But there's a lot of variability—some kids already know their letters and can even recognize words before pre-K, and others don't know any. So the idea was, because some kids don't have the early enriching stimulation at home, maybe we might need to do something about that. Not an unreasonable idea, but two things came out of that. First, it was the upper-middle-class parents who said, 'We need to do something!' ignoring the fact that they were already doing enough. Second, when the school systems got hold of this not-unreasonable idea, they decided to do with preschool kids what they do with first graders. So now we are seeing more direct instruction in pre-K out of fear."

There is no denying that sight words are important, in part because many English words don't follow the typical phonics rules and in part because if we had to sound out every word each time we picked up a book or opened a website, we would read very slowly. In fact, children who use only phonics sometimes read so slowly that they can't remember the beginning of a sentence or paragraph by the time they get to the end. Children read connected text faster and more easily when they recognize some of the words they encounter, especially irregular words like "thought" and "through" and high-frequency words like "the," "me," and "our." According to one study of over one thousand texts commonly used during the school years, one hundred of the most frequently used words make up half of what students read. Ten of them make up almost 25 percent! Given that, it's easy to see the benefits of teaching children to recognize those words so they don't have to constantly puzzle them out or "decode" them, in the language of reading researchers.

But children who only recognize sight words have the same problems with speed and fluency, yet sight words have developed an outsized influence in some classrooms, becoming if not the be-all-end-all of reading as in Lisa Gross's former classroom, then at least the most emphasized component of reading instruction. The problem is that children who know one hundred sight words can still be missing another key part of reading: comprehension. Isolated from their context, words don't mean much. That's why it's harder for adults to remember a list of random words than a grocery shopping list or a group of words paired with visual representations. It's also why it's hard for children exposed to random sight words to use them correctly. Boston Public Schools' early childhood coach Abby Morales told me about watching young children sit through a lesson on the words "gorgeous" and "unusual," repeating them back to the teacher but not applying them in any meaningful way. When a student later admired her skirt, Morales asked him if it was gorgeous or unusual; he gave her a quizzical look that suggested he had never heard the words before.

Kids learn from being immersed in the language, not from being taught a few words at a time, literacy experts told me. Through natural conversations, they not only gain a deeper knowledge of the words, they learn more of them. "Get rid of the list of words," one admonished. Reading expert Pani Kendeou, a professor at the University of Minnesota, agrees. Her studies show that readers understand words and sentences better when they are connected to some sort of context, whether it's their own real-life experience or a story they are hearing.

It is surprising that comprehension is sometimes left out of early reading instruction, because understanding is ultimately the goal of reading, but this is actually not a new trend. Educators and researchers used to think that the mechanics of reading had to come before comprehension, according to Kendeou. More recently, however, research has shown that's not the case. Comprehension and context help readers remember words, and, conversely, background knowledge like vocabulary and experience support comprehension. In fact, Kendeou has found that background knowledge is one of the most important factors in reading comprehension, more important than the mechanics of reading. I could see how this works as I watched my son learn to read. As he would sound out a new word, I could see and hear him trying to match it to words in the mental dictionary he had been building up since birth. He would begin sounding out the specific letters and then once he found a word that matched both the letters and the context, he would stop sounding out, and he would read the correct word and move on to the next one. Occasionally, he would start to sound it out and guess the wrong word, but then his teacher or I would ask him at the end of the sentence, "Does that make sense?" and he would go back and find the correct word. Kendeou says that what my son was doing was making inferences, or filling in information that is implied but not explicit. Her studies show that the ability to make inferences is a big part of reading comprehension, even for very young children.

Because multiple components of the reading process support one another, teachers have to build them simultaneously. "You need to scaffold the work of integrating the parts. You can't just teach vocabulary and phonemes and graphemes [word sounds and combinations] and expect them to get applied correctly," Kendeou advised. Neuroscience research supports this advice. Brain-imaging studies show that there are at least four separate parts of the brain that play major roles in learning to read. But they don't work in isolation. Neural connections called white matter pathways allow information to be shared among those different parts of the brain and help us make the necessary connections to recognize, decode, understand, and sometimes express what we read. Harvard researcher Nadine Gaab says that one of the most important pathways, or what she calls a "data highway," connects two areas of the brain: the "letter box," which recognizes letters and words and is located in the rear part of the brain associated with visual processing, and "the CEO," which is involved in reading comprehension and is located in the front part of the brain that is typically involved in executive functions. Reading requires a smoothly running network, just like a company, and the CEO keeps everything organized and goal-directed. The CEO helps us decide what information is important, filters out irrelevant information, and connects text with our existing body of knowledge. "Sight word people try to put as many objects in the letter box as possible early on and neglect the need to build the whole network," Gaab told me. You have to develop the CEO, too, if you want to succeed, she explained. "Otherwise, you can end up building a good product and a really fast highway, but the company will go bankrupt because nobody trained the CEO" to coordinate the functions.

To build the whole network, experts say that early childhood classrooms should be awash in language and literacy materials and activities, and that those should be embedded in organic ways throughout the whole day, including when children are playing, eating, and even lining up. Regardless of their background or the skills they bring with them on the first day of pre-K, all children can benefit from singing songs about the alphabet while they line up, finding the letters of their name in a sign they see on the playground, and "writing" customer orders while playing restaurant, even if they are just writing squiggles. Gaab says that it's particularly important for children to experience letters and words in multisensory ways, including touch and movement as well as sight and sound. And Morrison emphasized immersing children in lots of activities and lots of letters: "It's like learning to play the piano. You can't just learn one note at a time."

Building early literacy skills in an organic way might sound like a tall order, but good teachers make it look easy. "We're going to play a game where I'm going to sing a silly word that rhymes with something in the kitchen," said a teacher in Elizabeth, New Jersey, to her classroom of low-income, largely Spanish-speaking students. "What does a rhyming word mean?" she asked them. When a boy responded, after a pause, "Same sound," she went further. "It has the same sound where, at the beginning or the end?" "The end!" three other children replied. The teacher sang a little ditty about "What's cooking in the kitchen that rhymes with 'bapple'?" The children sang along, giggled, and exclaimed, "Apple!" The teacher smiled. "Right! Let's count out the syllables: *ap-ple*. How many? Two, right! What letter does it start with?" When a boy correctly supplied the *A*, she held up a card with the word "apple" and pointed to the *A*. Then the teacher and children all sang to the tune of "The Farmer in the Dell": "The *a* says *ah*, the *a* says *ah*, every letter makes a sound, the *a* says *ah*." She asked if any of the children's names started with *A*, and then asked for other words that start with the letter. For each response, she had an encouraging comment. As she went through other words and letters, students suggested a mix of English and Spanish words, all of which she understood and encouraged.

In this short, engaging activity, the teacher covered rhyming, letter sounds, vocabulary, syllables, and even counting. What's Cooking in the Kitchen is listed in a guide the Elizabeth early childhood department created of activities to build children's phonological awareness, or their ability to understand and use language sounds and concepts. Phonological awareness is a fundamental building block for reading, because children need to understand that language can be divided into smaller parts: sentences, then words, then syllables, then letters. Wordplay in the early years helps build these concepts. It works partly because it's fun. The children I saw giggled, sang, clapped, and stayed attentive enough to learn the concepts the teacher was explaining. Effective teachers have all kinds of strategies like these. They help children form letters out of yarn, clay, or dough that they can bake and eat. They introduce letters and the sounds they make not in an alphabetical or arbitrary order but in a context that is meaningful to a child: her name. They encourage children to write frequently and freely, with "invented spelling" that follows a strictly phonetic logic.

But perhaps the most important thing is for young children to be exposed to lots of language. "One of the most powerful predictors of a child's ability to learn to read and succeed in school is vocabulary size at kindergarten entry," wrote Harvard educational psychologist Meredith Rowe in a 2012 paper, citing decades' worth of studies. And the way to build children's vocabulary is to expose them to lots of new and varied words in daily conversations. Children learn and remember words more easily when those words are meaningful and connected to real life, rather than presented on flashcards. That means that teaching children vocabulary also means teaching them to be curious about and interested in the world around them.

One way to build curiosity and vocabulary is for adults and children to read books together and discuss them. Most parents and teachers have heard about the importance of reading to young children, but children pay more attention and learn more when adults read in a particular way: with lots of opportunity for questions, discussion, and interaction. Children who are engaged in what they are seeing and hearing often have questions and ideas, and they make more connections and better retain new information when they have the space to explore them. Skillful teachers (and parents) know how to encourage and respond to that engagement without getting derailed or losing the thread of the book. (For example, by asking specific questions about what children notice, gently redirecting them if they start to share an unrelated anecdote, or explaining a plan to take two more questions before moving on to the next page.) But it takes practice, because it's not always easy, and not necessarily intuitive. As a Harvard researcher I know pointed out, simply telling parents to read doesn't give them a sense of why or how they can expand their children's thinking. He recalled giving a talk to a group of low-income parents and hearing a mother ask, "I'm supposed to let him ask questions? He keeps trying to talk during the book and I always say, 'Shh! I'm reading! Pay attention!'" Her reaction to her child's questions was completely logical, because all she knew was that it was important for her child to hear the words of the book.

In almost all pre-K classrooms, read-aloud with book discussion is a component of the day, but the quality of the discussion varies widely, largely according to how skilled the teacher is at facilitation. Boston's K1 curriculum helps teachers with facilitation by suggesting specific questions about the text and links to other parts of the curriculum. The prompts help teachers like Nurtury's Herminia Santiago get in the habit of making those kinds of connections so they can come up with their own. Early one morning, with the children gathered around her in a close circle, Santiago read a picture book in a quiet but enthusiastic voice. "'Douglas built a bridge,'" she read sideways so that all her children could see the picture book she was holding out to them. "Oh, I hear the word 'bridge'!" she exclaimed, with an air of genuine surprise and delight. A little boy piped up: "*B* for 'bridge'!" Santiago smiled. "Yes. I'm thinking about two kids who made bridges. Roqeeba and Jonathan. What did you use to make bridges?" They reminded their classmates how they had used pipe cleaners and a shoe box to make an impressive replica of Boston's iconic Zakim Bridge, a complicated suspension bridge that took years and renowned engineers to build. Santiago continued reading but stopped again when she read the words "violets and dandelions." "Oh! Doesn't that remind you of the things we made in the classroom, when we were learning about things that grow? We made a garden, bridges. I remember when some of you made the Boston Public Garden after we went to visit it."

The K1 curriculum also encourages teachers to read books multiple times, especially books that are core to the curriculum and its center activities. This way, the teacher can read through the book fully and get through the whole story before going back and allowing space for questions and comments (some of which may have been addressed by getting a full reading of the book). Teachers also have the option to have their class act out parts of the book, because the more the children interact with the themes and words, the better they can understand and use them. And as many parents know, young children delight in repeated readings of books. It can drive parents crazy with boredom when children ask for the same bedtime book all week or cry "Again! Again!" at the conclusion of a favorite story. But experts advise parents to have patience and indulge the requests, because repetition helps children learn, reinforcing new vocabulary words and ideas and cementing neural connections as children link concepts together.

Of course, parents don't typically have the kind of training and experience that teachers do, and the environments children experience before
they come to school do matter. Children whose parents read to them in
an interactive way and have engaging conversations with them are at an
advantage when they start pre-K. Unfortunately, studies suggest that low-
income babies, toddlers, and preschoolers tend to have less exposure to
stimulating language and conversations at home. In a now famous study
published in 1995, Betty Hart and Todd Risley followed forty-two
parent-child pairs for several years, recording their conversations once a
month. When Hart and Risley compared children from different social
classes, they found that children from professional families heard an average of 487 words per hour, compared with children from working-class
families who heard 301 words per hour, and from welfare-recipient families who heard 176 words per hour. When the researchers extrapolated
those numbers to what would happen if the patterns persisted until children turned four, they estimated that the children from professional families would hear an astounding *thirty million more words* than their
lower-income peers. Importantly, the researchers found that differences
in parent-child conversations predicted differences in children's vocabularies: by age three, children from professional families had vocabularies
with about 1,100 words, compared to children from welfare-recipient
families who had about 525 words.

More recently, Rowe's research has shown that it's not just the number
of words parents use that matter but the types of words and conversations between adults and children. When parents of infants and toddlers
use more sophisticated and abstract words, have back-and-forth conversations with their children, point to things when they talk about them,
and ask "wh" questions like "where" and "why," their children go on to
have larger vocabularies and more sophisticated syntax, grammar, and
verbal reasoning a year later. The "wh" questions appear to be particularly important, because they encourage children to think critically and
produce verbal responses. For example, asking a child, "What animal do

you see?" elicits a more complex thought and speech process than asking, "Do you see the dog?" (Interestingly, research finds that fathers are more likely than mothers to ask "wh" kinds of questions.) Rowe has found that parents of different income and education levels vary on some of these dimensions but not others.

The growing body of research on the importance of parents talking with young children has driven investment in programs that teach parents of very young children how and why to talk with their children in their homes. In Providence, Rhode Island, home visitors have outfitted almost seven hundred low-income parents with a wearable device that records the quantity and quality of their utterances. The home visitors then sit down with parents to review their data and suggest ways they can improve their children's exposure to rich language. The results are encouraging, but the process can be complicated. Parent-child interactions are embedded in generations of cultural traditions, while schools tend to value one culture—a white, middle-class one. As Howard University professor Hakim Rashid has pointed out, "For those raised in a world where 'children should be seen and not heard,' finding the fine line between children who 'talk' and children who 'talk back' is difficult. In addition, it may be reasonable to remember that highly interactive, language-rich conversations are more difficult to come by in families overwhelmed by deep and persistent stressors who are trying, above all, to simply keep their children safe."

Some experts have also pointed out that many African American children grow up hearing and speaking an English variety known as African American Vernacular English (AAVE), Black English, or the more polarizing term Ebonics. Language experts have pointed out that AAVE follows a set of distinct rules, just like any language or dialect, but some of them are different than Standardized American English. For example, in AAVE it is common to convey a habitual action by employing the verb "be," as in "I be working hard in school" and to construct the past tense by using the word "ain't," as in "I ain't done it yet." The appropriate role of AAVE in schools has been highly controversial. Some Americans believe that it is not correct or proper English and therefore should be discouraged by schools. Others argue that it operates much like a dialect, that it should be respected along with Standardized English, and that schools do a disservice to African American children when they dismiss it. It should be noted that these advocates are generally not arguing for teachers to actually teach AAVE, but rather to respect its use and encourage children to be able to engage both forms of the language in different contexts. Regardless of one's position, it is obvious that all children do need to be competent in Standardized American English in order to succeed in school. But for complex reasons, including those previously stated, a language gap persists at kindergarten entry, as does a correlation between kindergarten vocabulary and later school success.

For all children, but especially for those who come to school with limited vocabulary, saturating pre-K classrooms with conversation, books, and experiences that invite curiosity and questioning is important. "When you look at the hours and hours of rich experiences and talk some children get at home, how do we do that in a classroom? It's hard, but the least we can do is not make it barren and boring," literacy expert Judy Schickedanz advised. The goal for all children should be to make language and reading fun, interesting, and accessible. That is best accomplished through shared book reading, conversations, and teachable moments. But for some children, reading in pre-K looks very different.

Eight

Skills and Drills

In DC's Ward 8, east of the Anacostia River, sits the Parklands campus of AppleTree Early Learning Public Charter Schools. The bright, welcoming school is a part of the Villages of Parklands, a well-groomed complex of apartment buildings, town houses, and youth facilities that belies the deep-rooted poverty of many of the residents and the violence in the neighborhood. On a beautiful spring day, I felt safe waiting on the sidewalk for a ride until a school administrator came out and told me, "Even I don't stand out here like that." Just a few blocks away, a young teenager had been shot and killed in a dispute over sneakers a few years back.

Inside, four-year-olds were watching a video with an upbeat narrator singing a hip-hop-inflected tune about the letter *u*. "*U, u, u* is a letter in the alphabet. *U* says *uh*, *U* says *uh*. *U* for 'umbrella'! *U* for 'umbrella'!" The children chanted along with the video and, when prompted, held their fingers up to draw phantom *u*'s in the air. After the video, their teacher asked a boy to stand up and help her "segment the word 'fun.'" She held out her arm with the palm facing up, as if she were about to have her blood drawn. She pointed to her upper arm and prompted him to do the same while saying, "*Fff*." Next she asked him, "Where does the *u* fall?" Seeing his blank look, she guided him through the exercise: *fff* for the upper arm, *uuhh* while touching the spot just about the elbow, *nnn* while touching the forearm, and finally blending the sounds together while running her hand down her arm: "*Ff-uh-nn*. 'Fun.'" Then the class rehearsed a poem they would be reciting for their parents at an end-of-year ceremony in a few days. The poem was about moving on to kindergarten and included lines like, "We're not scared, we were made for this."

After the children headed off to the bathroom to prepare for recess, the teacher told me apologetically, "They struggle with segmenting. They don't know the difference between syllables and segmenting. Or they get confused about the difference." I hadn't seen preschoolers use either the word or the concept of segmenting before (it refers to breaking down each sound of a word in order to sound it out), so I asked her why those skills are important to have before kindergarten. "Well, they don't have to have them, but it's very helpful," she explained. "My friends who are kindergarten teachers tell me it's so helpful when they come with those skills already."

AppleTree's mission is to close the achievement gap before kindergarten. Its eight campuses serve three-, four-, and five-year-olds who are predominantly low-income students of color. At Parklands, 100 percent of the children are African American and almost all of them are eligible for free or reduced-price lunches, an indicator of low family income. Charter schools just for preschoolers are rare, but if you wanted to find one, DC would be a good place to look. Nearly 40 percent of public school students in DC attend a charter school, and they are popular among low-income parents, because they represent an opportunity to try new educational strategies in a city that had a notoriously dysfunctional school system when those parents were young.

AppleTree is the brainchild of Jack McCarthy, a passionate and gregarious former entrepreneur who left his career in real estate to found charter schools for high school students. But after several years of watching the high schoolers struggle to read, McCarthy realized his schools were starting too late. He decided to take a step back, way back, and create a preschool. So in 2001, he started a free laboratory preschool in a church basement, funded with private dollars so that it could serve children from low-income families. "I never thought I'd be doing this," he says with a laugh, "but I'm happy I am," and it shows. He speaks with an almost religious sense of mission about education for low-income kids, and he is noticeably sympathetic to the huge challenges their families face, which, he says, "not even a highly educated person could navigate successfully." When he opened the first AppleTree classroom in 2001, which served thirty-six children in that church basement, it was a labor of love. Just before the school opened, the terrorist attacks on the World Trade Center and the Pentagon spurred AppleTree's main funders to redirect the grants and McCarthy couldn't pay the bills. He kept the school alive with passion and shoestrings.

In 2006, AppleTree applied for charter status and opened its first early childhood charter school, receiving public funding based on the number of students and the city's per-student allotment. In the early years, AppleTree was an experiment, with a small staff who tinkered with its model, trying out curricula and instructional practices as they went. Then in 2011, AppleTree began developing its own academic curriculum, which is called Every Child Ready and is overseen by the AppleTree Institute, the organization's research and development arm. With support from a philanthropic community enamored of charter schools, federal grants to develop the new curriculum, and a lot of interest from parents who wanted to steer their children out of failing public schools, AppleTree grew quickly. Today it serves almost nine hundred children and is, according to its website, "a $14 million enterprise with 175 staff and a growing impact on policy and practice." It disseminates its curriculum to several other pre-K–8 charter schools in the city, widening its sphere of influence in DC's early childhood sector.

Education director Anne Zummo Malone says that AppleTree's model is "true instruction, as opposed to what you see in some community preschools. It's not that we don't have fun, but it's not about having fun all day." That focus on instruction and school readiness, like the phonics and segmenting activities I saw, are a draw for many of the schools' families. They appealed to Jackie Taylor and her niece, Kenyona, when they were looking for a preschool for Kenyona's four-year-old daughter, Kennedy. Jackie, who raised Kenyona and sees Kennedy as a granddaughter, was so impressed when she read about the school's curriculum that she didn't see a need to look at any other preschools. She wanted to be sure that Kennedy was ready for kindergarten, and AppleTree promised that on their website. She also liked that each classroom had two teachers to work with the kids, and the fact that AppleTree serves only preschoolers. Kennedy, who has sickle cell anemia, is tiny and has trouble with stairs. "We were afraid that she would get lost in a bigger school with bigger kids," said Jackie, who takes Kennedy to and from school every day.

In Kennedy's classroom, the day starts off with breakfast and an educational TV show like *Sid the Science Kid*. That's followed by a video with a yoga instructor leading a deep-breathing and calming-down exercise, and then a greeting song in which children stand up and jump when the teacher calls out the color of their squares on the rug (undoing the calm they had achieved a few minutes prior). Next, one of the two teachers leads morning meeting. "What is today? What will tomorrow be?" a teacher asked one of Kennedy's classmates one morning. She had chosen him by randomly selecting a Popsicle stick with his name on it out of a cup—a strategy for making sure that students get called on randomly and fairly. The boy answered the first question correctly ("Thursday"), but struggled with the second one. The teacher tried to give him a clue: "It's the best day of the week, or the school week, anyway." That hint didn't resonate, so the teacher said to the class, "Everyone say, 'Tomorrow will be Friday.'" The children obliged, repeating as if they were one especially loud four-year-old, "Tomorrow will be Friday." She then asked the boy to lead the class in counting the days on the calendar up to the current date. "What voice should we count in today?" she asked the little boy. He chose Batman, so the class counted from one to twenty-six in deep, raspy voices. But when the teacher said, "So today is the . . . ," the boy needed his classmates to call out "Twenty-sixth!" When she got to the month, she prompted, "It is May. What letter does May start with?" He paused and then supplied the *m* she was looking for. "Good job!" she told him. "Everyone say, 'Good job, James,'" and his classmates repeated, "Good job, James."

Chanting and repeating the teachers' words are big parts of Apple-Tree's teaching approach. Some researchers believe this strategy is beneficial in African American communities because they have a strong tradition of oral storytelling and teaching. At AppleTree, adults use chants to establish routines and help children remember, make sure all children are participating, and build vocabulary. Building vocabulary is a central goal. "It is a challenge when we are reading them books, because they don't have the vocabulary and context and we have to scaffold that for them," said Nikeysha Jackson, the Parklands campus principal. Teachers hope that by prompting children to use specific words, not just hear them, children are learning them for future use. The children have a chant for everything, it seems, including counting forward and backward by tens and transitioning from the rug to centers.

But sometimes it feels like orderly transitions are more important than what children are learning. One day toward the end of the school year, before the children made the transition to centers, a teacher told her class what was available in each station. "Today in Investigation Location, you can count with cubes, or you can do these puzzles," she said, holding up two Ziploc bags containing paper puzzles, which, I discovered later, required children to match a piece with a letter on it to a piece picturing an object starting with that letter. (I had to take them out of the bag, because they had been ignored by the children.) "In Art Studio, you can use the markers and draw a picture of whatever your little heart desires; Mommy and Daddy, whatever," she continued. "We also have iPads today." The kids cheered. As they waited to be called on to choose their centers, the other teacher told me that "some of the centers are related to a theme, but we always have two that are real skills," by which she meant writing, reading, counting, and simple addition. "Sometimes we can tie in writing to the theme a little better . . ." she said, and trailed off. Later in the day, her colleague told me that centers sometimes include strategies like using word searches, where children find and circle words from a field of letters, in order to familiarize them with sight words. She acknowledged that sometimes it's hard to convince children to participate in the more academic centers, so she requires them to do those centers before others like blocks and dramatic play.

During centers every morning and afternoon, teachers pull a few children at a time to do small group instruction, a major focus of the Every Child Ready curriculum. Throughout the year, all children progress through a set of sequenced activities designed to build their literacy and math skills. The activities are what educators sometimes call "backwards mapped"—they are derived from standards and assessments of those standards to align what children are doing with what they should be learning. McCarthy told me the curriculum is designed this way because, "It only makes sense to start with the third-grade reading test, and the standards including Common Core and DC early learning standards, and backwards map from there." To him, it's common sense that you determine what kids need to know, teach it to them, test them on it, and if they don't get it, reteach and retest it. His philosophy is logical, especially for someone with a background in business. But I didn't hear McCarthy or any of his colleagues talk about how young children learn, or about how they decide which skills children really need to have at ages three and four to make sure they meet benchmarks at age eight.

"Riiiing," sang a teacher as she clapped her hands over her head one January morning. "Siiiiiing," she sang, and clapped again. The teacher was sitting on one side of a small table, facing three children as she talked and clapped. Administrators had identified rhyming as a weak skill among Parklands' four-year-olds. At the beginning of the year, teachers give children a comprehensive assessment to diagnose their skills in areas like identifying letters, recognizing letter-sound correspondence, and understanding rhymes, all of which are stepping-stones toward reading. The test is then given four more times during the year to assess children's progress. Administrators and teachers use the data to create small groups of children with similar skills and to pinpoint where in the curriculum they should focus with each group.

"Riiiiing, siiiing," the teacher repeated several more times. "Now you do it," she instructed the three students brightly. The goal seemed to be to clap on the "ing" part of the words, but the children were uncertain, as was I. Next she held up three cards with pictures of a ring, a bird, and a boat, and asked each child which two cards rhymed. When they looked at her blankly, she asked, "Which ones go together?" The children continued to look baffled, so she pointed to the bird and the boat and said, "Do they sound the same?" One boy nodded uncertainly. "Nope," she corrected him. "Boat and sing do not sound the same. Which ones sound the same?" Then she pointed to her wedding ring as a clue, followed by the card with the bird, which I slowly realized had its mouth open, apparently to sing. "R-iiiing, s-iiiing," she said a few times. "They sound the same. You say it. Ring, sing. Ring, sing." The little boy repeated with a quiet voice and a perplexed look. Perhaps he was even slower than me to realize the card was supposed to represent "sing" rather than "bird." Perhaps boat and bird sounded "the same" to him because they have the same first sound. Perhaps he was unclear that rhyming words have the same ending sound. Whatever the reason, the boy didn't appear to reach an aha moment.

At the conclusion of each day's small group activity, children are given a kind of quiz: three questions that are designed to show whether they have mastered the concept they are supposed to be learning on that day. If they "pass," as a group of teachers from another AppleTree campus explained it to me, they move on to a new activity the next day. If one or more of the children "fail," the whole group repeats the activity the following day. The cards with the singing bird, the ring, and the boat were part of this daily quiz. As the struggling boy wiggled in his chair, the teacher eventually guided him to the right answers and he bounded off to find a center, as if he were afraid she was going to ask him more questions he couldn't answer. He was probably not the only one who was relieved. One of the teachers I talked to said it can be hard on the whole group if one child fails. "Sometimes the other kids will say 'We have to do this *again*?' and they tell you the answers to the questions before you even ask them," she reported. And she said she didn't get much guidance from the curriculum or her supervisors on how to help children who failed. "Last year, I just kept doing the same thing every day because that's what I thought I was supposed to do. Of course, I got the same result every day. But then I realized you have to use your creativity to try something new," she explained.

Large group instruction is another central part of the curriculum. In Kennedy's classroom one day, a teacher sat in a chair in front of her children, who were gathered on the rug. "We're going to play a memory game," she announced, and began holding up cards with numerals printed on them. As she held up each card, the children chorused, "Ten," "Thirty," "Eighty." She applauded their answers, all of which were correct. Then she moved on to a matching game, placing two of each numeral card facedown on the floor in a version of the old Hasbro game Memory. "When you find a match, I'm going to call on a friend to write the number up here on the whiteboard," she explained to the children.

Later that day, the teachers eschewed their usual small-group time, opening up centers for a second time. It was the second-to-last week of school and the children had just finished taking their final assessment, which is administered through a combination of computer prompts, audio stories, and teacher questions. Looking around at the children playing in centers, some of whom were bashing each other's block towers or tearing up paper in the dramatic play area, the teacher told me, "They just finished testing, so we're just letting them be four-year-olds."

At AppleTree and many other preschools serving low-income children, there is a strong focus on making sure children know the basics like letters, numbers, and colors. Creativity, critical thinking, and executive functioning seem to take a back seat. AppleTree's high academic expectations for its children are in many ways aspirational. But they are also narrow, missing the focus on the whole child that makes some other programs successful. That worries many child development experts, and it raises questions about whether the children will develop the full range of skills and strengths they need to be on par with the middle- and upper-class children who tend, on average, to outperform them in school.

"Our kids are lacking in exposure to so many things that we need to start with very discrete skills," Malone told me when I asked how the organization has developed its instructional approach. She and other staff were clearly concerned that AppleTree's children wouldn't get those fundamental skills any other way than with repeated instruction and drilling, despite the fact that most early childhood experts say this is not the most effective way for young children to learn. AppleTree founder Jack McCarthy, who is passionately committed to closing achievement gaps, says, "We want all children to get to the same point by kindergarten, but you need different things and different dosages to get different kids there."

That opinion is hotly contested. "There are a lot of kids who are not getting exposed to the kinds of things that will help them get ready for school. We have to make sure they're not missing out so that when they hit the doorstep of school they're not forever behind. But the response has been 'Oh my God, we need basic skills,' and it ends up looking like first grade," says developmental psychologist Kathy Hirsh-Pasek. "We need to know *how* to deliver the information children are missing so we can ensure all kids are on equal footing. It's very easy to have kids sit at desks and memorize words," she warns, but that isn't how children make meaning of information or integrate it into their knowledge for the long term.

It also may not be the best way for them to learn to read, according to Kathleen Roskos and Susan Neuman, who wrote in a guidebook for educators: "Here's the tragic irony [of compensatory reading programs focused on basic letters and sounds]. Reading achievement in the earliest years may look like it's just about letters and sounds—but it's not. Successful reading, as will become abundantly clear by grades three and four, consists of knowing a relatively small store of unconscious procedural skills, accompanied by a massive and slowly built-up store of conscious content knowledge." In other words, it's important for children to learn the rules of sounding out the word "Arctic," but they won't be able to understand the word unless they have learned that there are different parts of the earth with different climates that are hospitable to certain forms of life and not others. It's important for them to learn that an exclamation point conveys excitement or emphasis, but it's even more important for them to understand why a person in Florida might use one when reporting that the temperature is predicted to be forty degrees in April. Roskos and Neuman go on to point out that interesting content and connections with real life are what drive children to *want* to read. That's why early childhood leaders like those in Boston know it's important to use books that are interesting and relevant to children's lives, whether it's *Peter's Chair* or *Tito Puente, Mambo King.*

The debate raises a crucial question: Are basic skills enough to close achievement gaps? Is being able to count to one hundred and recognize words, which AppleTree children do very well, enough to get them to achieve on par with their more affluent peers as they progress through school?

Parents I talked to at AppleTree seem to think the answer is yes. Many families come to the school specifically because of its intense focus on academics. Parent Samantha Bryan worried about low expectations and negative influences in traditional schools in her neighborhood, and she wanted to make sure that her son, Dylan, developed the skills she had seen her own classmates fail to master when she was a student. "Anything that makes him in the higher percentile is something I want for him," she explained to me, as she described her high expectations for Dylan and how hard she worked to be involved in his schooling. "There are stereotypes people put on black males, and I don't want people to do that to him. I don't want him to be known for sports but for his brain."

Jackie Taylor is happy with what her grand-niece, Kennedy, is learning, especially when she compares Kennedy's experience to that of her three-year-old cousin, who is enrolled in pre-K at a traditional DC public school. "In her first year at AppleTree, the teacher was teaching them two- and three-letter words, and this year, she's learning five-letter words. She's also learning the alphabet, counting, and how to learn to read and write," although Jackie pointed out that could be in part because Kenyona works on those skills with Kennedy at home for thirty minutes every night. In contrast, she was disappointed with what her grandson was learning at his school: "They don't teach him as much. They're teaching him the alphabet, how to count to one hundred, simple words like 'stop' and 'go,' but no five-letter words like 'night.'" She thinks the difference is largely a function of class size. At his school, "the classes are bigger and the teachers can't devote enough attention to the kids who need it. AppleTree is a smaller setting so the teachers can give children more attention. They taught Kennedy how to put together words and sentences and things like that." Her satisfaction is understandable. It's logical to think that more is better, especially when you are getting constant messages about how important it is for children to be "ready for kindergarten." The question, though, is what it really means to be ready. Do four-year-olds really need to recognize five-letter words?

In Boston, leaders like Jason Sachs and Marina Boni don't think so.

They believe low-income children need and deserve opportunities for reflection and creativity, the kinds of opportunities that middle-class children get as a matter of course in private preschools. Child development experts tend to agree. When I asked Judy Schickedanz about the argument for basic skills, she framed it as the difference between achievement gaps and opportunity gaps. "If we say, 'Well, direct instruction is better than they would be getting elsewhere,' then we're not talking about real opportunity." In today's knowledge economy, giving children the opportunity to enter (or stay in) the middle class means ensuring that they have abilities like curiosity, creativity, and critical thinking. AppleTree's Jack McCarthy rightfully pointed out, woefully, that we live in a society where "the rich get richer and the poor get poorer." But the poor can't get richer without the learning opportunities their more affluent peers have.

In conversations I've had with teachers, there seems to be an undercurrent of fear. One teacher told me she wanted her children to know "at least forty to fifty" sight words before leaving AppleTree because she believed they would be expected to learn about 125 by the end of kindergarten. She also wanted her children to leave with the ability to write sentences so that "by the winter of kindergarten, they can be writing three-sentence paragraphs." Writing paragraphs is something that many kindergarteners would struggle to achieve, even in the most affluent schools and high-ability groups. In fact, many parents in those wealthier communities cringe at the focus on sight words and preschool reading instruction, instead wanting their children to explore, think creatively, and develop social skills. When I asked the teacher why it was important for kids to know so many sight words and to write sentences before kindergarten, she told me, "They don't have to have them, but it's very helpful. My friends who teach kindergarten tell me it's so helpful," echoing what her colleague had told me earlier about making things easier on kindergarten teachers. I talked to pre-K teachers from Florida to California who are feeling a downward push of expectations from later grades. Most experience it as an unwelcome pressure, a sort of passing of the buck, in which teachers fear losing their jobs if their students don't perform up to par. And public discussion about pre-K as a strategy for closing achievement gaps across race and class has perhaps increased that pressure.

But there also seems to be a fear for children, that they will get swallowed up and spit out by kindergarten if they don't come already knowing how to read and write, especially among parents and teachers who had negative school experiences themselves. Samantha Bryan went to public schools in DC and saw some of her classmates passed from grade to grade even though they couldn't read, eventually graduating from high school without functional literacy skills. She didn't want to see Dylan end up in that situation. She knew firsthand the consequences of not being able to read. Bryan owns a carry-out Jamaican restaurant with her family, where she has supervised many employees, including one who used to start fights. "He was so angry all the time, causing conflicts with people," she remembers, and she wanted to understand why. She eventually discovered that he was frustrated and embarrassed because he couldn't read, but he didn't want to ask for help, even though he couldn't move up in the restaurant without the ability to read the menu or customers' orders. Bryan taught him to read, because she wanted to make sure he learned. But she also wanted to make sure Dylan learned much, much sooner. As he wrapped up his year at AppleTree, poised to start kindergarten at a new charter school in DC, she was happy with how he was doing in reading: "He knows how to sound out words and he can break them down. He was reading with [his twenty-year-old sister] and he put his hand over the different parts of the word, so he knows how to teach himself to pronounce a word. That's not something I taught him." She attributed his progress to the focused instruction he got at AppleTree.

The concerns of parents like Samantha Bryan and Kenyona Taylor about whether their children will get what they need in school are often sadly warranted, because low-income children and children of color tend to get lower quality instruction throughout schooling. While some middle- and upper-class parents stress about gaining admission to the most prestigious preschools out of worry about whether their children will be able to compete later and ultimately get in to elite colleges, the pressures are different and arguably less acute. And many middle-class parents, like Maria Fenwick in Boston, aren't concerned with either extreme of that spectrum—whether their children will get into elite schools or whether they will learn how to read. When I asked Fenwick what she valued about Luca's experience at Charlestown Nursery School, reading and writing were not on the list. "I know he's going to learn to read," she explained. "He doesn't need to do it this year." In Luca's world, everyone knows how to read and takes it for granted that he will, too. In Dylan's world, his family and friends also expect him to read, but his parents are more aware of people who haven't had the opportunity or support to learn that skill, so perhaps it's more on their minds. Schickedanz told me that she has seen parents from low-income families and neighborhoods have particularly high hopes and expectations for their young children's academic learning. For one of her projects, she conducted a preschool literacy program in several different neighborhoods in Boston and nearby Cambridge, known for being home to both Harvard and MIT. During the project, one member of the steering committee, an African American mother from a low-income Boston neighborhood, spoke up during a meeting. "She told me, 'You're not teaching enough. I want my kids to learn what those other kids are learning and I want them to have the same opportunities,'" referring to the more affluent children in Cambridge. "I told her that they were doing the exact same things as her children," Schickedanz recounted, describing the play-based, interactive approach of the project's teaching. "She didn't believe me. So I took her and some other parents on a visit" to a site on the MIT campus. "She was shocked. I told them, 'To be fair, these kids are getting a lot of experiences and resources at home, too, but this is what [preschool] looks like on the other side of the river.'"

There are downsides to the basics-only approach. One is that it is focused on children's deficits, on making up for what children lack rather than building on what they have. In a report called *Being Black Is Not a Risk Factor: A Strengths-Based Look at the State of the Black Child*, scholar Wade Boykin called this "the stance of benevolent pathology." Despite best intentions, he believes, education reformers often view poor and minority children as the victims of life experiences that threaten their ability to learn and succeed in school, a risk that "must be compensated for through remediation, extra learning time, or other benevolent interventions." He argues that a focus on those kinds of interventions will not lead to a real and lasting closing of achievement gaps. Instead, he advocates for a "human capacity building" approach, which looks at how schools can build on the assets and valuable life experiences of low-income children and students of color. Those assets sometimes look different than the assets of middle-class families, but Boykin believes African American and low-income families' strengths are too often overlooked. His approach to education would focus on authentic learning and student engagement, involving students in conversations and activities that value what they "say, do, understand or feel with regard to lessons, learning activities and subject matter . . . on an everyday basis." Real engagement means students being interested and invested in what they are learning. When children are engaged, they learn material more deeply, apply it to their lives, and seek out more knowledge. Observers sometimes confuse good behavior with high engagement. But just because children comply with the rules and participate in activities doesn't mean they are processing what they are learning or storing it in a way that will be useful later. They might be like a middle schooler quoted in the educational blog *MindShift* who said, "I learned how to fall asleep with my eyes open" when teachers thought he was engaged.

As I watched AppleTree students during center time, I wondered about whether they were really engaged or just compliant. I approached one little girl standing in front of an easel that was outfitted with a black-and-white outline of the earth, with the letter *g* on all the land masses and *b* on the bodies of water. On the tray were two containers of paint—one blue and one green. "What's this? What are you doing here?" I asked the girl, who looked at me blankly and shrugged. "It's a globe," she told me. I asked her what a globe is. When she clearly didn't know the answer, a teacher strode over and said brightly, "The globe is a picture of the earth, like we talked about this morning, remember?" The child did not remember. I asked the little girl what she was supposed to do with the drawing. The teacher reminded her to paint the *b* spots with blue and the *g* spots with green. "And why are you going to do that?" I asked. Again she didn't know. She didn't understand that the blue was for water and the green was for land. In another classroom, I saw three children happily playing at a water table. But when I asked what they were doing and why, their answers were vague. "We're squeezing water," they said, but they didn't notice what was happening when they put water in the top of the watermill toys. They were surprised when I pointed out that the water made the wheels move down below.

Perhaps the clearest illustration of the classroom's focus came on another visit toward the end of the school year. An outgoing little boy held up a complicated circular pattern he had made with large, interlocking plastic links. When I asked him what it was and what he was going to do with it, he told me it was a ring and he was going to give it to his mom to wear. When I asked what it was made out of, he told me, "Water." I considered. "How do you make a ring out of water?" I asked him. "You put it in water and it makes a rainbow!" he told me, and then with barely a beat, he added, "I know two words that start with *d*: 'dog' and 'duck.'" One of his classmates chimed in, "And 'door.'" Anyone who has spent time with young children knows that they are masters of the non sequitur, and they love to show off what they know. Yet the little boy's focus on letters and his confusion about the purpose of his activity closely mirrored the patterns I saw in the curriculum and the teaching. At the least, he had internalized that when an adult interacted with him, she wanted to know, above all else, if he knew his letters and vocabulary.

Low-income preschoolers and children of color like that little boy are more likely to get the kind of skill-and-drill instruction found at Apple-Tree than their higher-income peers, studies suggest. Researcher Rachel Valentino looked at the types of instruction and program quality experienced by preschoolers from varied backgrounds in eleven states and found striking differences. Black and poor children experienced more time in didactic instruction while white and non-poor children spent more time in scaffolded, interactive instruction, and teachers had less back-and-forth or "elaborated" conversations with black students. Black, Hispanic, and poor children spent more time doing individual tasks like worksheets and computer time and spent less time on free-choice activities. They also spent more time on basics like letters and sounds, and even on fundamental things like toileting and cleanup.

Despite these differences, Valentino did not find any differences in structural quality across race or class. In other words, even though adult–child ratios, materials and space, and health and nutrition routines were of equal caliber, the type of adult–child interactions and the kind of teaching varied for different groups of children. Valentino speculates that state and federal regulations about program quality, which tend to focus on structural characteristics, have reduced or even eliminated gaps in those program features. But although structural quality can enable positive relationships and effective teaching, it doesn't guarantee it. Indeed, Valentino's data suggest that there is something else driving differences in the kind of teaching preschoolers receive: teachers' beliefs about how children learn and should be taught. In her study, poor children and children of color were more likely to have teachers who believed in an adult-centered, top-down approach to child-rearing—and those teachers tended to be people of color themselves. The prevalence of those beliefs explained the vast majority of the difference in the kind of instruction received by children from different ethnic groups, suggesting that differences in instructional quality and type may be driven by mind-set more than other factors like teachers' education or academic knowledge.

These results are striking, but they aren't completely new. Instructional quality has historically been lower in classrooms serving children from low-income families, while direct instruction is higher, along with a philosophy that teachers should drive learning rather than children. What is not clear is whether this direct instruction is problematic or beneficial. Valentino is aware that her results raise some complicated issues about race, class, and teaching. She writes: "It is unclear that all of these gaps in classroom process are problematic. The magnitude of these gaps may rather be indicative of differences in racial and cultural norms of how children learn." She points out that studies suggest minority and low-income parents are more likely than white, middle-class parents to use "didactic and directive" strategies for teaching children, and to use an approach some psychologists have called authoritarian but others have labeled "no-nonsense." There are logical and adaptive reasons for this "Do what I say or else" philosophy, scholars say. As one put it, "The emphasis on social conformity in African American parenting style may have grown in particular due to the parents' own experiences with discrimination and institutionalized racism, for they know that the cost of misbehavior in the larger social context may create dire consequences for their children." Many African American parents stress the importance of compliance because they feel that their children get fewer chances to make mistakes and are more strictly and harshly punished for misbehavior, whether in the classroom or on the street—and there is statistical evidence that they are right. Given that, Valentino wonders whether it may be helpful for schools to use similar teaching strategies because it establishes consistency for children. Her study didn't have the data that would have allowed her to examine whether different teaching styles work better for children of different backgrounds, and the results of previous studies on that question are mixed. Many studies find that children from all backgrounds benefit from scaffolded play and exploration, especially on outcomes like vocabulary and problem-solving. On the other hand, some find that low-income children do better in discrete math and reading skills when they have either individualized or whole-group direct instruction in preschool. The findings are not necessarily contradictory, because they have looked at different kinds of outcomes. Valentino cautions that the results supporting direct instruction focus on a narrow set of achievements. "We tend to use such discrete measures of success," she told me. "Direct instruction is a really good way to improve test scores and technical skills in the short term, but it's not at all clear that is the right thing in the long term. There could be other negative consequences," she reflected.

One of those negative consequences is a lack of focus on self-regulation and the social-emotional skills that are so important for kindergarten and later grades. Powell teacher Jason Harris, who previously taught at a charter school with a strict focus on literacy and math, pointed out that children come to school with self-regulation gaps as well as academic ones, especially when they have experienced trauma or instability, and he argues that the self-regulation gaps are just as important and even harder to remedy later. At his former school, he says, the children weren't developing the social and emotional skills they needed to be successful in a classroom. "I remember one preschooler who could read on a first-grade level, but she couldn't handle her emotions at all. She would get angry and melt down. She wasn't going to be successful in school no matter how good a reader she was." Research shows that kindergarten teachers tend to agree with Harris, rating self-regulation skills as the most important school-readiness skills, well ahead of basic academic ones. But those skills may be getting lost in some preschools. "The focus is on preparation, but what are we preparing them for?" Harris lamented.

At AppleTree, teachers focus a lot on children's behavior, but not on their self-regulation. They rely on what psychologists would call "other regulation"—adults managing children's behavior by giving directives and enforcing rules. AppleTree's approach to student behavior is called a token economy, a strategy based on B. F. Skinner's behaviorist principle of operant conditioning that uses rewards and punishments to shape behavior. Token economies are often used in group homes and hospitals for the mentally disabled and substance addicted, and they are also used in some schools, as in the popular Good Behavior Game program. Throughout the day, teachers or administrators watch for good behavior and reward it with a token like a plastic poker chip or a checkmark on a chart, and at some determined interval, people with enough tokens receive a reward. (Some systems also give demerits.) At AppleTree, every component of the day (morning meeting, centers, outdoor time, etc.) ends with the teacher and her students sitting in a circle while the teacher marks off on a chart which children do, and don't, deserve a checkmark for good behavior. Children get ten or twelve chances a day to earn a token. At the end of the school day, children with enough checkmarks get a reward like a brief dance party or blowing bubbles. Those who don't get enough checkmarks sit and watch.

The first time I visited Kennedy's classroom, I asked a little girl about the chart I saw on the wall, filled with Ks in small boxes. "If I get a K for being good, I get something nice at the end of the day," she told me. "What does it mean to be good?" I asked, and she shrugged. "And why is it a K on the chart?" I asked, genuinely curious, and she didn't know that either. It turned out that K was the letter of the week, a strategy for familiarizing children with letters that literacy experts discourage, because it doesn't embed letter learning in play or meaningful life contexts, like the child's name or a letter that pops up frequently in a favorite book.

On another visit, I observed how the teachers brought children to the rug after each part of the day to discuss their status on the chart, or "token board." When a teacher gathered the children after centers, she said, "Some of our friends had to leave their centers and come back to the rug. Do they get a token?" The kids shook their heads and chorused, "Noooo." "And some friends didn't keep their hands to themselves. Do they get a token?" "Noooo." Then she ran down the list of names, one at a time, and as she said each child's name, she said things like "Jackson did a good job" or "Jason had to come out of centers. He doesn't get a token." One way to fail to earn a token is to be sent to "sit and watch"—a chair where students are sent for what parents and teachers traditionally call a time-out. I had heard a frustrated teacher tell a child, "Max, go to sit and watch! This is your third one today!" Max surely wasn't going to get a token. "Let's do a cheer for the friends who earned a token for centers," she wrapped up, and reminded the children that they needed to have eight tokens (out of ten opportunities) in order to participate in the celebration at the end of the day. Then before she dismissed the children to get ready for recess, she pointed out to two boys that since they didn't even have four tokens, they had to stay inside for the beginning of recess.

When the end of the day came, the teacher reviewed the token board with the class, pointing out who had enough tokens and who didn't. Kennedy and her classmates with eight or more tokens gathered on the rug for their reward—watching a movie called *The Adventures of Shark Boy and Lava Girl*—while two children who didn't have enough tokens sat at tables in the back of the room, one staring straight ahead and the other with his head down. "When they are left out, they learn quickly," Principal Jackson had explained to me. She went on to tout the fact that because the end-of-day celebration is a daily routine, the children get to "start fresh" every day. It doesn't cause them any harm, she reasoned, because everyone has the chance to do better the next day.

Jackson and many of the teachers think of the token economy as a positive approach, because it focuses on rewards rather than punishments. But when you are four years old and you are denied a Popsicle or a bottle of bubbles, that *is* a punishment, even if the teachers don't call it one. It's also pretty humiliating when your teacher publicly points out that you didn't earn one. Shame has a host of negative consequences for young children, including internalizing problems like anxiety and externalizing ones like aggression, especially when the shaming experience is frequent. Even when children theoretically get to start fresh every day, some struggle with behavior on an ongoing basis, and it doesn't take long for them, and their peers, to decide they are bad kids. Once children feel stigmatized, they tend to act out even more, because they are hurt, angry, confused, or don't believe they can do better. When I saw Max go to sit and watch, he was already so far behind that he couldn't get enough tokens to participate in the celebration. Maybe he had assumed eight tokens to be an impossible goal even before he walked in the door at 8:00 a.m. And since the end-of-day reward was the only incentive to behave, what was to stop him from acting out the rest of the day?

The token economy makes things clear and easy for teachers, and it allows them to keep control of their classrooms so they can teach and children can learn. But it doesn't give children tools for *how* to behave. Jackson told me the token economy is so effective that teachers don't need any other behavior-management strategies. That may be true in the moment, but it doesn't build the self-regulation skills children need to control their own behavior in the future. Young children need to learn why their behavior is problematic. (I did see some AppleTree teachers explain why negative behaviors disrupt the class or make children unsafe.) They also need strategies to change the behavior, like taking deep breaths, using a signal to stop and think, or following a protocol for solving conflicts with classmates. These kinds of self-regulation skills take time to learn, but they have a long-term payoff, because children will be called on to use them throughout their schooling. (Children, especially those with self-regulation challenges, also need a chance to run around and use their energy constructively, which is why many experts cringe when they hear about children being denied part or all of recess.) I asked a few AppleTree teachers and administrators what would happen to the children's behavior in kindergarten if their schools didn't provide tangible rewards for meeting expectations. How would they know how and why to behave? All of the staff I talked to offered variations on the same theme: they trusted that kindergarten teachers would have similar behavior strategies to motivate and manage students. None of them said anything about trusting children to have developed their own strategies.

One potential benefit of the token economy is that it gives teachers a clear way to communicate with families about their children. "Many parents replicate it at home and there is a partnership," Jackson told me. "Parents love it because it's tangible. We give them a chart for them to take home, like sitting through dinner without crying or having a tantrum. Or getting through bath time without having any aversion to being told no. Parents also like to have a way to know how their children did during the day." Jackie Taylor agreed with that. "I tell [Kennedy] every day in the car: 'Make sure you get ten tokens, mind the teacher, do what you've got to do.' But sometimes kids see the bad things other kids do and they want to do it, too. So sometimes, she'll say, 'Nana, I didn't get ten tokens today.' I'll ask her why and she says, 'Because I was talking when my teacher was talking.' And I tell her, 'Well, you're going to do better tomorrow.'" To reinforce that, Taylor takes away the privilege of eating out on the way to school and gives Kennedy breakfast at home if she didn't earn enough tokens the previous day. "She needs to know that if you do bad things, you get things taken away from you," Taylor explained.

But not all parents like the token system. Samantha Bryan says the teachers seem to be inconsistent about enforcing the system, and sometimes it doesn't seem fair. "There was an incident with Dylan," she recalled. "They had a birthday party at school and he didn't get to have birthday cake [because he didn't get enough tokens]. I didn't like that." Dylan was "deflated when he got in the car" at the end of the day, so Bryan immediately asked him what was wrong. "Everyone got a cupcake but me," he told his mother, and when she asked him why, he said he didn't know. "I wouldn't have minded if it was bubbles or something," Bryan said, but a cupcake is a very big deal to a five-year-old. "This was so upsetting and he didn't understand it," she said. When she talked to the teacher later, she was told that those were the rules, and "Besides, there are other times I reward him when he shouldn't be rewarded." For Bryan, that suggested that the system is inconsistent and uncertain, and she wasn't surprised that Dylan was confused.

Indeed, Dylan's teacher told me that she likes the token economy but that there is a constant "teacher battle" in her head, because she feels bad about denying certain rewards to children. For example, she will sometimes send kids who don't have four tokens out to recess anyway if it is the first sunny day in a week and they really need to get outside. (She seemed to intuitively understand research on the benefits of recess.) In another case, according to Bryan, the teacher relented after Dylan was nearly denied participation in a field trip he had long been looking forward to. Bryan went to the teacher and told her that she found the punishment "not appropriate because you've gotten him excited for weeks about this trip. He had even picked out his red shirt." Dylan got to go on the field trip.

Inconsistency is not the only weakness in the token system. Bryan pointed out a bigger problem: punishing kids doesn't get to the root of their behaviors. "One time, I found out [Dylan] was misbehaving because he had an ear infection in both ears and we didn't realize it. When we finally took him to the doctor, the doctor asked me if his behavior had changed and I said, 'Oh yes, actually.' If someone hit him and it hurt him, he lashed out. Then after the medicine he started getting ten tokens every day." In another case, Dylan had been acting out because of a stressful family situation that kept him from seeing his half siblings. "He was being very aggressive and selfish at school, he didn't want to share, he pushed people away," Bryan recalled. Meanwhile, at home, he kept saying that he missed his brothers. "Before you judge or punish the kids, find out what's going on," Bryan admonished.

Psychologists agree that should be the first step to addressing challenging behavior. One of the most effective strategies for classroom behavior management is something called an ABC chart. Teachers use it to identify and map the Antecedents of a child's difficult behavior (when it happens and what the triggers seem to be), the specific Behaviors that are causing problems, and the Consequences (whether the child gets some sort of desired outcome from the behavior, like getting attention from a tantrum). The chart allows teachers to make a plan that addresses one or more of the antecedents and consequences and change strategies accordingly. Sometimes that means setting up the classroom differently or giving the child a different kind of feedback when she acts out.

The type of feedback students get from adults matters. Many teachers and parents use time-outs, in which misbehaving children are sent to a time-out chair for a specific amount of time, like five or ten minutes, and are required to observe the class or family rather than participate. But time-outs are actually not very effective as commonly used, research shows. One of the problems is that they can actually reinforce the misbehavior; for example, if a child wants to avoid a difficult math game or a tough social situation, he may learn that acting out will get him removed from the situation. In some cases, a child like Max may get so many time-outs that he just gets accustomed to spending much of his day in the chair. Another problem is that a time-out doesn't actually teach children anything. It's important to note that a time-out chair is different from an effective strategy many teachers use called a calming-down corner or a safe space, where children can go to calm down and reflect, often with the use of materials like posters reminding them to take deep breaths and "glitter jars" that help them switch mental gears by focusing on glitter falling in a tube for a minute.

There are better ways to handle challenging behavior that focus on building children's coping skills rather than punishing them for not already having them. Stuart Ablon directs Think:Kids, a program at Massachusetts General Hospital that helps children with aggressive and explosive behaviors. He has found that time-outs aren't useful for kids with consistently challenging behaviors, and he warns against token systems like the one used at AppleTree. "Rewards and consequences work for some things but not others," he explains. "They are good for teaching very basic lessons about right and wrong. But they weren't intended to build complex skills," like coping with anger or sitting quietly and paying attention. "When we use them for the wrong things, we make things worse," he adds, because rewards and punishments penalize the kids who simply don't know how to change their behavior.

Too often, Ablon says, educators like those at AppleTree are overly focused on motivation—they believe that kids do well if they *want to*. Research shows, however, that "kids do well if they *can*," he says. Many adults fail to recognize that kids struggle because they don't have the skills to behave differently, especially if they have experienced trauma or toxic stress that literally causes their brain development to lag in important areas like executive functioning. Ablon and his colleagues work with teachers around the country to educate them about these patterns and help them change their approaches. "Today, schools can't get away with telling a kid who has a reading disability, 'that's no excuse' for not reading. We need to do the same thing with discipline and behavior," he believes.

Ablon's team uses a method they developed called Collaborative Problem Solving (CPS), which helps adults and young people build relationships and learn the skills to resolve problems in alternative, collaborative ways. When they step back and look at what's happening, adults see that sometimes children are aggressive because they misinterpret ambiguous social cues as being intentionally hostile, for example a child who shoves a classmate because she thinks he knocked over her milk on purpose when it was really an accident. Sometimes children falsely think that acting aggressively will make their peers like them more. Sometimes they simply don't know that there are other alternatives. In the CPS process, the child first states his concern, then the teacher or parent states her concern and invites him to find a solution. They discuss the possible solution together and try it out.

Ablon showed me a video of a young African American boy he aptly described as "smart, adorable, and really, really challenging," who was having persistent troubles sitting still during class. He distracted not only himself but the other children with his wiggling, bouncing, and moving around the room. In the video, his teacher was trying out the

CPS method, sitting with him in the hallway outside the classroom while her assistant teacher took over the class for a few minutes. As I watched them talk, it was obvious that the boy literally could not sit still, even if he wanted to. It was also clear that the teacher wanted to help him and cared about him. The boy talked about why he needed to move, and the teacher shared her concern that he would distract himself and others from learning. Together, they came up with a solution for him to sit at a table behind the circle during class meeting time, where he could listen and participate in a place where his fidgeting wouldn't bother others. As he heard his teacher understand his concerns and listen to his suggestions, he visibly calmed down. He began to make eye contact with her and settle his body movements. The conversation turned out to be a big success. No one had yelled or felt badly about themselves, and they found a solution that addressed the problem and allowed the teacher to focus on teaching the whole class. To some teachers and parents, the process might seem overindulgent or time-consuming. But it was neither—and it worked. It addressed the teacher's concern, and it taught the boy that he could come up with solutions and that his teacher cared about him.

There is an important philosophical difference between the CPS approach and a token economy: the former builds self-regulation while the latter focuses on compliance. As Ablon pointed out, one of the reasons adults focus on compliance and control is that they often take children's misbehavior personally; they think children misbehave to "push our buttons or disrespect us." But that's not usually the case, especially with young children. And focusing on control and authority actually discourages both the skills and the motivation to cooperate. It can be particularly problematic for children with histories of trauma, Ablon says, because "uses of power and control are completely dysregulated in these kids," causing them to either explode or shut down completely.

One AppleTree teacher I talked to was very focused on respecting authority and told me that's why she likes the token system. "At a lot of schools, there are no real consequences for behavior," she reasoned. "We have to teach them to connect their actions with consequences. Because in real life there are consequences. If I don't do my job, there are consequences." Her point is a valid one, but it may not be the most helpful one for three-, four-, and five-year-olds, especially when they can be sanctioned for infractions like talking when the teacher is talking or not facing forward during instruction. Many early childhood experts point out that although those kinds of misbehaviors are not ideal in a classroom, they are quite normal reactions that children often outgrow, and furthermore, they are not truly challenging behaviors because they don't harm other children or put the child at real risk. They can often be addressed with more effective classroom organization, routines, and teaching strategies, and more reasonable age-appropriate expectations.

When I watched children fail to earn tokens for minor misbehavior, I was reminded of Jason Harris's question about his former school: "What are we preparing them for?" At AppleTree's Parklands campus, that question especially resonated for me the first time I saw children transition from one activity to the next. When it was time to clean up at centers, the teacher gave children a warning and then she began counting down from ten. When she reached zero, she chanted, "Everybody stop, hands on top," and the children, all of them African American, stopped what they were doing and froze with their hands on their heads. Shocked, I looked around the room, half expecting someone to read them their Miranda rights. But no one, not the African American teachers, their African American principal, or a white administrator, appeared to register the symbolism of a roomful of African American children complying with the authority figure by freezing and putting their hands on their heads. In fact, when I asked about it later, the school's principal told me, "As an African American, it has never stood out to me or bothered me."

Early childhood educators told me that stopping and putting hands on the head is a strategy borrowed from special education, which encourages the practice as a visual and sensory approach for children who struggle with language processing or comprehension. Indeed, visual cues are very helpful for all young children, and "freezing" can help build their executive functioning. But in other classrooms, I had seen kids freeze in a pose of their choosing or "become Popsicles" by clasping their hands together up above their heads and then "melting" by exhaling and shaking out their arms as they brought them down. At Charlestown Nursery School, Luca Murthy's private Reggio Emilia–inspired school in Boston, teachers used to play a soothing chime and then call out "Freeze, please," guiding their children to put their hands on their heads to focus their brains and bodies, but they changed the practice in 2014, after teacher Carly Reagan had the same reaction to it that I did.

Reagan grew up in Ferguson, Missouri, and she started teaching at CNS about a month after riots broke out there following the police shooting death of Michael Brown, an unarmed African American teenager. That fall was a time of heightened awareness about race, authority, and vulnerability, and although her students were white and affluent, Reagan was concerned about the message the hands-up strategy sent to them about power and control. Standing with hands on one's head is a vulnerable, powerless position, regardless of how old you are. Teachers have to have a level of authority over students, but it shouldn't be a physically controlling one, Reagan believes. "I definitely see the benefit of having a school-wide strategy for getting group attention," she told me, but she and the other teachers wanted their messages to be about cooperation rather than intimidation. So they came up with a new strategy: after playing the chime, teachers sing "Peace, please" and hold up their fingers in the V-shaped peace sign, and students respond in kind. (If it sounds precious, it doesn't feel that way when a group of four-year-olds does it.) The children still stop what they are doing and look to the teacher for instruction, but it feels more about cooperation.

The freeze example is a reminder about how important, and how thorny, issues of race and class are in classrooms. Civil rights advocates worry about the nation's "school-to-prison pipeline," through which too many at-risk children, especially African Americans, are swept into a cycle that starts with labeling and severe punishment for misbehavior at school; leads to problems like disengagement, dropping out, or expulsion; and increases the likelihood of crime and incarceration. Even for young people of color who don't become part of that pattern, tense interactions with authorities are a daily reality. "Stop and frisk" policies allow police to interrogate and search people they view as suspicious, usually young African American men, without specific cause, and the Black Lives Matter movement has raised national attention to the problem of police violence against African Americans. Certainly the pre-K teachers who I met were not trying to prepare their students to be stopped and frisked. But they were unintentionally sending messages about power and their students' place in society, perhaps because their intense focus on teaching reading and writing clouded other crucial details. Stuart Ablon believes they were missing an important opportunity to teach their students how to deal with charged situations if they do someday get stopped by the police. "You need to be compliant in the world sometimes, but you need skills to do that," he explains. "That's the part a lot of people don't get. You need to be able to manage your anger and frustration, to think calmly and flexibly, and problem-solve" to address the situation, especially if it's an unjust one.

"I'll be the first to say AppleTree schools still have a lot of work to do on the social and emotional component, because we are really focused on the academic skills," education director Anne Malone told me after my visits. That focus is laudable, and critics might say that it's unreasonable to build all of children's skills at once. But it is possible to integrate academic skills with social and emotional ones, regardless of children's backgrounds. The question shouldn't be whether to do both, but how.

The freeze strategy is also a reminder of how thoughtful early childhood educators need to be about everything they say and do in the classroom. Young children are sponges not just for facts about dinosaurs and new vocabulary words but for the messages adults send them, both overtly and unintentionally, about the world and their place in it.

Nine

Money Matters

Pre-K programs and their teachers do not operate in a vacuum; they are part of a complex political and financial landscape. When it comes to making pre-K programs work, money matters, and there is no way around the fact that quality is expensive. To hire and support great teachers, provide adequate materials, and guarantee supplemental supports like social workers and behavior specialists, programs need to have sufficient funding, whether it comes from state subsidies, public school dollars, family tuition, or some combination. Finding the money often leads to heated political battles, but pre-K without quality isn't worth a dime. That is one of the lessons from New Jersey's groundbreaking pre-K effort, which has become a model for the nation. Its standards and requirements, including generous per-student funding and higher-than-average teacher pay, have strongly influenced how Boston and other cities have shaped their programs. But New Jersey has taught an equally important lesson that has been taken to heart in Boston: generous funding benefits children only if it is used well and overseen by thoughtful, strategic leaders.

New Jersey is home to the Abbott Preschool Program, created to serve three- and four-year-olds in thirty-one of the state's poorest cities and towns. The program has a unique origin story. Unlike most state pre-K programs that have been funded through ballot initiatives or legislative action, the Abbott program was created through the judicial system as a fundamental educational right for the state's poor children. In the 1990s and 2000s, a series of state Supreme Court decisions declared New Jersey's system of funding public schools through property taxes inequitable and unconstitutional. To redress the inequity, the court's ruling mandated that the state provide a number of educational improvements in low-income communities, including preschool. Those results were unprecedented, and the *New York Times* called the case the most significant lawsuit since *Brown v. Board of Education*. The thirty-one participating communities became known as the Abbott districts, from the case's name, *Abbott v. Burke*. (Fred Burke was the state commissioner of education when the case was filed, and Raymond Abbott was an eighth grader from Camden who was listed first among the plaintiffs convened by the case's sponsor, the Education Law Center.) The dedicated funding for preschool, and the oversight and support that comes with it, have made the Abbott districts a notable exception to the national pattern of lower-quality early childhood services in lower-income communities. The impact of their impressively high quality shows in a long-running study of the program, which has the preschool-friendly acronym of APPLES (Abbott Preschool Program Longitudinal Effects Study) and a crayon-colored logo that could have been drawn by any of the program's forty thousand participating children. The most recent report found that fifth graders who had been in the program at ages three and four still had significantly higher grades and test scores in math, literacy, and science than their peers, and scores were highest for those who had attended an Abbott preschool for two years rather than one.

But like the Boston program that would follow in its footsteps, the Abbott program didn't start out at the level of quality it boasts today. The program as it currently exists was built over many years, through the tireless efforts of New Jersey–based early childhood experts who seized an opportunity to change the program and the field. Alex Figueras-Daniel watched that process unfold over many years, and she knows how much of a difference money can make—when it is used effectively. Figueras-Daniel has seen how Abbott funding and support has transformed early education in her hometown and other New Jersey cities. She has also seen how high-tuition private programs don't guarantee quality, and how difficult it is for a middle-class family like hers to find preschool programs as good as the Abbott ones, even when paying out of pocket. A New Jersey mother of three, Figueras-Daniel has worked for over a decade across many sectors of early childhood education as a teacher, instructional coach, and researcher. She took her first steps into the early childhood field as an undergraduate at Rutgers a few years after the start of Abbott preschool in districts including Elizabeth, where she grew up. Elizabeth is a mid-sized industrial city about fifteen miles south of Manhattan, where the per capita income is around $19,000 a year and about 20 percent of the population lives in poverty. Three-quarters of residents over age five speak a language other than English at home, most frequently Spanish. Figueras-Daniel had grown up in one of the city's few middle-class neighborhoods and attended private school because of her family's concerns about the quality of the public schools. But she felt an affinity for her hometown even after she went off to college.

When she arrived at Rutgers, Figueras-Daniel wasn't sure what career path she wanted to pursue, but she heard that a university research center was conducting a study of quality in Abbott preschools and needed bilingual observers to collect data in classrooms. A native speaker of both English and Spanish, she figured she had a good shot, and she might even have an excuse to go home to Elizabeth on a regular basis. When she called about the job, the center's codirector, Ellen Frede, answered the phone. Frede, a developmental psychologist who would later become a major force in creating quality in the Abbott districts, informed her that it wasn't an undergraduate position, but Figueras-Daniel must have made a good impression, because she got a call a few days later offering her an administrative job. The center quickly became a second home and Frede a devoted mentor, and it wasn't long before Figueras-Daniel got trained to be one of the classroom observers after all.

By the time they finished the study, Frede, Figueras-Daniel, and their colleagues discovered that the Abbott program, for all its promise, wasn't living up to the vision of its advocates. Despite the court mandate, quality was lower than national averages (which weren't impressive to start with). The study showed that less than 10 percent of children in Abbott districts were getting quality programs, and 20 percent of them were in classrooms so poor that researchers concluded they "might even be harmful to children's development." (When Jason Sachs would take over the Boston program several years later, the disappointing results of the program's initial evaluation would be among the many striking parallels between the Abbott trajectory and Boston's.) There were problems with everything from basic space needs to a surprising lack of books to teachers' failure to use rich, descriptive language to help children extend their thinking. "It was a mess," one state administrator told me. In one classroom she visited, she found mouse droppings in the bins for children's personal items. In others, there were broken heating systems or leaky faucets that ran constantly. "I wouldn't have put my dog in there," she said of one center. Most of the centers with those kinds of conditions lost their state contracts and ultimately shut down, but there was still a long way to go to get to quality.

One of the major problems, Frede and other early childhood experts believed, was a lack of adequate funding and services. At the time, centers provided half-day programs, funded at a little less than $3,000 per child. It can be difficult to provide meaningful education in a three- or four-hour program, especially when large sections of time are taken up by meals and meeting children's basic needs, and it is always difficult to hire great teachers when funding necessitates low salaries. Frede and colleagues, including her husband, Steven Barnett, an economist and head of the National Institute for Early Education Research (NIEER), crafted a set of recommendations for increasing funding and improving the program, and Abbott lawyers returned to court. Barnett's research-infused testimony ultimately convinced the judge to increase per-student funding (it is now around $14,000 per child), mandate full-day programs, and require that programs meet stringent new quality standards that would later become the gold standard of quality criteria adopted in Boston and other successful pre-K initiatives.

The increased funding enabled major changes to be implemented on an impressive scale and timeline. Classrooms were now required to have certified teachers who were paid commensurate with their K–12 counterparts, and to use one of several approved curricula. They received family-engagement specialists, English Language Learner specialists, and social workers and intervention teams to deal with behavior problems and other needs, which were high among the largely poor, stressed populations served by the Abbott districts. In addition to money, there was another key factor in making sure the funds were used effectively: Ellen Frede. In 2002, the state's new governor made the Abbott districts a high priority, appointing an education chief focused specifically on the Abbott districts and asking Frede to oversee the early childhood component. Before the governor's call, Frede had never envisioned herself working for the state or in politics, but she knew an opportunity to help thousands of children when she saw it, and it wasn't a chance she could pass up. Frede is a crusader for children's needs, a former Head Start teacher, researcher, and professor who has always adored children and remembers "flirting with children in the restaurant booth behind me instead of my date when I was a teenager." (She is now deputy director for early learning at the Bill and Melinda Gates Foundation.) She is a straight shooter who some find brash but brilliant, and she has a laser-like focus on what's best for children, even when it means angering adults who are used to shaping policies around their own needs.

When Frede began working for the state, some of the basic structural issues like cleanliness and safety had improved, but the more nuanced, and critical, process-quality features were often lacking. "When I got there, there were no guidelines for budgets, [and] no data" on how centers were using their resources, she told me, still incredulous more than a decade later. When asked to submit a budget, one director handed in some calculations hastily penciled over an Excel printout that were so ill-informed that Frede estimated the total proposed budget wouldn't cover half the cost of the classrooms. Many a government bureaucrat would see such a mistake and start firing employees, but Frede was no bureaucrat, and she saw a systemic problem that needed a systemic solution. "My philosophy is that you have to give people support to meet the standards," she says, just like a great pre-K teacher would say about her children. She created budget guidelines, instituted audits, and then hired fiscal specialists to help each center or school complete the audit. That support was invaluable for center directors, some of whom had never written a budget before. If programs didn't know how to allocate their resources, Frede reasoned, all the funding in the world wouldn't give children what they really needed.

Frede saw a similar human capital issue with teachers and handled it in a similar way. When she started visiting classrooms, she saw some excellent teachers, but many others who needed a lot of work. She watched one checked-out teacher tell children "I can't wait to get out of here" for vacation and spend the day on activities about Florida, because that was her destination the following day. In another classroom, a teacher held up a rhombus and called it a triangle. One teacher attempting reading instruction pointed to the letter *e* at the end of a word and asked the children, "Do you know what the *e* does?" When they looked at her blankly, she asked a little girl to stand up. Pointing to the quiet girl, she said, "There, that's what the silent *e* does—nothing." (A silent *e* does do something—it indicates that the previous vowel uses a long sound, as in the word "late," where the final *e* determines that the *a* makes the long sound *aaay* rather than the short sound *ahhh*.)

As she had done with the budgeting problems, Frede used some of her funds on staff and structures for improving teacher practice. Drawing on her past as a university faculty member, she knew that teachers needed support in at least two different stages: before they entered the classroom and once they had been teaching but were ready to increase their skills. When Frede first started working for the state, the Abbott program had recently instituted a requirement that pre-K teachers have college degrees, just like their counterparts in K–12 classrooms. But many teachers didn't have their degrees. In fact, only two four-year colleges in the state offered majors in early childhood education. Frede quickly tackled those barriers. She led the effort to create a new early childhood teaching certification that, within months, increased the demand and therefore the supply of college programs. She also made sure that people already teaching had both time and financial help to get their degrees. Under her direction, the state provided tuition subsidies directly to the universities, so that preschool teachers didn't have to pay out of pocket and wait to be reimbursed—a big deal for a workforce that is constantly teetering on the edge of financial crisis. The New Jersey officials addressed that issue, too, becoming one of the first places in the country to require that all the teachers, even those in community centers, be paid on the same scale as public school teachers.

Frede and her colleagues also took on the massive task of creating a coaching infrastructure that could reach all thirty-one of the districts, so that teachers would receive the continuous training and support that are so beneficial for teaching and learning. Through a model in which districts hired coaches and the state trained them, everyone from the state officials to the classroom teachers began to get training and mentoring on a regular basis. The Abbott program was providing pre-K on an unprecedented scale, and Frede wanted to make sure that quality was consistent so that children would get a good experience no matter where they went to school. The Abbott districts have what is known in the policy lingo as a mixed delivery system: some of the classrooms are in public schools, some in stand-alone early childhood centers, and some in private facilities with state and district support, but all receive state funding and coaching coordinated by the state and run by the local school district. In Elizabeth, I visited some of each type of classroom, and the content and quality was strikingly consistent across classrooms.

All of this infrastructure for building and maintaining quality took a significant amount of funding, money that the public typically either doesn't see or derides as government bloat. But the leaders' strategic approach was essential to making the program work. In fact, a lack of investment in leadership and support can foil education reform efforts, as New Jersey would prove a decade later, when an unprecedented gift of $100 million to the Newark Public Schools by Facebook CEO Mark Zuckerberg achieved almost nothing due to a lack of adequate planning and community involvement. As a result of the investment in the Abbott program, there was steady quality improvement in pre-K classrooms, according to NIERR's ongoing evaluation, and children's achievement scores rose. By the time Alex Figueras-Daniel graduated from Rutgers in 2003, things looked very different than they had when she first started visiting classrooms. She was eager to step into the shoes of a teacher and have a pre-K classroom of her own. With the help of a family friend, she found a teaching position in Elizabeth. Since her childhood, the public schools there had improved but still struggled. Yet she found the pre-K classrooms to be a "hidden gem," well resourced, supported by knowledgeable leaders, and well matched to the developmental needs of young children, which she had studied intensively at Rutgers. She vividly remembers the days she spent setting up her first classroom. The school principal brought her a stack of supply catalogs and told her that she had $4,000 to order whatever materials she needed for her classroom, funded by the state, thanks to the Abbott mandate. She knew it was a boon; even her friends teaching in suburban and private schools didn't have that kind of money. She was also supported in her first years of teaching by coaches, knowledgeable principals and vice principals, and specialists who helped her cope with children who displayed challenging behaviors, giving her teacher friends even more reason to be envious.

After initially teaching in a public school annex, Figueras-Daniel moved to one of Elizabeth's beautiful new early childhood centers, a dedicated facility housing thirty classrooms for three- and four-year-olds and overseen by the public school district. The center, and two others like it, operate in a dual-immersion model in which children switch every two weeks between an English-speaking classroom and a Spanish-speaking one. When you walk through the centers, you hear children delightedly talking and singing in both English and Spanish, and their work in both languages is beautifully arranged on bulletin boards that cover the hallways. Teachers function in teams of two (one of whom teaches in each language) and their classrooms form a small suite, with an observation room in the middle. The observation room provides a space where the teachers can meet regularly to plan and observe each other's classrooms so that they can make sure children's learning is cumulative and no content is repeated in the other teacher's classroom and language.

The observation rooms are also helpful for the centers' Preschool Intervention and Referral Teams (PIRTs), which help children with challenging behaviors. Abbott leaders know that behavior problems in young children are influenced by a variety of factors, and they also know that many challenges can be fully addressed if targeted early enough. Children who act out may be experiencing stress at home, they may have maladaptive habits because their parents haven't learned how to effectively manage their behavior, they may have developmental or mental health issues or be acting out of frustrations caused by difficulty learning or speaking a new language—or some combination of the above. Such needs are best addressed holistically. So when a child in an Elizabeth preschool needs support, center leaders form a PIRT with all the potential helpers, for example a social worker, a special education expert, a teacher, and, most important, a parent. Together, the PIRT can observe the child from the observation room through a one-way mirror and discuss ways to help him or her. Their focus is on finding solutions and trying them out, both at school and at home, and reevaluating until the concern is adequately addressed and the child is no longer struggling.

The results of this comprehensive approach are impressive and often prevent the need for future behavior services. The principal of the center I visited stressed the importance of the PIRTs for getting children on the right track. She told me about a student named Carlos who had a very tough year when he was three, hitting other children, yelling, throwing things. Working together, the PIRT established that he needed a more structured classroom with a different teacher, and they gave his mother strategies to help him manage his anger and frustration at home. By the following year, he seemed like a different child, happy, calm, and learning, according to the director. Kindergarten and first-grade teachers would probably be surprised and delighted to know that they had one less behavior challenge to address because of the PIRT. "The PIRT team allows us to address these problems early," Carlos's principal explained. "We approach it as 'let's work together to help this child,' not as a punishment. In kindergarten, kids would get suspended for these behaviors. That's why it's so important for us to have the time and staff to work on the problems here." It was a striking illustration of economist James Heckman's point that it is more effective to intervene early than to utilize vast resources and intensive effort to remediate problems later.

This kind of collaboration sometimes occurs in other states in a more informal way, but the Abbott districts are relatively rare in formalizing the process. One national organization trains early childhood centers how to form teams and use what they call a pyramid model to identify and address children with varying levels of behavioral needs. The pyramid is a visual representation of a model in which teachers provide certain social and emotional supports to all children, constituting the base level of the pyramid; intensive targeted services to a small number of at-risk children at the top of the pyramid; and a range of mid-level services in between. In centers that use the model, a team of program leaders and staff convene on a regular basis to identify the behavioral needs of children as a group and as individuals, find root causes of behavior issues, and make targeted efforts to reduce the problems by eliminating triggers, changing consequences of children's behaviors, and other strategies. Thousands of teachers have been trained, but early childhood experts I talked to told me that the model is often not fully implemented, because "it comes down to personnel," and that comes down to funding, as one explained. "You need an explicit commitment from the state or the district or somewhere, because a lot of centers don't have the funds for a social worker or other support staff. Many directors are completely consumed with having enough teachers," she said.

Unfortunately, that's even becoming the case in Elizabeth. Although the district's pre-K program has been going strong for over a decade, it has started to struggle with financial sustainability. The district still receives the $14,000 per child granted in the court decisions, but as the program matures, the costs of providing it go up, because teacher salaries and benefits increase. That means that even if none of the classroom materials needed to be replaced, the program would still get more expensive. Elizabeth has kept the problem at bay for many years because its steadily increasing enrollment has allowed it to open new classrooms every year, each of which brings in more funding. But the preschool population is leveling off. And although the district has stepped in to take on some of the program's costs (like children's bus transportation to and from school), its capacity is limited because it is facing major budget shortfalls across the board.

As a result of these pressures, the Elizabeth early childhood department has had to make some significant cuts. In 2015, it reluctantly eliminated half of the coaching positions, sending some staff back into classrooms and displacing newer teachers. It also had to eliminate schools' early childhood vice principals and shift social workers to cover multiple schools. That has impacted the PIRTs, because there are fewer staff to draw from, and those who remain have larger caseloads and less time for each needy child. "I wish we had a video of then and now, so you could see the difference," the principal I met told me, referring to the decrease in staff support in her building since she started. She and other leaders in Elizabeth say they don't think the cuts have adversely affected children yet, but she and her staff are worried about how they will continue to serve children like Carlos, who was turned around thanks to his PIRT. The cuts are "stretching everyone thin and stressing everyone out," she said.

The stress could get worse. In 2016, New Jersey governor Chris Christie proposed a bill that would seriously curtail funding in the Abbott districts. Per the court mandate, the state has been providing more school funding to low-income districts than other communities, in order to create more equitable access to good schools across the state. Almost half of the state's $9 billion education budget goes to about 30 school districts, out of more than 550. As a result, property taxes in the wealthier communities are among the highest in the country, and there has long been opposition from suburban homeowners to contributing so heavily to urban schools. Christie's plan would provide the same amount of funding per student in every district in the state, whether in Elizabeth or in its wealthier surrounding towns, like the one where Figueras-Daniel and her family reside. That change would undermine the decades-old Abbott mandate to create equitable access to good schools. It would increase many suburban districts' funding by nearly 100 percent, allowing them to rely more on state funding and reduce local property taxes. Affluent Teaneck, where the median household income is nearly $100,000, would see an almost 400 percent increase in state aid. Meanwhile, the Abbott and other low-income districts would see their state funding drastically reduced. (The number of districts receiving supplemental aid, and implementing state-funded pre-K, has increased from 31 since the original Abbott case, based on a newer state funding formula that accounts for the percentage of low-income children in each district.) Elizabeth would lose more than 50 percent of its state funding (around $7,500 per student). It and the other low-income districts would probably have to cut services, because they would be hard-pressed to make up the funding decrease by raising property taxes for already-strapped residents. The universal pre-K classrooms that are considered some of the best in the country could be at risk.

Regardless of where you fall on the political spectrum, questions about how to fund pre-K and for whom are thorny. It's not a stretch to feel for both low-income parents with few options and more affluent parents with sky-high property tax bills. As a result, sustainability is a persistent challenge, even in some of the country's most established programs. In New Jersey, the funding has been in question for decades, challenged and then saved multiple times in court. Just to the north, in New York City, the original plan to fund universal pre-K with a tax on the city's wealthiest residents was sunk by political opposition. Even with the state funding that has enabled the program, some critics have claimed that it is irresponsible to use public funding to educate middle-class preschoolers whose families could theoretically afford private pre-K. In Boston, there have been some cuts to pre-K classrooms in the district-run early childhood centers, and funding for the partnership that is bringing K1 to community centers is tenuous, based largely on a federal grant that is subject to annual approval by Congress. Although the mayor and superintendent have called for universal pre-K for all children in Boston (possibly through a model similar to the one being piloted at the Roxbury YMCA and elsewhere), state government has been silent on whether and how it will support that goal.

But one of the important lessons from the Abbott program is that public pre-K funding is essential to enable quality-assurance measures like standards, training, and research. Alex Figueras-Daniel says, "There are no words to compare the quality of the Abbott districts [with other programs]. The Abbott communities have become so knowledgeable about developmentally appropriate practice and what's right for kids. When I go out of state, I remember that things are different here—more resources, structure, how the networks and systems of leadership work with each other."

When she had her own children, Figueras-Daniel was surprised to discover just how different things are even within New Jersey—and what happens when there is no system in place for building and monitoring quality. She explored her town's low-cost half-day public preschool program, but the hours and logistics didn't work with her schedule, which includes juggling a full-time job, doctoral program, and three children. So she looked to private programs, enrolling in and then leaving three of them. She quickly found that funding doesn't always guarantee quality. Expensive programs that are poorly run or don't have their priorities straight don't serve children well, and many private programs do not have the kind of central support and oversight that she and her colleagues had been providing to the Abbott districts. At the first school where she enrolled her son, an expensive cooperative school where parents help provide staffing and other volunteer support, she felt the supervision was insufficient and led to children being aggressive, and she was disappointed that the staff were less qualified and trained than in the Abbott districts. "They were basically babysitting," she remembers, not providing the kind of engaging experiences she had provided when she was a preschool teacher. At the next center, she put down a large deposit and then asked to conduct an observation. After getting past the center's resistance with a "What do you have to hide?" attitude, she was unhappy with what she saw and with the scores she recorded on the research tool she had brought along. Staff were "strict and mean" with kids, inappropriately requiring toddlers to stand in straight, quiet lines. Classrooms didn't have enough materials, which led kids to argue and become aggressive. Starting to feel desperate, she and her husband took the plunge to pay the high tuition at a private pre-K–12 school. "It was expensive, but I rationalized that the tuition was about the same as what New Jersey pays in the Abbott districts," she recalls. But she and her husband could only afford to send their son three days a week.

At first, things seemed to be going well. The teacher had gotten a master's degree with a professor Figueras-Daniel knew, and the classrooms were outfitted much like the Abbott ones. But it wasn't long before she realized that the program wasn't doing the developmentally appropriate practices she was looking for. "When I went in for the first teacher meeting, I pushed back on letter of the week. 'Can you tell me more about that and why you do it with three-year-olds?'" she asked. But the teacher couldn't. Then the teacher brought out her son's daily journal, clucking disappointedly about how he drew a rainbow almost every day, and his worksheets, complaining that he wasn't very interested in them. Of course he wasn't interested in them, thought his developmental psychologist mother; they wouldn't be interesting for anyone, certainly not a curious and active three-year-old. The teacher did mention that her son's verbal ability was amazing but neglected to expound upon that, focusing instead on the fact that he was refusing to write the letter T over and over. Figueras-Daniel left the meeting disturbed. But other parents didn't seem upset. "They were obsessed about organic, perfect snacks, and the board meetings were about fund-raising. I don't think anyone knew enough to be concerned about whether the classrooms were developmentally appropriate."

After a second disappointing teacher meeting, Figueras-Daniel's husband looked at her and asked, "Are you OK with this? Because we can't afford this if you're not happy with it." But she could only think of one other option. It was a lengthy drive from their house, and it was a long shot, because the school year was well under way and most good programs have already filled their spots by that point in the year. Plus, the place she had in mind—the early childhood center on the Rutgers campus—tended to have long waiting lists of university professors and staff, because highly educated parents knew that the center was staffed with the university's own early childhood experts. "Give me the number," her husband said, and he called the director immediately. Their son was enrolled shortly after, and his parents have been happy with the play-based, inquisitive way he, and now his two younger siblings, are learning at the center. Figueras-Daniel doesn't know if there was a waiting list when her husband called, and she believes they got a spot because he is "very good at charming people," she told me with a laugh. She does know that she had more options than many parents and yet still struggled to find a quality program. When neighborhood friends ask her where to send their kids, she has no recommendations.

For Figueras-Daniel, the contrast between the Abbott programs where she had taught and observed and the private programs where she enrolled her son was striking and frustrating. She is discouraged by suburban centers she has seen where teachers aren't certified, materials are inadequate, and children are doing too many worksheets. "I am shocked how unaware the suburban districts are about what the Abbott districts are doing," Figueras-Daniel says. "I live next door to an extremely wealthy town. If I told people there that they should look at the preschool classrooms in Elizabeth as models, they would look at me like I'm crazy." But while she hopes for more classrooms like those in the Abbott districts, even those programs are at risk, financially and politically. And if one of the nation's best pre-K programs can be at risk, that means that all the others could one day be, too.

Ten

Test Prep for Parents

Funding is an important part of the quality puzzle, but as Alex Figueras-Daniel discovered, money is not necessarily a proxy for quality. If families and policymakers can't assume a program is working just because it costs a lot, how can they judge quality? Most don't have the professional expertise that Figueras-Daniel does. This is where objective assessment comes in. Tools that measure the progress of programs and individual children can provide valuable information that can be compared across programs. Assessment has gotten a bad rap in recent years, largely because of concerns that children and teachers are undergoing so much testing that it's taking away from time for teaching and learning. Those are legitimate concerns, but there are times when assessment can be useful and even transformative. After all, evaluations highlighted serious problems in the early stages of pre-K programs in Boston and New Jersey, and then confirmed that administrators were on the right track after major quality improvement efforts. Those and other studies have helped establish which programs should serve as models for other cities and states. Other types of assessments that screen children for developmental delays can be life-changing for children and their families, and occasional measurements of children's progress can help teachers tailor activities to individual needs.

However, many early childhood teachers feel unprepared to conduct the assessments required of them, limiting the usefulness of the results. And just like programs, some assessments are developmentally appropriate while others are not. One of the most startling examples of a misguided approach occurred in Head Start in the early 2000s. In 2003, President George W. Bush's administration wanted a way to measure whether Head Start programs were educating children well enough to justify federal funding, so they created a standardized achievement test for four- and five-year-olds. The National Head Start Reporting System was a fifteen- to twenty-minute sit-down test of children's vocabulary, math, and other cognitive skills. (It did not include other crucial early childhood skills, like motor development or social and emotional competence, which are equally important goals of Head Start.) It was immediately clear that the test was not created by people knowledgeable about young children. Preschoolers were asked to name letters in a confusing, out-of-context way. Many math questions were actually assessing vocabulary knowledge. Vocabulary items were heavily biased toward people from privileged social classes, even though Head Start serves low-income children. For example, as one critic pointed out, "for the word 'vase' the incorrect illustrations, or test foils, include items that could actually all be used as vases." For many children, especially those in low-income families, it is probably common for a water glass or a jug to hold flowers, and they may never have heard the word "vase." It might be reasonable to expect a high school student, regardless of background, to recognize the word "vase," but the children being tested were only four years old.

Another item showed children four faces and asked them to choose the one that was expressing the word "horrified." "The facial features of all four images are Caucasian, ignoring the fact that facial expressions differ in different cultural and ethnic groups," the critical experts explained. "Also, by including this emotion, the test ignores extensive research indicating that the depiction of the facial expression for *horrified* (which researchers note is often confused with the expression of anger or rage) is not recognized by most children until much later in life."

The backlash from early childhood experts was swift, but the ill-conceived test was not dropped until 2007. And its lessons haven't been universally learned; some schools are still following its lead in their attempts to evaluate preschoolers and their teachers. One teacher I talked with had been teaching pre-K and kindergarten in Florida for twenty years when she began to feel frustrated and helpless as testing took over her school and her classroom. When the trend started, she would close the door of her kindergarten classroom and refuse to do the testing other teachers were doing. But that became more difficult as her once-supportive principal began to feel pressured by the district. Frustrated, she moved to a district-run pre-K center in the hope that there would be less emphasis on testing in a classroom for four-year-olds, but she was disappointed. The principal required teachers to use worksheets and drill a set number of sight words, and the assessments began coming fast and furious. The teacher estimates that the assessments now take about ten total weeks of instructional time. That's almost half the school year, she points out.

She and other teachers in her district feel that what they are required to do is not in the best interests of children. One overheard the principal telling a parent that his child wouldn't be ready for kindergarten because he wasn't reading at age four. (This is clearly not true, as statistics reported in chapter 7 show that less than 10 percent of children are reading at the beginning of kindergarten.) And the Florida teacher sent me a disheartening photo she took in her classroom: during pretend play, students had seated a teddy bear at a computer with headphones on, simulating the computerized testing to which they had become accustomed.

In Cambridge, Massachusetts, long-time early childhood teacher Suzi Sluyter made a national splash when the *Washington Post* published her resignation letter, which detailed her complaints about how her classroom had become too focused on assessment. "I have watched as my job requirements swung away from a focus on the children, their individual learning styles, emotional needs, and their individual families, interests, and strengths to a focus on testing, assessing, and scoring young children, thereby ramping up the academic demands and pressures on them," she wrote. Sluyter told me that she had started spending so much time out of the classroom for one-on-one assessments that she was no longer able to build the kinds of relationships with children that are key to learning. She found herself envious of her assistant teacher, who still had those kinds of relationships with the children.

These teachers' experiences are alarming but extreme, and they are not the norm everywhere. For example, the Boston Public Schools early childhood department has eschewed evaluation of children beyond a brief, low-stakes literacy screening.* But they have caused some parents to take the equally extreme position that assessment has no place in early childhood classrooms. In between there is a sweet spot, in which teachers, parents, and policymakers have valuable opportunities to better serve children. But navigating the world of assessment can be challenging for everyone, especially parents, who are often left in the dark about whether and how children and teachers are evaluated. When is assessment appropriate and helpful? What kinds of tests and evaluations should parents expect, and when should they be worried about too much testing?

Pre-K assessment generally falls into two categories: measurements of program quality and assessments of individual children's needs and skills. Program assessment is often mandated, for example by state licensing bodies, school districts, or in the case of Head Start, the U.S. Department of Health and Human Services. It can include checklists of program features like staff–child ratio and physical safety, evaluations of teacher performance, and observations of how staff members interact with children. Child assessment, on the other hand, measures what children are

---

* For research studies like the one published in *Child Development*, outside evaluators randomly select small samples of students and get permission from parents to test them.

capable of doing and how they are progressing. It can cover everything from social skills to vocabulary development. Among the many different types of child assessments are screeners, which identify whether children have any learning or developmental delays that should be addressed; achievement tests, which examine how much children have learned; behavior checklists; and research tools that allow evaluators to measure programs' success according to how much children have improved their skills. Programs vary enormously in which, if any, of these tools they use. Some use a combination, while others (usually private programs) conduct no formal assessment at all. Some keep up to date with the latest guidelines for evaluation, while others push down assessments designed for older students that are inappropriate for pre-K.

The best assessments of young children's skills don't involve pencil-and-paper or computer tests, which are not only boring and sometimes stressful for children, but also not very accurate. More than with older students, preschoolers' performance on any given task is likely to vary from day to day or even hour to hour. Scores tend not to be stable, because they are heavily influenced by children's moods, current interests, attention spans, and other unpredictable factors like what color the paper is or whether a dog barks outside the window. In addition, it is normal for young children to develop the same skills at different rates. Just as some babies walk first and others talk first, some preschoolers may be tuned to first master basic addition while others are focused on painting detailed pictures that develop the fine motor skills that will become essential for writing.

The better way to assess young children is with authentic assessments, in which the teacher observes the children in their daily activities and records whether they have seen each child use a skill like counting to ten, building a stable tower out of five blocks, or identifying the letter *L*. Teachers can record these skills when they occur naturally, or create opportunities to bring them out while simultaneously providing a learning opportunity. Teachers make their observations over a certain period of time, rather than setting a day to take children out of the classroom to answer questions on a computer. At Powell Bilingual Elementary in Washington, DC, where pre-K teachers use a popular assessment called Teaching Strategies GOLD, I watched Jason Harris upload notes and photographs documenting children's skills on specific tasks to a smartphone app designed to accompany the assessment. Harris told me that the app was a huge help, allowing him to do assessments quickly and relatively easily while he was teaching. Later he would sit down to review his notes and figure out which children he still needed to observe using or developing certain skills. Harris and other Powell teachers told me that assessment still takes a lot of time and attention and can sometimes be frustrating, but they don't feel that it takes away from teaching and learning. (Although, during one visit, Harris and his colleagues did tell me they were finishing an assessment cycle and hadn't gotten to every child, so they had specifically incorporated some classroom activities to capture which letters children knew. But it never felt to the children or to me like they were being tested.) Harris and his colleagues frequently meet as a team to review their children's scores and figure out what they need to focus on next—for example, whether they need to spend more time emphasizing letters with puzzles and games or whether they can move on to silly songs that illustrate the sounds letters make. That kind of assessment and "reflective practice," as those in the field call it, is advantageous for children, because it focuses on what a specific group of children needs at a given point in time, rather than what a curriculum publisher decided children should be doing in, say, November. (At Powell, teachers do follow the curriculum, but it is flexible and designed to allow them to choose the most appropriate activities for their students.)

In some rare instances, authentic assessments are not possible and sit-down tests are actually the best option, but these situations are the exception to the rule. When I met with reading expert Nadine Gaab, she was advocating for passage of a Massachusetts state law that would mandate a reading screener for kindergartners to diagnose early indicators of dyslexia and other reading problems. Many states already have these laws, but Massachusetts was not among them at the time. In the test, an assessor sits down with a child and asks her to do things like identify rhymes, letters, and the sounds that letters make. Explaining her rationale for the brief assessment, Gaab showed me a slide with a timeline of a child's reading development. On the right side, from grades two to five, was a block of color showing the age at which students are typically diagnosed with reading disabilities—around eight or nine, after they have struggled with reading for several years. On the left side, from grades pre-K to two, was another block of color that represented the most effective age for interventions that address dyslexia, according to research. The mismatch was striking. Studies show the surprising fact that indicators of reading problems emerge early, even before children are reading per se, when they are building the foundation. And when young children get help with those basic skills right away, they improve much faster than students who get intervention later in elementary school. In fact, Gaab told me, many of those children make such major strides that they don't even get a diagnosis later in elementary school, when other students' problems are just being identified despite years of feeling frustrated and demoralized. Her case for a brief kindergarten assessment was compelling, especially when she told me that a surprising number of teachers don't know how to spot early reading problems. When she surveys her graduate students, many of whom are experienced teachers, asking what surprised them most during her course, the most common answer is learning that dyslexia is not a visual problem with seeing letters backward (as commonly thought) but a more complex neurological processing issue. Although Gaab believes that "teacher education programs need to change" to better prepare teachers to spot and address reading difficulties, she believes there will still be an important role for a specific and universal early assessment.

Some skills are not so quick and easy to measure. Social, emotional, and executive functioning skills are among the most important skills for children to develop during pre-K. And in recent years, policymakers'

growing recognition of the importance of those skills has led to a movement to assess them. As of the 2015 reauthorization of the federal Elementary and Secondary Education Act (ESEA), schools are now required to
incorporate at least one indicator of students' development outside of
standard achievement measures, like student engagement, social and
emotional learning, or school climate. Traditionally, some teachers have
used behavior checklists to rate students' social and emotional skills, or
simply written down their impressions when it was time to meet with parents or the child's future teacher for the subsequent school year. Those
kinds of assessments can be unreliable, however, based on the day on
which the form is filled out or on a teacher's personal bias about a child or
group of children. Recently, researchers have been using tools that directly tap into children's skills. For example, some ask children to respond to hypothetical social scenarios or perform a complex task, like
touching their shoulders when they hear the word "head" and touching
their head when they near the word "shoulders." However, these assessments have been developed for use in laboratory studies and it's not yet
clear whether they are good and feasible measures of children's skills in
the real world. Assessment of social and emotional skills in classrooms
remains an underdeveloped area, one where there is a clear need for more
research and knowledge.

In an ideal situation, parents are informed when their child is assessed
and have the opportunity to go over the results with teachers, so that all
parties can use the information to help children. But many programs never
share that information with families. So how can parents know whether
their children are being assessed appropriately and helpfully? The best
way is to ask teachers or program supervisors questions like these:

- How will my child's teachers know if he is progressing at the rate
  he is expected to? How will they know if he has any developmental delays, and will they inform me?
- Do teachers do any formal observations or notes on children?

- Will my child ever be tested in this program? If so, how and how often? What happens if a child seems anxious or upset during an assessment?
- How do you use the information you collect? Will it be shared with me?

Although different families may look for different responses to these questions depending on their priorities, there are some general rules of thumb for determining if a program's approach to assessment is appropriate. Programs should have a clear method (whether formal or informal) of identifying children at risk of developmental problems, and a policy for contacting parents. Parents should always be in the loop and offered multiple opportunities to learn about their child's progress (for example, through parent-teacher conferences, home visits, at pickup time, or via text message). Children's results should never be shared publicly, like on a bulletin board. Parents should recognize red flags if young children are being assessed often with a sit-down test, and they should ensure that their children are given permission to stop or take a break if they become upset during an assessment. Families should always know when their children are being tested and should talk with teachers if they notice any behavior pattern changes at home that might indicate anxiety (like difficulty sleeping or chewing hair more than is typical for that child). Even when programs choose to use data only for internal purposes, parents have every right to know how it is being used. It is a good sign if teachers or directors can give examples of how they use children's data to inform what they are teaching and how (for example, playing more math games if many four-year-olds in a group are struggling to count to ten).

Beyond knowing how their own children are doing, parents should also look at how well schools or centers are doing. Families might take it for granted that their child's pre-K program is being evaluated to make sure it is safe, nurturing, and educational. Although most programs do undergo some sort of evaluation, the processes vary widely, as do the results.

Programs rarely publicize their findings to parents, and most parents don't know to ask. Quality assessment is almost always required in publicly funded programs, like Head Start, state-run programs, and municipal initiatives like New York City's Pre-K for All. For example, Head Start programs are required to use an observation tool called the CLASS, which measures how well teachers interact with children. But even so, a recent study of Head Start programs found that there is huge variation across states in quality, and that may be partially explained by marked differences in staff qualifications, teacher turnover, and funding. "Adjusting for cost of living, the highest funded state received twice as much per child enrolled in Head Start as the lowest funded state," the authors noted. And while 90 percent of teachers in West Virginia and Washington, DC, held bachelor's degrees, only about 36 percent did in New Mexico. Instructional quality, though generally low across the board, was at a level considered adequate by early childhood experts in only a handful of states. The study didn't report on how programs conducted quality assessment or used the results, but it's not a big leap to assume that programs with less funding, less qualified teachers, and more staff turnover were less capable of comprehensive approaches to quality improvement.

If quality assessment varies in public programs, it is all over the map in privately run early childhood programs. These programs have to be licensed by states, of course, and the licensing requirements ensure that basic health and safety guidelines are followed. (While I was visiting classrooms for this book, some programs received warnings from their states because there were too many children and not enough adults in classrooms. And multiple parents told me their children had attended centers that were later shut down for repeated safety violations.) But licensing requirements don't typically include more nuanced measures of quality, like whether teachers provide emotional support and stimulating instruction to children, because it is difficult to collect and monitor that kind of intensive data on a state-wide scale. That means it is up to programs to decide whether and how to monitor those detailed aspects of quality, and many choose not to because it can be a costly and time-consuming endeavor.

States have looked for other ways to monitor and improve quality, and nearly all of them are currently using a market-based approach called a Quality Rating and Improvement System (QRIS). With a QRIS, the state sets a series of benchmarks and then rates programs on how well they achieve them. Each program gets a star rating (usually zero to five stars), which is supposed to make it easier for parents to choose high-quality programs. (Some states also use the systems to determine which programs are worthy of public funding, or to tailor training and support to help low-quality programs improve.) But so far, QRIS programs have been of limited utility. Few parents know about them, and a large national study called into question the reliability of the systems. It found that in most states, the star ratings don't predict children's outcomes, probably because the ratings tend to be based on structural features like staff–child ratio and class size, which establish only base levels of quality. Furthermore, the study found that states have very different expectations for quality: for example, in one state, 85 percent of programs were able to receive the highest rating, but using another state's standards, *only 10 percent* of those same programs would have gotten that rating. That kind of variability has to make parents wonder if the ratings really tell them anything about where to send their children.

Some programs and schools choose to go through a voluntary process of quality certification through the National Association for the Education of Young Children (NAEYC). NAEYC assesses how well programs meet its standards, which include positive relationships, effective instruction and curricula, and communication with parents. Accreditation is an intensive, multiyear process; programs do a self-assessment, submit evidence of how they are meeting the standards, and get observed by NAEYC assessors. In Boston, early childhood director Jason Sachs encourages schools to pursue accreditation because it helps them stay focused on developmentally appropriate practice in their early childhood classrooms. Coaches from his department help teachers and principals with the process. But even though more than seven thousand programs and schools across the country have been accredited by NAEYC, most of the nation's two million early childhood educators have not gone through the process. Many small private programs find the process too expensive, especially if they are already filling their spots and don't need the seal of approval to attract parents.

If it sounds confusing to sort out which programs are great and which aren't so hot, that's because it is. As early childhood expert Marcy Whitebook pointed out to me, "People have a lay of the land in K–12 education about how it works, [like how] it's financed, organized, etc.," but they are lost when it comes to pre-K. She compared K–12 to the geography of New York City, which is mostly organized in a logical grid that you can follow on a map. "Early childhood is much more like Los Angeles," she continued; it's sprawling and not always clearly labeled. "Navigating early childhood is kind of like trying to navigate L.A. without a car." To put it differently, most parents aren't trained in child development or public policy, and many don't even know how their child's program is funded. Some centers slot children into different classrooms based on whether they qualify for Head Start or a public school program. Others use a sliding fee scale, in which families who can afford it pay tuition while those who can't receive state vouchers that cover the cost. These basic inner workings tend to be opaque, never mind whether a program has any quality requirements.

For many families, selecting a program comes down solely to cost and convenience. But even for those who can afford choices, formal quality measures are rarely a contributing factor. Many of us rely on friends' experiences and recommendations. I know one family who didn't even visit schools but instead ranked the same schools in the same order as a neighbor who works in education. And many parents simply don't know that programs vary so widely, explains University of Massachusetts–Boston professor Monica Yudron. For a lot of families, especially from certain ethnic and cultural groups, it is natural to assume that schools do what is right for children, and it is even disrespectful to question what teachers do in their classrooms. But quality is so inconsistent that parents should ask questions, talk to teachers, and visit classrooms if at all possible, Yudron advises. Around the country, schools are trying to make it easier for parents to learn about schools even if they can't visit during the day. For example, in Washington, DC, Powell Bilingual Elementary and other public schools are partnering with a local nonprofit to film virtual tours that families can view on computers or mobile devices at home or in family resource centers. But overall, schools have a long way to go to normalize that kind of accessibility. Even families with resources and flexible schedules typically get little time in the classrooms they are considering; the standard pre-K tour includes a brief informational talk with the director followed by a walk-through of the classrooms, with five to ten minutes in each one (or outside the door).

What can parents learn in that amount of time? A surprising amount, actually, especially if they can be there when programs are in session and they can observe how teachers and children interact with each other. These are some helpful things to look for and ask about that can be covered relatively quickly:

- Does the center seem to be basically safe and clean? (For example, are playground areas fenced in and are children expected to wash their hands before eating?)
- How do adults talk to children? Do they bend down to their eye level, use their names, and talk to them in a warm, nurturing way (positive signs) or do they yell, sigh, or roll their eyes at children (red flags)?
- Do staff members seem to enjoy their jobs, or do they seem exhausted and frustrated?
- Do teachers receive benefits, and how often do staff members turn over? (This is usually a question for the director.) Frequent turnover can be a warning sign of teacher burnout and indicate that children don't have enough opportunity to build stable relationships with

adults. Health benefits and paid vacation time, on the other hand, are good signs, because they attract more qualified staff and lead to less turnover.

- Are children engaged in the classroom? Do they have opportunities to choose their activities, and are they enjoying them? Do they laugh and sing? Do they play with other children?
- How do teachers handle conflicts between children? Are they patient and able to explain an alternative behavior and why it is important, or do they yell at children and send them to a corner?
- Do the walls of the classrooms have student work (e.g., art, writing, projects) hanging on them? Are there books at children's eye level and arm length?
- If a child has special needs, does the center provide special services like speech therapy or supports for autistic children?

Quality centers can look and feel very different, but they all meet children's needs in nurturing and developmentally appropriate ways. The diversity of pre-K choices is important, because families and children have different needs and preferences. But Yudron cautions parents that what they and their children need can be very different in infancy and in pre-K. Many families, like the Coker family in Boston, begin at one center for childcare in the earliest months and days and simply stick with it until kindergarten. Yudron suggests that parents take a closer look at the pre-K classrooms as their children reach ages three and four, so they can make a change if necessary.

Of course, many families don't have the option to shop around, and they take what they can get. That's why quality assessment should be systematic and not left up to families alone. We can't simply depend on the free market to sort out the best programs from the worst, because some children will lose out. With their futures at stake, no child should have to be a canary in a coal mine for an ineffective program. Ultimately, we need to ensure quality programs for everyone.

Eleven

The Myth of the Silver Bullet

High-quality pre-K has changed the lives of children, families, and communities across the country. But even the best pre-K programs can't guarantee lifelong success. Children need great learning opportunities from birth to adulthood. Pre-K is a crucial link in that chain, and as economist James Heckman has shown, it is more cost-efficient than later remediation. But learning can't start or end at age three. Pre-K programs are often expected to bear an unreasonable burden, like teaching all children to read or erasing achievement gaps. Results from Boston and elsewhere suggest that good pre-K programs can in fact help narrow achievement gaps, but it would be foolish to expect them to solve entrenched, systemic barriers to success by themselves.

Children's brains develop rapidly from birth (and in some ways, even before). In the first years of life, babies' brains develop seven hundred new neural connections *per second*. Nurturing and stimulating environments pave the path for those connections to form. Meanwhile, neurological pathways that are not encouraged atrophy and fade away, in a kind of "use it or lose it" pattern. From the very beginning, children's abilities build on one another, and on availability to enriching experiences. "Houses are not built starting on the second floor," as one early childhood director in Brooklyn frequently points out to policymakers in her city. "They have to have a solid foundation if you don't want the upper floors to fall down."

Meg Hackett's preschoolers were already behind their more advantaged peers when they walked into her classroom at the Roxbury Y in Boston. Most had unmet basic needs that took priority for Hackett. She brought in extra food for children who were always hungry and bought clothing for some who needed it. "It took us almost the full year to get the kids to feel safe," she reflected after the children had gone on to kindergarten. "In the eyes of some people, we wasted a whole year not teaching things. But our kids weren't healthy kids yet. We had to meet their basic needs. We couldn't always focus on words and definitions." Classroom teachers should not have to meet children's basic needs, but in many cases they do, because families lack a wider safety net.

The stress of meeting basic needs also means that young children from low-income families tend to get less cognitive stimulation at home. Parents who are struggling to put food on the table don't always have the time or the mental energy to teach their children about the alphabet and don't have as many opportunities to place them in costly activities like music classes. Certainly many low-income families do find opportunities to engage their children in learning at home, including some I have met and profiled in this book who have made enormous efforts to give their children the best possible start. But others have work schedules that severely limit their time with their children, suffer from depression that affects their ability to engage, or are consumed with the many other stresses of poverty. There are sometimes social and cultural factors at play, too. For example, in some cultures, it is not the norm to encourage children to ask questions or it is commonly believed that teachers should be responsible for education and it is a sign of respect to defer to them.

It pays to help parents of infants and toddlers understand the value of helping young children learn at home and to suggest strategies for doing that. Studies show that there are tangible benefits to offering home visits, in which nurses or social workers help families learn positive parenting strategies and how to help children learn through play and conversation. And children like Jeremiah Hilton, who had difficulty speaking in his toddler years, benefit from early intervention programs to work on specific skills, whether they be cognitive, emotional, or physical. These kinds of investments in the earliest years are essential if children are to benefit equally from pre-K, but most of them (except for early intervention) are not available to all families.

Of course, many infants and toddlers like Jeremiah's little sister are cared for in center- or home-based childcare programs, and the quality of those programs is every bit as important as the quality of pre-K. But it is difficult to achieve. Childcare workers are paid even less than pre-K teachers and tend to have less training. Caring for young children has always been undervalued in our society, largely because it is seen as "women's work" and therefore not worthy of respect or compensation. Early childcare settings also lack the kind of centralized infrastructure that has grown up around pre-K programs to build and monitor quality. State licensing is important, of course, but as with pre-K, it is limited in its ability to assure that children get the kind of cognitive stimulation that will help them realize their parents' dreams for them.

When children get the kind of support they need in the earliest years, they come into pre-K ready to work on their social, emotional, and academic skills, and that helps them get "ready for kindergarten," as so many policymakers and educators have been pushing for. But kindergarten and elementary school quality matter, too. "We tend to think of pre-K as a silver bullet or an inoculation, but it isn't," developmental psychologist Fred Morrison points out. "An early good start is better than an early bad start. But you still need to have stimulating experiences in first, second, third grades, and beyond." Parents and early childhood experts are increasingly concerned about the quality and age-appropriateness of later grades, especially kindergarten. Kindergarteners shouldn't be sitting at desks all day or learning by rote, experts say. They should be involved in active, exploratory learning, and they should have plenty of opportunities to play. But some research has found that kindergarten is looking more like "the new first grade," with too much structure and expectations for reading and writing that are higher than they need to be. Many parents are also understandably concerned about the disappearance of recess and play.

The varying quality of kindergartens is a problem not only for six- and seven-year-olds. It can also mask the positive effects of pre-K programs. A study of a program to build preschoolers' executive functioning skills found that although participating children did better at the end of the year than their peers, only some were still doing well a year later. The successful children had gone on to high-quality kindergarten classrooms after pre-K. In contrast, children who were attending low-quality kindergartens ended up doing even worse than their peers who hadn't participated in the pre-K intervention. The research team hypothesized that was because the children had grown accustomed to supportive, developmentally appropriate practices and experienced a kind of culture shock when they encountered kindergarten teachers who were harsh or unsupportive. The study is an important lesson for the early childhood field, because when it looked at all the participants together, it seemed that the program had no effect a year later. If researchers hadn't looked at the kindergartens, the study might have led some policymakers to conclude that it wasn't worth investing in the pre-K program.

These kinds of masking effects have been around for decades, some scholars believe. They may help explain why Head Start has often failed to find long-term results for participants. Steven Barnett of the National Institute for Early Education Research believes that the notorious fadeout effect in Head Start evaluations is actually a "catch-up effect." Kindergarten classrooms serving predominantly low-income children typically have some students who participated in Head Start and some who were in lower-quality preschools or not in school at all. That means the children come in with varying levels of social skills and academic basics, so teachers may have to go over the same things the Head Start children have already learned. That could lead the Head Start children to show little gain during kindergarten, Barnett suggests. If all children had high-quality pre-K, that kind of repetition wouldn't be necessary and the benefits of pre-K would be more obvious, he and other advocates believe.

This is one of the reasons so many cities have decided to locate pre-K programs in public schools. It allows teachers and administrators to align what children are doing in pre-K and the later grades, and to communicate with one another about what each child and group of children is able to do. But policymakers and school administrators will have to pay close attention to make sure that their pre-K classrooms are appropriate for young children and are not simply imposing a third-grade model on three- and four-year-olds. That requires training, not just for teachers but for support staff and administrators. A 2015 study by the National Association of Elementary School Principals found that only one in five new principals felt well trained in early childhood teaching methods. That can lead to confusion and inappropriate expectations for pre-K classrooms. An early childhood coach in New Jersey told me that one day she received a call from a panicked principal, who told her, "I need you to get down here right away. The pre-K classroom is completely out of control!" She rearranged her schedule and hurried to the school, only to find that the classroom "looked exactly like what it should look like. Children were talking and laughing and moving around the room." The principal had expected them to be sitting quietly at tables like third graders. Some cities are beginning to provide early childhood training for principals, but so far, those programs have been voluntary, and, of course, they add to the cost of pre-K. (Boston and DC have solicited the help of local philanthropy and nonprofit organizations to pay for such training.)

Some early childhood experts have been calling for a pre-K–3 approach that creates intentional alignment across the early grades. Schools and communities that have adopted that approach have coordinated learning standards, curricula, and teaching practices between each grade level and the next, so that each year builds on what was learned in the previous one, with no gaps and little repetition. For example, in New Jersey, teachers in training can get a "P–3" certification that allows them to teach any of those grades, and aims to provide an understanding of how the developmental stages from ages three to eight are connected. One of the benefits of a pre-K–3 approach is that it can reduce the likelihood of elementary school teachers and principals "pushing down" unreasonable expectations to preschoolers. In some places that I visited, it is even providing an opportunity for pre-K to "pull up" effective practices, like learning centers and hands-on exploration. In Boston, the district's early childhood department developed its own kindergarten curriculum to build on the skills and successes of K1. After tackling pre-K, director Jason Sachs was worried children's gains would be lost because of thin, boring kindergarten curricula. He was inspired to have his department write and coach the new curriculum when he visited a kindergarten classroom and found himself telling an educator, "You're too good a teacher to be teaching this." Recently, BPS has been piloting a first-grade curriculum as well, and Sachs hopes to see his department work up to third grade.

But the quality of kindergarten and first grade is still uneven in Boston, as it is in many places. For Ayannah Hilton, getting her son into a good kindergarten proved just as difficult as getting him into a good pre-K program. When I saw Hilton at the Roxbury YMCA's preschool graduation ceremony in June, dressed up and grateful for a few hours off from her new temp job, she still didn't know where Jeremiah would be going to kindergarten. She had skipped the first registration period in January, because she still hadn't figured out how to deal with the logistics of coordinating her work schedule with the children's school schedules. She hadn't realized that waiting until the second-round lottery would mean there were fewer choices available, because most of the spots at highly rated schools would already be taken. But she was still hopeful and had done some research on schools before listing her choices. "I wanted it to be convenient, but I didn't want it to be all about that. I wanted him to go to a good school, so I looked at the numbers," meaning test scores, how many students get promoted on time from one grade to the next, and the amount of enrichment opportunities available. Hilton grew quiet as a portable speaker began to play a funky version of "Pomp and Circumstance," and she beamed as her son walked up to a podium to receive his pre-K diploma, wearing a small black cap and gown and a huge smile. Some of his classmates paraded around the room while a grandmother cheered, "Show that diploma! Tell everybody you got a di-*plo*-ma!" In between snapping the photos she had promised to her new coworkers, Hilton repeated nervously, "I want Jeremiah to be in a good school."

In early August, Hilton still hadn't heard, so she called BPS. She was disappointed when she learned of the school assignment Jeremiah had received. "It's at the bottom for academics," she told me, referring to the fact that it had been designated by the state as a Level 4 school, which means that it has low test scores and is far from hitting its improvement goals. She requested that Jeremiah be put on the waitlist for other schools, but she was told their chances were small this late in the process, and her hopes did not come to pass.

In mid-September, Jeremiah started at his new school and at its after-school program, which was run by a nonprofit organization out of the school's basement. On the second day, Jeremiah fell off the monkey bars during the after-school program and broke two bones in his arm. His mother was furious, because when she arrived minutes later to pick up her son, she observed that the children were not being supervised on the playground. She believed that the staff were negligent and the situation could have been avoided. She became even angrier because of the response from the staff, who she felt treated it "lightly, like it was just a cut that needed a Band-Aid," rather than a serious injury that resulted in an overnight hospital stay and weeks in a cast.

Meanwhile, Hilton was in the middle of a dispute with her landlord and was trying to relocate. The landlord had failed to address numerous health and safety hazards in her apartment, so when the ceiling collapsed, revealing mildew and mold, she called inspectional services and started looking for a new place when the building failed inspection. Hilton found an apartment in a small city about thirty miles south of Boston and pulled Jeremiah out of school. He never went back after his second day, because his mother didn't think he was safe there. She held the school partially responsible for his injury, because she felt the principal should have been monitoring the quality of the after-school program in the school building. "They know I'm mad at them," she said, but "since we are relocating anyway, I didn't want to deal with BPS anymore."

But Hilton and her children weren't able to move right away, so Jeremiah spent more than a month out of school, alternating between his grandmother's and great-grandmother's houses about forty minutes away from Boston during the day, when his mother was at work. Hilton knew it was a priority to get him back to kindergarten, but she was just keeping her head above water. Between finishing up her temp job, looking for another one, dealing with the apartment situation, and talking with a lawyer about taking legal action for Jeremiah's injury, she hadn't had time to look into the schools in their new town. "It's been a lot to deal with. And it's just me. I'm just doing the best I can," she sighed.

Fortunately, Jeremiah hadn't lost what he had learned in the Roxbury Y's K1 classroom. One day at home he asked his mother, "Mom, do you know what one plus one is? It's two!" Hilton was surprised, because she hadn't been doing math with him at home. He told her he had learned it at school, even though he hadn't been to the Y in months. His vocabulary kept growing, and he loved books. "He still can't read them, but he loves to look at them, or at tablets," Hilton told me. She added that he loves to write, "but he can't write right now, because of his arm." She paused for a minute and then added, "He's missing his education."

There is another important way in which continuity from pre-K to elementary school matters: parents' choices about which schools are a good fit for their families. In many communities, free pre-K is a strong incentive for parents to select a public school with early childhood classrooms. And the reverse is also true: the reputation and quality of the later grades has an impact on whether and where parents decide to take pre-K spots. No matter what their choices are, parents often have an eye toward elementary school long before their children get there.

That was the case for Maria Fenwick in choosing where to send her son, Luca, to pre-K. In early March, I got an email from Fenwick with the subject line "K1 results are in!" Despite the enthusiastic headline, her news was mixed. Luca had not gotten into the Eliot, Fenwick's top choice school where he might have been in Jodi Krous's classroom, but he had gotten a K1 spot at her second choice, Harvard-Kent. She was conflicted. Should she jump at the chance for a year of free pre-K and the peace of mind that would come with having one of her choices for the rest of elementary school? Or should she stick with her trusted but expensive private preschool for another year and try again for the Eliot in the kindergarten lottery?

Fenwick went back to visit the elementary school and talk with the principal again. She and her husband attended an open house, where she met dedicated teachers and an enthusiastic literacy specialist who came in a Harriet Tubman costume to demonstrate how she tries to get kids excited about reading. Fenwick was impressed enough that she decided to accept the spot. Twelve other children from their neighborhood also accepted spots at Harvard-Kent, which seemed to Fenwick like good news for Luca and corroboration of her impression that the school was improving.

As the summer came, more and more families got off the waitlists at other schools and decided to take the spots based on the schools' reputations around the neighborhood. Fenwick was disappointed. She had already begun volunteering to help Harvard-Kent with its marketing and parent outreach efforts and she had been organizing playgroups among the dozen incoming families in her neighborhood. She had also served on the school's committee to hire a new K1 teacher, and she was feeling excited. She believed the other parents (all white and middle class) were buying into stereotypes that schools serving mostly low-income children wouldn't provide a good education for their own families. When I accompanied Fenwick to the Harvard-Kent's back-to-school night, we heard a parent start a conversation with Luca's new teacher by explaining in a haughty tone that his child probably wouldn't be there on the first day because he was high on the waitlist at another school. By the time school started, Luca knew only two other children. The others had all gotten spots at Harvard-Kent's competitor school up the hill, which middle-class parents tended to prefer but which Fenwick, with her knowledge of education, had found lacking in creativity and innovation.

Fenwick was now sold on the school, but she was still a little nervous about Luca's transition, as pre-K parents tend to be. By the end of the first week, however, her fears had been put to rest. Luca liked his new teacher and told his mother all about his classmates. He loved being a "big kid," and even the large, imposing school building wasn't a big deal. One day after school, Fenwick heard Luca proudly tell his little sister: "You can't go to this school yet, because you're little. I get to go to this big school because I'm a big kid—I'm four." Another day when Fenwick picked him up from his classroom, he pointed to a staircase and told her in a hushed, reverent voice, "Those stairs go to the computer lab!" For her part, Fenwick loved that the early childhood wing had a wide hallway that teachers used for indoor recess during rainy days and the many wintry days Boston was sure to see in the months ahead. It was crucial for her that the teachers understood how much Luca and the other four-year-olds needed that time to jump, move, and be silly.

Within the first month, she could tell that Luca was learning many of the things she had been hoping for. He suddenly had new strategies for dealing with his sister, saying things like, "Marin, in my classroom we only use gentle touches." After reading a book from the K1 curriculum called *Oonga Boonga*, he modeled how the boy in the story helped his baby sibling, making silly "oonga boonga" noises to get Marin to stop crying. "He's also writing way more," Fenwick told me. "I didn't know he could write his name! He's never been interested when I've asked him. I could never get him to even write the letter *L* at home. But now when I drop him off, he signs in all by himself." She also started seeing him engage in new kinds of play, like playing store with a pretend cash register. "He writes down the prices of items—they are nonsensical, mostly squiggles—but he gets it. This is new. We've never done this at home or seen him do it."

Then in late September, Harvard-Kent was named a Level 1 school, the state's highest academic rating, based on steady improvement in student achievement. The school had jumped two levels, surpassing the rating of its competitor school up the hill. Fenwick was proud and felt vindicated, especially when neighborhood parents about to enter the lottery would approach her on the playground and ask her about the school. "Didn't they just win some kind of award?" one asked.

Around the same time that Luca started K1, the private preschool he had been attending announced that it would raise its already-high tuition rates. As more and more of its four-year-olds left for public pre-K classrooms, it needed to cover the costs of teacher salaries and professional development that were so essential to its model. Fenwick understood the rationale, but it didn't change the fact that she and her husband wouldn't be able to afford the new tuition for their younger child. Luca had started preschool when he was two, but Marin would have to wait until she turned four and was eligible to join her brother, tuition-free, at his public school. Even Fenwick, who had the time, resources, and knowledge to look for a great pre-K program, couldn't guarantee a high-quality classroom for her youngest child.

Across town in Hyde Park, Folashade Coker was also on pins and needles about where her children would spend the next school year. Unlike Fenwick, she had decided to forgo the stressful BPS lottery altogether, hoping her twins, Roqeeb and Roqeeba, would follow in their older brother's footsteps and attend a suburban school through the METCO busing program. She had worried about how the twins would fare in their METCO interviews and entrance tests because she had been initially unimpressed with the quality of their early childhood education. But after the BPS K1 partnership had revamped the twins' classroom at Nurtury, she had felt reassured, and when she and the twins returned from their METCO interviews, her optimism about the program had been confirmed. "When we went to the METCO interview, I was so surprised [by] all the things Roqeeb knew. And he could read!" she gushed in the spring. "I came back [to Nurtury] after the interview and I said [to the teachers], 'I don't know what to do for you. I'm so grateful.' From the bottom of my heart, these teachers are doing a great job."

When I talked to Coker in October, the twins were doing well at their new school in Brookline, an affluent town just outside of Boston. Roqeeb was having a little trouble adjusting to riding the METCO bus with older kids, but once he and his sister arrived at the school's beautiful, well-manicured campus, there were no problems. Their mother told me, "I have no concerns. I always talk to the teachers and they say the kids are doing great." She wasn't surprised. "They are used to adjusting," she told me of her first-generation American children, and they had solid social and cognitive skills after their year in Herminia Santiago's Nurtury classroom. She couldn't point out one thing that had been particularly helpful from the K1 classroom, but she reiterated her gratitude for the teachers and told me she had already promised the twins to bring them back to visit Ms. Herminia and Mr. Clif.

Coker, Fenwick, and Hilton all discovered that there is marked variability in early childhood classrooms, even within a city, a neighborhood, or a school. They wanted the very best opportunities for their children, as all parents do and as all children deserve. And they were acutely aware that the high stakes of inequity begin in the earliest years. The roots of that inequity are many, but they often flow through teachers. Those who teach low-income children tend to have not only the lowest pay and least benefits but the least support in the classroom, from materials to professional development to emotional and logistical support from other staff and society at large.

Around the time that Boston parents were making their decisions about schools for the following year, teacher Meg Hackett was making a big decision of her own. When I visited her classroom at the Roxbury YMCA in early March, the children were happily engaged in their curriculum activities and the walls had been transformed with the children's work. On one bulletin board were numerals made out of Cheerios, which children had glued over yellow highlighter outlines of the numerals—a low-pressure, fun way to help children work on math and writing that Hackett had learned from her coaches. On another was the word "architecture" in handmade bubble letters, with photographs of buildings and bridges interspersed with children's drawings of similar structures. And children were regularly writing their names on their drawings and other work. Jeremiah Hilton had made several of the signs. "Whenever I need something written, I ask Jeremiah to do it," Hackett told me, explaining that he was the strongest writer in the class and she could see she needed to give him extra challenges to keep him engaged.

But although the children's tension had started to melt away, Hackett's had ramped up. The classroom was finally fully staffed, but because of the need to cover ten hours a day, Hackett still didn't have dedicated planning time during the day. She was staying late and coming in on weekends to prepare the activities and set up the appropriate materials. Even her coaching sessions were getting squeezed in during the children's naps, when it was hard to focus. Two nights a week, she was attending a class on children's social and emotional development that the Y required of all its teachers, even though Hackett said she had taken it before at another job. And she was still trying to help some of the parents get special education services outside the Y, despite the fact that that was now officially someone else's job. She adored the children and was frustrated that she could do only so much to help those who had few resources and stressful home lives. When she got home from work, she would take a shower and then curl up in bed, barely spending time with her family.

Hackett was exhausted, and she felt unsupported. She was frustrated that she didn't have access to the full range of resources that a BPS teacher would. And her relationships with supervisors at the center were growing more strained by the day. She felt that they weren't providing the logistical or emotional support she needed to teach her challenging class, and they were so focused on compliance they would call her out of the classroom during instructional time to scold her for minor administrative matters. For their part, her supervisors seemed worried about meeting the numerous state and federal regulations that governed their classrooms with a long and sometimes contradictory list of requirements, and staffing was a constant challenge that got even harder when Hackett had had to take a lot of time off for personal reasons. They also worried that Hackett's classroom-management skills, though vastly improved, still weren't up to the level needed by the children.

On the day I visited in March, Hackett was having a particularly tough day. She had recently spent a few days out of state dealing with a family emergency. When she came back to her classroom, she says her supervisors scolded her for missing work, gave examples of other staff members who had come to work even during family medical emergencies, and told her she was expected to do the same. Because she had used up all her vacation and sick time and her supervisors were concerned about coverage and consistency in the classroom, they called her out of her classroom during a lesson and required her to sign a written commitment that she would miss no further days of work, even though the family emergency had not yet been resolved. Without her having to say it, I could tell this might be the last straw for Hackett, and it was.

Leaving her classroom was a wrenching decision. Hackett told me that she wanted to hang on for the rest of the school year, to see it through with the kids with whom she had formed a tight bond, especially the kids who badly needed a supportive and nurturing adult. Despite their troubles and the constant challenges they threw at her, the kids weren't the problem, she said. It was the working conditions and the lack of support she felt. Administrators also felt a lack of support, but from policymakers and the public. They were experiencing two sides of the same coin: Hackett was frustrated that she didn't have more resources in the classroom; administrators were frustrated that they didn't have more resources from the state, especially for the center's younger classrooms. Hackett wished she could teach in a BPS classroom; her supervisors fretted that those public school classrooms were making it ever harder for centers like theirs to find qualified teachers.

When Hackett left in early April, children and parents were disappointed to see her go. Jeremiah told his mother, "Ms. Meg is leaving and I'm going to be so sad." Even after she left, he continued to talk about her at home. Before his family moved into their new apartment, his mother told me she would try to enlarge a picture she had taken of Jeremiah and Hackett, so that she could hang it up in his bedroom. Another parent whose son was also very attached to Hackett worried about what the classroom would be like after she left. "For them to lose Meg . . . I don't know. I trust Ms. Meg. I wish I could take [my son] out of there today," she told me. For her part, Hackett tried to hold back tears and promised the children she would stay in touch. And she did. She came back to visit the classroom every few weeks, even after starting a new job, and arrived early for the students' pre-K graduation ceremony in June. As she greeted parents and hugged the kids, it was clear how much she missed them.

Hackett took a job working as a nanny for a young girl with autism. The child's wealthy parents, thrilled to find someone with a master's degree in special education, covered her health insurance and paid her a salary similar to her classroom salary, but for far fewer hours and much less stress. Hackett and her boyfriend immediately noticed her anxiety drop, and she stopped taking the sleeping pills. She enjoyed her new job and was grateful for the "breather" it gave her. But months after leaving the Y, she told me she was still having dreams about the children. "These kids will always be sitting back there in my mind," she explained.

Despite her passion for working with children, Hackett has no plans to go back into the classroom. She said she gets too emotionally involved with the children and gets angry when she sees a system that isn't working for them. Those qualities gave her the potential to be a great teacher, but without the support she needed, they also made it impossible for her to do the job. "I need to go into advocacy or somewhere where I have a larger voice," she decided, and was thinking about getting a PhD in school administration or education law. She wanted to help fix problems at a systemic level, because, as she told me ruefully, "there are too many kids like Jeremiah who can fall through the cracks."

Teachers are the fulcrum on which all the levers of quality pivot. Their jobs are challenging to a degree that most of us can't imagine. Higher wages are important for increasing the stability and competence of the early childhood workforce, but the solution to teacher quality isn't just about money. If it were, Meg Hackett would still be teaching at the Y. Working in a classroom with young children can be isolating; teachers need dependable coteachers or assistants and specialists for mental health and special education. They need lots of opportunities to talk about their classroom challenges and successes with other teachers and supportive supervisors and coaches. They need ongoing opportunities for training and professional development, because teaching young children is a complex task that is always changing and never fully mastered. Above all, they need respect, and not just from the children.

With all those pieces in place, amazing things can happen, as they did in the majority of community-based classrooms that participated in the partnership with the Boston Public Schools. But the existing financing structure of early childhood, particularly for community-based settings, makes it very difficult for organizations to create those conditions. Through the partnership with BPS, Hackett's classroom had many of the most essential supports, and they clearly helped. But the other classrooms at the center didn't, and that meant the whole system was strapped and stressed, from staff who seemed tense and consumed with paperwork to difficulty finding consistent teachers who could have freed up Hackett's coteacher to be in the pre-K classroom more consistently.

The Boston experience shows how important and how complex it can be to build the systems that improve quality. When I talked to Marcy Whitebook, the director of the Center for the Study of Child Care Employment who has been in the field for more than forty years, I asked her what she would do first if someone offered her the chance to improve early childhood education in America. "I would stop saying there is a silver bullet and we have to pick out one thing," she told me. "You can't think of it as a single ingredient. You have to do [all of the quality elements] simultaneously." She said her opinion has changed over the decades, from a focus on teacher training to an overhaul of the whole system. "The field had an assumption for many years that if you invest in [teacher] education and training, everything will follow. It won't. You have to improve the higher education system [for future teachers], but you also have to adjust the salaries and working environment, make sure that people have opportunities to grow in the job, and improve working conditions." To do that, she added, you have to figure out how to increase revenue.

Contrary to popular opinion, she said, "I don't think that's the biggest challenge. It's the will to do it. You have to make a decision that parents won't have to pay for this, or at the very least, parents don't pay more than a certain amount of their income so you make it more equitable."

Everyone I talked to about pre-K underscored that it takes significant financial resources to make programs that work for children. When former president Obama announced his proposal for a $75 billion investment in early childhood, he didn't shy away from the cost, but he also summed up the value. "What is required is a sense on the part of all of us that what happens to those [low-income] kids matters to me, even if I never meet 'em. Because my society's going to be better off . . . And over time, I'm confident that my children and my grandchildren are going to live a better life if those kids also have opportunity."

Because that kind of major investment has yet to materialize, the struggles of programs like the Roxbury YMCA and the cuts in Elizabeth, New Jersey, raise real threats to the sustainability of pre-K. Creating a stable workforce means providing not just competitive wages but the kinds of salary increases for cost of living and merit that are standard in other professions, including K–12 teaching. Community-based programs have been struggling with those cost increases for years, and now district-run programs like Elizabeth's are running into the same problem. Is it feasible for public funding to cover those increasing costs indefinitely? Perhaps not. But on the other hand, what is the alternative? Passing on the costs to families is not an ideal solution, because so many families are already struggling. Parents like Ayannah Hilton, whose children are subsidized by the state, simply can't afford to pay more. Even for middle-income parents like Maria Fenwick, the costs can be prohibitive. The strain is especially heavy for low- and moderate-income families who just miss the eligibility cutoff for Head Start but can't afford private programs. Their children, who often end up left out of pre-K altogether, are among those who most need the benefits it can provide.

What is clear is that we need to find a solution. Pre-K matters, especially for the most vulnerable children, the children who are on the losing end of opportunity and achievement gaps that start in infancy and widen as students get older. Pre-K may be just one or two years of a child's schooling, and most students won't remember those years when they graduate from high school or college. Yet those years are critical, setting children off on a long path toward a future of either security and success or difficulty and distress. Pre-K programs not only develop children's social and early academic skills, they also shape how children think and feel about education. When a young child has a nurturing teacher and a positive classroom experience, he comes to see school as a place that is fascinating, fun, and sometimes just a little bit frustrating in the best possible way. To be sure, he will continue to feel that way only if kindergarten and the many grades that follow are also effective, but it helps enormously to get off on the right foot. When a child has a positive experience with school in his earliest years, no one can take that away from him.

We owe it to our children to find a way for all of them to start off on the right foot. Creating effective pre-K programs is hard work for everyone, but the potential payoffs are big. As one elementary school principal told me, "Preschoolers are cute, but they're not babies. They love to hug and cuddle, but they're really, really smart. Push that. Now is the time for provocations and questions." Now is the time not just for the children but for the adults.

Acknowledgments

What a pleasure it is to have the opportunity for so many thanks. I am ever grateful to my agent, Alia Hanna Habib, for believing in this book and taking a chance on me, and for her invaluable advice, support, and good humor. My editor, Lucia Watson, is a true pleasure to work with and made this book stronger with every conversation. I extend my thanks to everyone at Avery and Penguin Random House, especially Matthew Martin, Nina Caldas, Megan Newman, Justin Thrift, Claire Sullivan, and Jennifer Eck. Nellys Liang's thoughtful cover design helped bring my vision to life.

This book would not have been possible without Monica Yudron, whose insights, introductions, and friendship have been instrumental and generous. As usual, Liz Murray stretched my thinking, challenged the status quo, and made me laugh all at the same time. Tobey Pearl, Nadine Gaab, Anna Goldsmith, and Greg Harris read sections of the book and provided helpful feedback at various stages. Helen Westmoreland, Nazli Parvizi, and Abby Weiss facilitated important connections and conversations. I am fortunate to have the mentorship of Nancy Walser, Stephanie Jones, Rick Weissbourd, and Nancy Etcoff.

I am grateful beyond words to the teachers, staff, families, and researchers who opened up their lives to me and found time in their busy schedules to answer my questions and share their experiences. I am particularly grateful to Jason Sachs, Marina Boni, Abby Morales, Anthony Valdez, TeeAra Dias, Carolyn Christopher, Meg Hackett, Kamilah Washington, Traci Griffith, Jodi Krous, Kayla Brennan, Maria Fenwick, Ayannah Hilton, Folashade Coker, Cliff Kwong, Herminia Santiago, Regina Walker, Melanie Mathieu, Mary Kinsella Scannell, Jason Harris, Amy Symonds, Lisa Gross, Kira Moore, Janeece Docal, Carla Ferris, Diana Suarez, Jackie Taylor, Kenyona Taylor, Samantha Bryan, Jack McCarthy, Anne Zummo Malone, Nikeysha Jackson, Kelly Pellegrini, Carly Regan, Tracy Crosby, Gissela Barnas, Kathie Priestley, and Alex Figueras-Daniel. Every one of them cares deeply about children—theirs, mine, and yours. I also extend my thanks to the many early childhood experts who answered my questions and shared their insights.

Many people supported me as I wrote the book. Tricia Seidler provided translation services, car parties, and a genuine friendship that transcends gaps in time and location. She and the rest of the Seidler clan—Doug, Maya, and Andre—were the most gracious hosts imaginable. Dee and Lou Angelakis helped on the home front and have been great cheerleaders. Megan Phillips was flexible and generous with her time and her smile. David Bouffard and Lucia Burns-Bouffard provided their reliable moral and logistical support. As always, I am especially thankful for my incredible parents, Don and Sandy Bouffard, who are the model of parental support and did everything from watching the kids and cooking to sending news articles and weighing in on the title.

Above all, I am grateful for the most wonderful husband and children a person could have. Chris—my best, my truest, my favorite—you make all the good things happen. Theo and Ellis, you inspired this book and continue to inspire me every single day.

Notes

Prologue

4 *Over one and a half million American children are enrolled in pre-K:* W. Steven Barnett, Allison H. Friedman-Krauss, Rebecca E. Gomez, Michelle Horowitz, G. G. Weisenfeld, Kirsty Clarke Brown, and James H. Squires, "The State of Preschool 2015: State Preschool Yearbook" (New Brunswick, NJ: National Institute for Early Education Research, 2016), http://nieer.org/research/state-preschool-2015.

4 *We rank twenty-eighth out of thirty-eight countries in the percentage of four-year-olds enrolled in programs:* Organisation for Economic Co-operation and Development, "How Do Early Childhood Education and Care (ECEC) Policies, Systems and Quality Vary Across OECD Countries?" *Education Indicators in Focus* (Paris, February 2013), http://www.oecd.org/edu/EDIF11.pdf.

4 *In countries like the United Kingdom:* Lillian Mongeau, "Why Britain Said 'Yes' to Universal Preschool," *The Atlantic*, August 23, 2016, https://www.theatlantic.com/education/archive/2016/08/why-britain-said-yes-to-universal-preschool/496919.

5 *Around 90 percent of parents believed that the preschool years are a critical period of development:* "Tuning In: Parents of Young Children Tell Us What They Think, Know and Need," Zero to Three, June 6, 2016, https://www.zerotothree.org/resources/series/tuning-in-parents-of-young-children-tell-us-what-they-think-know-and-need; "Early Childhood Educators: Advancing the Profession," National Association for the Education of Young Children, n.d., https://www.naeyc.org/files/naeyc/Executive%20Summary.pdf; "Essential for Children and Families: Voters Rate Early Childhood Education as a Top National Priority," First Five Years Fund, 2015, http://ffyf.org/2015-poll.

5 *More than forty states fund some sort of pre-K program at a cost of over $6 billion:* Barnett et al., "The State of Preschool 2015: State Preschool Yearbook."

5 *Government has supported tens of thousands of new slots via grant programs:* Lillian Mongeau, "Obama Administration Declares Its Early Education Initiatives a Success,"

Education Week, September 19, 2016, http://blogs.edweek.org/edweek/early_years/2016/09/obama_administration_declares_its_early_education_initiatives_a_success.html.

5 *The brain develops faster in early childhood:* "From Best Practices to Breakthrough Impacts: A Science-Based Approach to Building a More Promising Future for Young Children and Families," Center on the Developing Child at Harvard University, May 2016, http://46y5eh11fhgw3ve3ytpwxt9r.wpengine.netdna-cdn.com/wp-content/uploads/2016/05/HCDC_From_Best_Practices_to_Breakthrough_Impacts.pdf; National Research Council/Institute of Medicine, *From Neurons to Neighborhoods: The Science of Early Childhood Development,* edited by Jack P. Shonkoff and Deborah A. Phillips (Washington, DC: National Academies Press, 2000).

5 *Benefits of high-quality pre-K:* Hirokazu Yoshikawa, Christina Weiland, Jeanne Brooks-Gunn, Margaret R. Burchinal, Linda M. Espinosa, William T. Gormley, Jens Ludwig, Katherine A. Magnuson, Deborah Phillips, and Martha J. Zaslow, "Investing in Our Future: The Evidence Base on Preschool Education," Society for Research in Child Development, October 2013, http://www.srcd.org/sites/default/files/documents/washington/mb_2013_10_16_investing_in_children.pdf; Greg J. Duncan and Katherine Magnuson, "Investing in Preschool Programs," *Journal of Economic Perspectives* 27, no. 2 (Spring 2013): 109–32, doi:10.1257/jep.27.2.109; Vivian C. Wong, Thomas D. Cook, W. Steven Barnett, and Kwanghee Jung, "An Effectiveness-Based Evaluation of Five State Pre-Kindergarten Programs," *Journal of Policy Analysis and Management* 27, no.1 (2008): 122–54, https://www.sesp.northwestern.edu/docs/publications/13704553154e5523c50fb8c.pdf; Carollee Howes, Margaret Burchinal, Robert Pianta, Donna Bryant, Diane Early, Richard Clifford, and Oscar Barbarin, "Ready to Learn? Children's Pre-Academic Achievement in Pre-Kindergarten Programs," *Early Childhood Research Quarterly* 23, no. 1 (2008): 27–50, doi:10.1016/j.ecresq.2007.05.002; Lauren Bauer and Diane Whitemore Schanzenbach, "The Long-Term Impact of the Head Start Program," August 2016, http://www.hamiltonproject.org/assets/files/long_term_impact_of_head_start_program.pdf.

5 *Model preschool programs created in the 1960s:* Lawrence J. Schweinhart; Jeanne Montie, Zongping Xiang, William S. Barnett, Clive R. Belfield, and Milagros Nores, "Lifetime Effects: The High/Scope Perry Preschool Study Through Age 40," 2005, https://works.bepress.com/william_barnett/3; W. Steven Barnett, "Long-Term Effects of Early Childhood Programs on Cognitive and School Outcomes," *The Future of Children* 5, no. 3 (Winter 1995): 25–50; W. Steven Barnett, "Benefit-Cost Analysis of Preschool Education: Findings from a 25-Year Follow-Up," *American Journal of Orthopsychiatry* 63, no. 4 (October 1993): 500–08; Judy A. Temple and Arthur J. Reynolds, "Benefits and Costs of Investments in Preschool Education: Evidence from the Child-Parent Centers and Related Programs," *Economics of Education Review* 26, no. 1 (February 2007): 126–44, doi:10.1016/j.econedurev.2005.11.004; Arthur J. Reynolds, Judy A. Temple, Barry A. White, Suh-Ruu Ou, and Dylan L. Robertson, "Age 26 Cost-Benefit Analysis of the Child-Parent Center Early Education Program," *Child Development* 82, no. 1 (January 2011): 379–404, doi:10.1111/j.1467-8624.2010.01563.x; James J. Heckman, Seong Hyeok Moon, Rodrigo Pinto, Peter A. Savelyev, and Adam Yavitz, "The Rate of Return to the High/Scope Perry Preschool Program," *Journal of Public Economics* 94, nos. 1–2 (February 2010): 114–28; James J. Heckman, "Invest in Early Childhood Development: Reduce Deficits, Strengthen the Economy," *The Heckman Equation,* December 7, 2012, https://

heckmanequation.org/assets/2013/07/F_HeckmanDeficitPieceCUSTOM-Generic
_052714-3-1.pdf.

6 *High-quality programs run by cities and states:* W. Steven Barnett, Kwanghee Jung, Min-Jong Youn, and Ellen C. Frede, "Abbott Preschool Program Longitudinal Effects Study: Fifth Grade Follow-Up," National Institute for Early Education Research, March 1, 2013, http://nieer.org/research-report/201311apples205th20grade-pdf; Christina Weiland and Hirokazu Yoshikawa, "Impacts of a Prekindergarten Program on Children's Mathematics, Language, Literacy, Executive Function, and Emotional Skills," *Child Development* 84, no. 6 (November 2013): 2112–30, doi:10.1111/cdev .12099; Kenneth A. Dodge, Yu Bai, Helen F. Ladd, and Clara G. Muschkin, "Impact of North Carolina's Early Childhood Programs and Policies on Educational Outcomes in Elementary School," *Child Development*, November 17, 2016, doi:10.1111 /cdev.12645; Wong et al., "An Effectiveness-Based Evaluation of Five State Pre-Kindergarten Programs"; Deborah Phillips, William Gormley, and Sara Anderson, "The Effects of Tulsa's CAP Head Start Program on Middle-School Academic Outcomes and Progress," *Developmental Psychology* 52, no. 8 (2016): 1247–61, doi:10.1037 /dev0000151.

6 *Benefits of Boston pre-K program:* "Measuring the Effectiveness of BPS K1 Programs Using 3rd Grade MCAS Performance Scores BPS K1 Cohorts: 2007, 2008, 2009," Boston Public Schools, Office of Data and Accountability, http://drive.google.com/file /B3q KorUGb2mHZER zaWFIQm9zUWc/view; Weiland and Yoshikawa, "Impacts of a Prekindergarten Program on Children's Mathematics, Language, Literacy, Executive Function, and Emotional Skills."

6 *Kindergarten teachers report their biggest challenges are children's behaviors:* Sara E. Rimm-Kaufman, Robert C. Pianta, and Martha J. Cox, "Teachers' Judgments of Problems in the Transition to Kindergarten," *Early Childhood Research Quarterly* 15, no. 2 (2000): 147–66, doi:10.1016/S0885-2006(00)00049-1.

6 *Benefits of preschool program in New Jersey:* Barnett et al., "Abbott Preschool Program Longitudinal Effects Study: Fifth Grade Follow-Up."

6 *Benefits of North Carolina pre-K program:* Dodge et al., "Impact of North Carolina's Early Childhood Programs and Policies on Educational Outcomes in Elementary School."

6 *Graduates of Michigan's Great Start Readiness Program:* Michael P. Flanagan, Memorandum to State Board of Education, May 21, 2012, "Presentation on Great Start Readiness Program Evaluation," http://www.michigan.gov/documents/mde/GSRP _Evaluation_397470_7.pdf.

7 *Benefits of pre-K are particularly striking for children from low-income families:* Weiland and Yoshikawa, "Impacts of a Prekindergarten Program on Children's Mathematics, Language, Literacy, Executive Function, and Emotional Skills"; Yoshikawa et al., "Investing in Our Future: The Evidence Base on Preschool Education."

7 *Achievement gaps across income appear shockingly early:* Sean F. Reardon and Ximena A. Portilla, "Recent Trends in Income, Racial, and Ethnic School Readiness Gaps at Kindergarten Entry," *AERA Open* 2, no. 3 (July 1, 2016), http://ero.sagepub.com /content/2/3/2332858416657343.abstract; Sean F. Reardon, "The Widening Academic Achievement Gap Between the Rich and the Poor: New Evidence and Possible Explanations," in *Whither Opportunity? Rising Inequality, Schools, and Children's Life Chances,*

edited by Greg J. Duncan and Richard J. Murnane (New York: Russell Sage Founda-
tion, 2011), 91–116; Sean F. Reardon, "The Widening Income Achievement Gap,"
Educational Leadership 70, no. 8 (May 2013): 10–16; Valerie E. Lee and David T.
Burkam, *Inequality at the Starting Gate: Social Background Differences in Achievement
as Children Begin School* (Washington, DC: Economic Policy Institute, 2002); Emma
García, "Inequalities at the Starting Gate: Cognitive and Noncognitive Skills Gaps
Between 2010–2011 Kindergarten Classmates," Economic Policy Institute, June 17,
2015, http://www.epi.org/files/pdf/85032c.pdf; Tamara Halle, Nicole Forry, Elizabeth
Hair, Kate Perper, Laura Wandner, Julia Wessel, and Jessica Vick, "Disparities in
Early Learning and Development: Lessons from the Early Childhood Longitudinal
Study, Birth Cohort (ECLS-B)," Child Trends, June 2009, http://www.elcmdm.org
/Knowledge%20Center/reports/Child_Trends-2009_07_10_FR_DisparitiesEL.pdf.

7 *Achievement gaps are also evident across racial and ethnic groups:* Lee and Burkam,
    Inequality at the Starting Gate; George Bohrnstedt, Sami Kitmitto, Burhan Ogut,
    Daniel Sherman, and Derek Chan, "School Composition and the Black–White Achieve-
    ment Gap," National Center for Education Statistics, 2015, https://nces.ed.gov/nations
    reportcard/subject/studies/pdf/school_composition_and_the_bw_achievement
    _gap_2015.pdf.

7 *Achievement gaps are narrowing:* Reardon and Portilla, "Recent Trends in Income, Ra-
    cial, and Ethnic School Readiness Gaps at Kindergarten Entry."

7 *It could take another hundred years for the gap to close completely:* Sarah D. Sparks, "Are
    Poor Students More Prepared for Kindergarten?" *Education Week*, August 26, 2016,
    http://blogs.edweek.org/edweek/inside-school-research/2016/08/kindergarten
    _readiness_gap_closing.html?intc=main-mpsmvs.

7-8 *Obama on the benefits of early childhood education:* "President Barack Obama," *WTF
    with Marc Maron* (podcast), episode 613, June 22, 2015, http://www.wtfpod.com
    /podcast/episodes/episode_613_-_president_barack_obama.

8 *Obama proposed an unprecedented investment:* Lillian Mongeau, "Obama Budget
    Would Allocate $75 Billion over Next Decade to Preschool," *EdSource*, April 10, 2013,
    https://edsource.org/2013/obama-budget-would-allocate-75-billion-over-next
    -decade-to-preschool/30223.

8 *"Among the smartest investments that we can make":* "Early Learning," The White
    House: President Barack Obama, n.d., https://obamawhitehouse.archives.gov/issues
    /education/early-childhood.

8 *Pre-K saves the government somewhere between $3 and $8:* Arthur J. Reynolds, Arthur J.
    Rolnick, Michelle M. Englund, and Judy A. Temple, "Early Childhood Development
    and Human Capital," in *Childhood Programs and Practices in the First Decade of Life: A
    Human Capital Integration,* edited by Arthur J. Reynolds, Arthur J. Rolnick, Michelle
    M. Englund, and Judy A. Temple (Cambridge, UK: Cambridge University Press, 2010);
    Yoshikawa et al., "Investing in Our Future"; James J. Heckman, "Skill Formation
    and the Economics of Investing in Disadvantaged Children," *Science* 312 (2006):
    1900–02.

8 *Economists advocating for early childhood education:* Reynolds et al., "Early Childhood
    Development and Human Capital."

8 *Heckman and Yellen as advocates for early childhood education:* Heckman, "Skill For-
    mation and the Economics of Investing in Disadvantaged Children"; Janet L. Yellen,

"Perspectives on Inequality and Opportunity from the Survey of Consumer Finances," Conference on Economic Opportunity and Inequality, October 17, 2014, http://www .federalreserve.gov/newsevents/speech/yellen20141017a.htm#f42.

8 *Law enforcement officers advocate for early childhood education:* William Christeson, Sandra Bishop-Josef, Natasha O'Dell-Archer, Chris Beakey, and Kara Clifford, "I'm the Guy You Pay Later: Sheriffs, Chiefs, and Prosecutors Urge America to Cut Crime by Investing Now in High-Quality Early Education and Care," Fight Crime: Invest in Kids, 2013, http://cdn.fightcrime.org/wp-content/uploads/I'm_The_Guy _Report.pdf.

9 *Income inequality is at its highest rate in nearly a hundred years:* Yellen, "Perspectives on Inequality and Opportunity from the Survey of Consumer Finances."

9 *Percentage of parents working outside the home:* "Employment Characteristics of Families: 2015," Bureau of Labor Statistics, U.S. Department of Labor, 2016, https://www .bls.gov/news.release/pdf/famee.pdf.

9 *Early childhood care and education costs more:* Brigid Schulte and Alieza Durana, "The New America Care Report," New America Foundation, September 28, 2016, https://www.newamerica.org/better-life-lab/policy-papers/new-america-care-report.

9 *NYC parents say free pre-K allows them to work:* Westat, Metis Associates, and Branch Associates, "New York City's *Pre-K for All*: Family Perceptions," February 19, 2016, http://schools.nyc.gov/NR/rdonlyres/35669F51-084F-42D7-BCE0-457E0F27F067/0 /BranchAssociatesFamilyPerceptionsReport21916.pdf.

15 *It will take fifty years to serve all low-income children:* Barnett et al., "The State of Preschool 2015: State Preschool Yearbook."

15 *Long-standing ambivalence about women in the workforce:* Barbara Beatty, *Preschool Education in America: The Culture of Young Children from the Colonial Era to the Present* (New Haven, CT: Yale University Press, 1997).

15-16 *Savvy politicians passed Oklahoma pre-K legislation on the sly:* "Getting Away with It," *This American Life*, episode 477 (transcript), October 19, 2012, http://www.this americanlife.org/radio-archives/episode/477/transcript.

16 *Three-quarters of Oklahoma four-year-olds enrolled in state-funded pre-K:* Barnett et al., "The State of Preschool 2015: State Preschool Yearbook."

16 *Advocates for targeted pre-K:* Bruce Fuller, "Expanding Preschool in New York City: Which Communities Benefit from Gains in Supply?" University of California–Berkeley, Institute of Human Development, 2014, http://gse.berkeley.edu/sites/default/files/users /bruce-fuller/NewYorkCity-PreK-Distribution.pdf; Heckman, "Invest in Early Childhood Development: Reduce Deficits, Strengthen the Economy."

16 *Kindergarteners make greater gains when more of their classmates went to preschool:* Matthew Neidell and Jane Waldfogel, "Cognitive and Noncognitive Peer Effects in Early Education," *Review of Economics and Statistics* 92, no. 3 (August 2010): 562–76, doi:10.1162/REST_a_00012.

16 *Low-income children do better in economically mixed pre-K programs:* Andrew J. Mashburn, Laura M. Justice, Jason T. Downer, and Robert C. Pianta, "Peer Effects on Children's Language Achievement During Pre-Kindergarten," *Child Development* 80, no. 3 (May/June 2009): 686–702, http://onlinelibrary.wiley.com/doi/10.1111/j.1467 -8624.2009.01291.x/full; Laura M. Justice, Yaacov Petscher, Christopher Schatschneider, and Andrew Mashburn, "Peer Effects in Preschool Classrooms: Is Children's

Language Growth Associated with Their Classmates' Skills?" *Child Development* 82, no. 6 (November 2011): 1768–77, doi:10.1111/j.1467-8624.2011.01665.x; Carlota Schechter and Beth Bye, "Preliminary Evidence for the Impact of Mixed-Income Preschools on Low-Income Children's Language Growth," *Early Childhood Research Quarterly* 22, no. 1 (2007): 137–46; Jeanne L. Reid and Douglas D. Ready, "High-Quality Preschool: The Socioeconomic Composition of Preschool Classrooms and Children's Learning," *Early Education and Development* 24, no. 8 (2013): 1082–1111; Gary T. Henry and Dana K. Rickman, "Do Peers Influence Children's Skill Development in Preschool?," *Economics of Education Review* 26, no. 1 (2007): 100–112, doi:10.1016/j.econedurev.2005.09.006.

16 *Middle-income children benefit from economically diverse pre-K classrooms:* Weiland and Yoshikawa, "Impacts of a Prekindergarten Program on Children's Mathematics, Language, Literacy, Executive Function, and Emotional Skills"; Phillips et al., "The Effects of Tulsa's CAP Head Start Program on Middle-School Academic Outcomes and Progress"; William T. Gormley, "Small Miracles in Tulsa: The Effects of Universal Pre-K on Cognitive Development," in *Childhood Programs and Practices in the First Decade of Life: A Human Capital Integration*, edited by Reynolds et al., 188–98.

17 *Large variations in program quality, with most programs somewhere in the middle:* Yoshikawa et al., "Investing in Our Future"; Rachel Valentino, "Will Public Pre-K Really Close Achievement Gaps? Gaps in Prekindergarten Quality Between Students and Across States," Stanford Center for Education Policy Analysis, 2015, https://cepa.stanford.edu/content/will-public-pre-k-really-close-achievement-gaps-gaps-prekindergarten-quality-between-students-and-across-states; Andrew J. Mashburn, Robert C. Pianta, Bridget K. Hamre, Jason T. Downer, Oscar A. Barbarin, Donna Bryant, Margaret Burchinal, Diane M. Early, and Carollee Howes, "Measures of Classroom Quality in Prekindergarten and Children's Development of Academic, Language, and Social Skills," *Child Development* 79, no. 3 (May 2008): 732–49, doi:10.1111/j.1467-8624.2008.01154.x; Jennifer LoCasale-Crouch, Tim Konold, Robert Pianta, Carollee Howes, Margaret Burchinal, Donna Bryant, Richard M. Clifford, Diane Early, Oscar A. Barbarin, "Observed Classroom Quality Profiles in State-Funded Pre-Kindergarten Programs and Associations with Teacher, Program, and Classroom Characteristics," *Early Childhood Research Quarterly* 22, no. 1 (2007): 3–17, doi:10.1016/j.ecresq .2006.05.001; Robert Pianta, Carollee Howes, Margaret Burchinal, Donna Bryant, Richard Clifford, Diane Early, and Oscar Barbarin, "Features of Pre-Kindergarten Programs, Classrooms, and Teachers: Do They Predict Observed Classroom Quality and Child-Teacher Interactions?" *Applied Developmental Science* 9, no. 3 (July 2005): 144–59, doi:10.1207/s1532480xads0903_2; Barnett et al., "The State of Preschool 2015: State Preschool Yearbook"; Donna M. Bryant, Margaret Burchinal, Lisa B. Lau, and Joseph J. Sparling, "Family and Classroom Correlates of Head Start Children's Developmental Outcomes," *Early Childhood Research Quarterly* 9, nos. 3–4 (1994): 289–309, doi:10.1016/0885-2006(94)90011-6.

17 *Children benefit from pre-K only when the programs they attend are rated as good or great:* Howes et al., "Ready to Learn? Children's Pre-Academic Achievement in Pre-Kindergarten Programs"; LoCasale-Crouch et al., "Observed Classroom Quality Profiles in State-Funded Pre-Kindergarten Programs and Associations with Teacher,

Program, and Classroom Characteristics"; Pianta et al., "Features of Pre-Kindergarten Programs, Classrooms, and Teachers"; Mashburn et al., "Measures of Classroom Quality in Prekindergarten and Children's Development of Academic, Language, and Social Skills"; Yoshikawa et al., "Investing in Our Future"; Wong et al., "An Effectiveness-Based Evaluation of Five State Pre-Kindergarten Programs."

17 *Quality differences in programs:* Diane M. Early et al., "How Do Pre-Kindergarteners Spend Their Time? Gender, Ethnicity, and Income as Predictors of Experiences in Pre-Kindergarten Classrooms," *Early Childhood Research Quarterly* 25, no. 2 (2010): 177–93, doi:10.1016/j.ecresq.2009.10.003; Steve Barnett, Megan Carolan, and David Johns, "Equity and Excellence: African-American Children's Access to Quality Preschool," National Institute for Early Education Research, November 2013, http://nieer.org/wp-content/uploads/2016/08/Equity20and20Excellence20African-American20ChildrenE28099s20Access20to20Quality20Preschool_0.pdf; Daphna Bassok, Maria Fitzpatrick, Erica Greenberg, and Susanna Loeb, "The Extent of Within- and Between-Sector Quality Differences in Early Childhood Education and Care Center on Education Policy and Workforce Competitiveness," *CEPWC Working Paper Series*, no. 17 (December 2013), http://curry.virginia.edu/uploads/resourceLibrary/18_Bassok_Sector_Quality_Differences.pdf.

Chapter 1: The Art and Science of Teaching

22 *Connection between social, emotional, and academic skills:* C. Cybele Raver and Jane Knitzer, "Ready to Enter: What Research Tells Policymakers About Strategies to Promote Social and Emotional School Readiness Among Three- and Four-Year-Olds," National Center for Children in Poverty, July 2002, http://www.nccp.org/publications/pdf/text_485.pdf; Joseph A. Durlak, Roger P. Weissberg, Allison B. Dymnicki, Rebecca D. Taylor, and Kriston B. Schellinger, "The Impact of Enhancing Students' Social and Emotional Learning: A Meta-Analysis of School-Based Universal Interventions," *Child Development* 82, no.1 (January 2011): 405–32, http://onlinelibrary.wiley.com/doi/10.1111/j.1467-8624.2010.01564.x/full; C. Cybele Raver, Pamela W. Garner, and Radiah Smith-Donald, "The Roles of Emotion Regulation and Emotion Knowledge for Children's Academic Readiness: Are the Links Causal?" in *School Readiness and the Transition to Kindergarten in the Era of Accountability*, edited by Robert C. Pianta, Martha J. Cox, and Kyle L. Snow (Baltimore, MD: Paul H. Brookes Publishing, 2007): 121–47; Janelle J. Montroy, Ryan P. Bowles, and Lori E. Skibbe, "The Effect of Peers' Self-Regulation on Preschooler's Self-Regulation and Literacy Growth," *Journal of Applied Developmental Psychology* 46 (September–October 2016): 73–83, http://www.sciencedirect.com/science/article/pii/S019339731630082X; Stephanie M. Jones and Suzanne M. Bouffard, "Social and Emotional Learning in Schools: From Programs to Strategies," *Social Policy Report* 26, no. 4 (2012), http://www.srcd.org/sites/default/files/documents/spr_264_final_2.pdf; Megan M. McClelland, Claire E. Cameron, Carol McDonald Connor, Carrie L. Farris, Abigail M. Jewkes, and Frederick J. Morrison, "Links Between Behavioral Regulation and Preschoolers' Literacy, Vocabulary, and Math Skills," *Developmental Psychology* 43, no. 4 (July 2007): 947–59, doi:10.1037/0012-1649.43.4.947; Kimberly Andrews Espy, Melanie M. McDiarmid, Mary F. Cwik, Melissa Meade Stalets, Arlena Hamby, and Theresa E. Senn, "The Contribution of Executive Functions to Emergent Mathematic Skills in Preschool Children,"

Developmental Neuropsychology 26, no. 1 (August 2004): 465–86, doi:10.1207/ s15326942dn2601_6; Clancy Blair and Rachel Peters Razza, "Relating Effortful Control, Executive Function, and False Belief Understanding to Emerging Math and Literacy Ability in Kindergarten," *Child Development* 78, no. 2 (March 2007): 647–63, doi:10.1111/j.1467-8624.2007.01019.x.

22 *Kindergarten teachers' reports of behavioral challenges:* Rimm-Kaufman, Pianta, and Cox, "Teachers' Judgments of Problems in the Transition to Kindergarten."

22 *Teachers don't have to choose between academics and social-emotional skills:* Edward F. Zigler and Sandra J. Bishop-Josef, "The Cognitive Child Versus the Whole Child: Lessons from 40 Years of Head Start," in *Play = Learning: How Play Motivates and Enhances Children's Cognitive and Social-Emotional Growth*, edited by Dorothy G. Singer, Roberta Michnick Golinkoff, and Kathy Hirsh-Pasek (New York: Oxford University Press, 2002); Maurice J. Elias, "The Connection Between Academic and Social-Emotional Learning," *The Educator's Guide to Emotional Intelligence and Academic Achievement* (Thousand Oaks, CA: Corwin Press, 2006), https://us.corwin.com/sites/default/files/upm-binaries /8299_Ch_1.pdf; Jones and Bouffard, "Social and Emotional Learning in Schools from Programs to Strategies"; Roger P. Weissberg and Jason Cascarino, "Academic Learning + Social-Emotional Learning = National Priority," *Phi Delta Kappan* 95, no. 2 (2013), http:// journals.sagepub.com/doi/full/10.1177/003172171309500203.

24 *Head Start has had multiple goals:* Edward Zigler and Susan Muenchow, *Head Start: The Inside Story of America's Most Successful Educational Experiment* (New York: Basic Books, 1992).

25 *Community-based preschool teachers paid almost $14,000 less than public school pre-K teachers:* Marcy Whitebook, Deborah Phillips, and Carolee Howes, "Worthy Work, *Still* Unlivable Wages: The Early Childhood Workforce 25 Years After the National Child Care Staffing Study," Center for the Study of Child Care Employment, 2014, ffyf .org/wp-content/uploads/2014/11/Child-Care-Employment-Report-11.18.14.pdf.

25 *Higher turnover among community-based preschools than public school pre-K:* W. Steven Barnett, "Low Wages = Low Quality: Solving the Real Preschool Teacher Crisis," *Preschool Policy Matters* 3, no. 3 (2003); Whitebook, Phillips, and Howes, "Worthy Work, *Still* Unlivable Wages"; Daphna Bassok and Eva Galdo, "Inequality in Preschool Quality?: Community-Level Disparities in Access to High-Quality Learning Environments," *Early Education and Development* 27, no. 1 (January 2, 2016): 128–44, doi:10.1080/10409289.2015.1057463.

28 *Children learn less in unstructured play:* Nina C. Chien, Carollee Howes, Margaret Burchinal, Robert C. Pianta, Sharon Ritchie, Donna M. Bryant, Richard M. Clifford, Diane M. Early, and Oscar A. Barbarin, "Children's Classroom Engagement and School Readiness Gains in Prekindergarten," *Child Development* 81, no. 5 (September 2010): 1534–49, doi:10.1111/j.1467-8624.2010.01490.x.

30 *Approximately half of preschool teachers do not have a college degree:* Whitebook, Phillips, and Howes, "Worthy Work, *Still* Unlivable Wages."

30 *Studies suggest that preschool teachers with a bachelor's degree are more effective:* Marcy Whitebook and Sharon Ryan, "Degrees in Context: Asking the Right Questions About Preparing Skilled and Effective Teachers of Young Children," *National Institute for Early Education Research* 22 (April 2011): 1–16; Yoshikawa et al., "Investing in Our Future."

Chapter 2: Getting Connected

34 *National median salary for preschool teachers:* Whitebook, Phillips, and Howes, "Worthy Work, *Still* Unlivable Wages."

34 *Early childhood educators' financial stress and eligibility for public assistance programs:* Ibid.

35 *Turnover occurs in about half of early childhood centers every year:* Daphna Bassok, Maria Fitzpatrick, Susanna Loeb, and Agustina S. Paglayan, "The Early Childhood Care and Education Workforce from 1990 Through 2010: Changing Dynamics and Persistent Concerns," *Education Finance and Policy* 8, no. 4 (Fall 2013): 581–601, http://www.mitpressjournals.org/doi/abs/10.1162/EDFP_a_00114; Marcy Whitebook and Laura Sakai, *By a Thread : How Child Care Centers Hold on to Teachers, How Teachers Build Lasting Careers* (Kalamazoo, MI: W. E. Upjohn Institute for Employment Research, 2004); Marcy Whitebook and Laura Sakai, "Turnover Begets Turnover: An Examination of Job and Occupational Instability Among Child Care Center Staff," *Early Childhood Research Quarterly* 18, no. 3 (Autumn 2003): 273–93, http://www.sciencedirect.com/science/article/pii/S0885200603000401; Whitebook, Phillips, and Howes, "Worthy Work, *Still* Unlivable Wages."

35 *Teachers' wages as a strong predictor of quality:* Julie Kashen, Halley Potter, and Andrew Stettner, "Quality Jobs, Quality Child Care," Century Foundation, June 13, 2016, https://tcf.org/content/report/quality-jobs-quality-child-care.

38 *When classrooms have too much decoration, it can be distracting:* Anna V. Fisher, Karrie E. Godwin, and Howard Seltman, "Visual Environment, Attention Allocation, and Learning in Young Children: When Too Much of a Good Thing May Be Bad," *Psychological Science* 25, no. 7 (2014): 1362–70, doi:10.1177/0956797614533801.

40 *Strong and positive teacher-child relationships:* Mashburn et al., "Measures of Classroom Quality in Prekindergarten and Children's Development of Academic, Language, and Social Skills"; Robert C. Pianta, Michael S. Steinberg, and Kristin B. Rollins, "The First Two Years of School: Teacher-Child Relationships and Deflections in Children's Classroom Adjustment," *Development and Psychopathology* 7, no. 2 (April 1995): 295–312, doi:10.1017/S0954579400006519; Bridget K. Hamre and Robert C. Pianta, "Early Teacher-Child Relationships and the Trajectory of Children's School Outcomes Through Eighth Grade," *Child Development* 72, no. 2 (March 2001): 625–38, doi:10.1111/1467-8624.00301; Yoshikawa et al., "Investing in Our Future"; Bridget K. Hamre, "Teachers' Daily Interactions with Children: An Essential Ingredient in Effective Early Childhood Programs," *Child Development Perspectives* 8, no. 4 (December 2014): 223–30, doi:10.1111/cdep.12090; C. Cybele Raver, Stephanie M. Jones, Christine Li-Grining, Fuhua Zhai, Molly W. Metzger, and Bonnie Solomon, "Targeting Children's Behavior Problems in Preschool Classrooms: A Cluster-Randomized Controlled Trial," *Journal of Consulting and Clinical Psychology* 77, no. 2 (2009): 302–16, doi:10.1037/a0015302.

40 *"Serve and return" interactions:* "From Best Practices to Breakthrough Impacts," Center on the Developing Child; "The Foundations of Lifelong Health Are Built in Early Childhood," Center on the Developing Child at Harvard University, 2010, http://developingchild.harvard.edu/resources/the-foundations-of-lifelong-health-are-built-in-early-childhood. .

41 *Coaching for early childhood teachers:* Bridget K. Hamre, Laura M. Justice, Robert C. Pianta, Carolyn Kilday, Beverly Sweeney, Jason T. Downer, and Allison Leach, "Implementation Fidelity of MyTeachingPartner Literacy and Language Activities: Association with Preschoolers' Language and Literacy Growth," *Early Childhood Research Quarterly* 25, no. 3 (2010): 329–47, http://www.sciencedirect.com/science /article/pii/S0885200609000428; Jason T. Downer, Marci E. Kraft-Sayre, and Robert C. Pianta, "Ongoing, Web-Mediated Professional Development Focused on Teacher–Child Interactions: Early Childhood Educators' Usage Rates and Self-Reported Satisfaction," *Early Education and Development* 20, no. 2 (2009): 321–45, http://www .tandfonline.com/doi/abs/10.1080/10409280802595425.

42 *Classroom Assessment Scoring System (CLASS):* Bridget K. Hamre, Robert C. Pianta, and Karen M. La Paro, *Classroom Assessment Scoring System (CLASS) Manual, Pre-K* (Baltimore, MD: Paul H. Brookes Publishing, 2008).

42 *Conscious Discipline:* Becky A. Bailey, *Easy to Love, Difficult to Discipline: The Seven Basic Skills for Turning Conflict into Cooperation* (New York: William Morrow and Company, 2000).

45 *"Field-experience placements" are less often required for future early childhood educators:* Whitebook and Ryan, "Degrees in Context."

46 *Preschool expulsions:* Walter S. Gilliam, "Prekindergarteners Left Behind: Expulsion Rates in State Prekindergarten Systems," Foundation for Child Development, Policy Brief Series no. 3, May 2005, http://challengingbehavior.fmhi.usf.edu/explore/policy _docs/prek_expulsion.pdf.

47 *African American preschoolers over three and a half times more likely than white children to be suspended:* "2013–2014 Civil Rights Data Collection," U.S. Department of Education, Office for Civil Rights, June 7, 2016, https://www2.ed.gov/about/offices/list /ocr/docs/2013-14-first-look.pdf.

47 *School hands out 68 suspensions in kindergarten:* Peter Balonon-Rosen, "What Discipline Looks Like at a Boston School with 325 Suspensions," *Learning Lab*, WBUR, March 9, 2016, http://learninglab.legacy.wbur.org/2016/03/09/what-discipline -looks-like-at-a-boston-school-with-325-suspensions.

47 *Massachusetts preschoolers and kindergarteners were suspended over six hundred times:* Peter Balonon-Rosen, "Mass. Had Hundreds of Suspensions Last Year—in Kindergarten and Pre-K," *Learning Lab*, WBUR, February 3, 2016, http://learninglab.legacy.wbur.org /2016/02/03/mass-had-hundreds-of-suspensions-last-year-in-kindergarten-and-pre-k.

Chapter 3: Beautiful Little Puzzles

52 *Evaluation report found K1 program struggled with quality:* Nancy L. Marshall, Joanne Roberts, and Linda Mills, "Boston Public Schools K1 and K2 Programs Needs Assessment: Internal Report to the Department of Early Childhood, Boston Public Schools," Wellesley Centers for Women, 2006, http://www.academia.edu/29853675 /Boston_Public_Schools_K1_and_K2_Programs_Needs_Assessment._Internal _Report_to_the_Department_of_Early_Childhood_Boston_Public_Schools.

53 *Front-page story about the dangerous and low-quality pre-K classrooms:* Tracy Jan, "Boston Preschools Falling Far Short of Goals, Study Says," *Boston Globe*, April 7, 2007, http://archive.boston.com/news/local/articles/2007/04/07/boston_preschools _falling_far_short_of_goals_study_says.

54 *Curricula are sometimes chosen based on political connections:* Michael Grunwald, "Billions for an Inside Game on Reading," *Washington Post*, October 1, 2006, http://www.washingtonpost.com/wp-dyn/content/article/2006/09/29/AR2006092901333.html.

55 *Success of Boston curricula:* Weiland and Yoshikawa, "Impacts of a Prekindergarten Program on Children's Mathematics, Language, Literacy, Executive Function, and Emotional Skills"; Christina Weiland, M. Clara Barata, and Hirokazu Yoshikawa, "The Co-Occurring Development of Executive Function Skills and Receptive Vocabulary in Preschool-Aged Children: A Look at the Direction of the Developmental Pathways," *Infant and Child Development* 23, no. 1 (January 2014): 4–21, doi:10.1002/icd.1829.

55 *Boston K1 teacher salary higher than national average:* Jason Sachs and Christina Weiland, "Boston's Rapid Expansion of Public School-Based Preschool: Promoting Quality, Lessons Learned," *Young Children* 65, no. 5 (2010): 74–77.

63-64 *History of Reggio Emilia schools:* Carolyn Edwards, *The Hundred Languages of Children: The Reggio Emilia Approach to Early Childhood Education* (Norwood, NJ: Ablex Publishing, 1993), http://eric.ed.gov/?id=ed355034.

64 *Malaguzzi quotes:* Loris Malaguzzi, "History, Ideas, and Basic Philosophy: An interview with Lella Gandini," in *The Hundred Languages of Children: The Reggio-Emilia Approach-Advanced Reflections*, edited by Carolyn Edwards, Lella Gandini, and George Forma (Greenwich, CT: Ablex Publishing Corporation), 49–98.

69 *Home-School Study of Language and Literacy Development:* David K. Dickinson, Roberta M. Golinkoff, and Kathy Hirsh-Pasek, "Speaking Out for Language: Why Language Is Central to Reading Development," *Educational Researcher* 39, no. 4 (2010): 305–10, doi:10.3102/0013189X10370204; David K. Dickinson and Patton O. Tabors, "Fostering Language and Literacy in Classrooms and Homes," *Young Children* 57, no. 2 (2002): 10–18, https://eric.ed.gov/?id-EJ656300; David K. Dickinson and Michelle V. Porche, "Relation Between Language Experiences in Preschool Classrooms and Children's Kindergarten and Fourth-Grade Language and Reading Abilities," *Child Development* 82, no. 3 (May 2011): 870–86, doi:10.1111/j.1467-8624.2011.01576.x; David K. Dickinson and Patton O. Tabors, *Beginning Literacy with Language: Young Children Learning at Home and School* (Baltimore, MD: Paul H. Brookes, 2001).

Chapter 4: Doing the Math

73 *Teachers of young students not confident about their own math skills:* Carrie R. Leana, "The Missing Link in School Reform," *Stanford Social Innovation Review* 9, no. 4 (2011): 30–35, http://ssir.org/articles/entry/the_missing_link_in_school_reform.

73 *Long-term math achievement affected by early messages and early skills:* Douglas H. Clements, Arthur J. Baroody, and Julie Sarama, "Background Research on Early Mathematics," National Governors Association Center for Best Practices, November 20, 2013, http://www.nga.org/cms/home/nga-center-for-best-practices/meeting--webcast-materials/page-edu-meetings-webcasts/col2-content/main-content-list/strengthening-early-mathematics.html; Sharon Ryan, Marcy Whitebook, and Deborah Cassidy, "Strengthening the Math-Related Teaching Practices of the Early Care and Education Workforce: Insights from Experts," Center for the Study of Child Care Employment,

March 1, 2014; Nilanjana Dasgupta and Jane G. Stout, "Girls and Women in Science, Technology, Engineering, and Mathematics: STEMing the Tide and Broadening Participation in STEM Careers," *Policy Insights from the Behavioral and Brain Sciences* 1, no. 1 (October 1, 2014): 21–29, doi:10.1177/2372732214549471; Nancy C. Jordan, David Kaplan, Chaitanya Ramineni, and Maria N. Locuniak, "Early Math Matters: Kindergarten Number Competence and Later Mathematics Outcomes," *Developmental Psychology* 45, no. 3 (June 2009): 850–67, doi:10.1037/a0014939; Sara Edelstein, Heather Hahn, Julia B. Isaacs, Ellen Steele, and C. Eugene Steuerle, "Kids' Share 2016: Federal Expenditures on Children Through 2015 and Future Projections," Urban Institute, September 20, 2016; Alex M. Moore, Kristy van Marle, and David C. Geary, "Kindergartners' Fluent Processing of Symbolic Numerical Magnitude Is Predicted by Their Cardinal Knowledge and Implicit Understanding of Arithmetic 2 Years Earlier," *Journal of Experimental Child Psychology* 150 (October 2016): 31–47, doi:10.1016/j.jecp.2016.05.003.

76 *Math skills at kindergarten entry predict later achievement:* Ibid.

76 *U.S. ranking in global math achievement:* Jill Barshay, "U.S. Now Ranks Near the Bottom Among 35 Industrialized Nations in Math," *Hechinger Report*, December 6, 2016, http://hechingerreport.org/u-s-now-ranks-near-bottom-among-35-industrialized -nations-math; "Program for International Student Assessment (PISA)—Mathematics Literacy: Average Scores," National Center for Education Statistics, Institute for Education Sciences, U.S. Department of Education, 2015, https://nces.ed.gov/surveys/pisa /pisa2015/pisa2015highlights_5.asp.

76 *The United States doesn't have enough STEM grads to fill all jobs:* Sian L. Beilock and Erin A. Maloney, "Math Anxiety: A Factor in Math Achievement Not to Be Ignored," *Policy Insights from the Behavioral and Brain Sciences* 2, no. 1 (October 1, 2015): 4–12, doi:10.1177/2372732215601438.

77 *Young children's surprising mathematical understanding:* Sara Cordes and Rochel Gelman, "The Young Numerical Mind: When Does It Count?," in *Handbook of Mathematical Cognition*, edited by Jamie I. D. Campbell (New York: Psychology Press, 2005): 127–42; Rochel Gelman, "The Nature and Development of Early Number Concepts," *Advances in Child Development and Behavior* 7 (1973): 115–67, doi:10.1016/ S0065-2407(08)60441-3; Rochel Gelman, "Logical Capacity of Very Young Children: Number Invariance Rules," *Child Development* 43, no. 1 (March 1972): 75–90, doi:10.2307 /1127873; Tamar Kushnir and Alison Gopnik, "Young Children Infer Causal Strength from Probabilities and Interventions," *Psychological Science* 16, no. 9 (2005): 678–83; Tamar Kushnir and Alison Gopnik, "Conditional Probability Versus Spatial Contiguity in Causal Learning: Preschoolers Use New Contingency Evidence to Overcome Prior Spatial Assumptions," *Developmental Psychology* 43, no. 1 (January 2007): 186–96.

77 *Learning trajectories:* Douglas H. Clements and Julie Sarama, "Learning Trajectories in Mathematics Education," *Mathematical Thinking and Learning* 6, no. 2 (April 2004): 81–89, doi:10.1207/s15327833mtl0602_1; Douglas H. Clements and Julie Sarama, *Learning and Teaching Early Math: The Learning Trajectories Approach* (New York: Routledge, 2004).

78 *Building Blocks math curriculum:* "Building Blocks," McGraw-Hill Education, 2015, http://www.mheducation.com/prek-12/explore/building-blocks.html.

85 *Lowest teacher salaries had the worst working environments:* Marcy Whitebook, Caitlin McLean, and Lea J. E. Austin, "Early Childhood Workforce Index 2016," Center for the Study of Child Care Employment, University of California–Berkeley, 2016, http://cscce.berkeley.edu/files/2016/Early-Childhood-Workforce-Index-2016.pdf.

87 *High levels of depression among Head Start staff:* Robert C. Whitaker, Brandon D. Becker, Allison N. Herman, and Rachel A. Gooze, "The Physical and Mental Health of Head Start Staff: The Pennsylvania Head Start Staff Wellness Survey, 2012," *Preventing Chronic Disease* 10 (October 31, 2013): 130171, doi:10.5888/pcd10.130171.

88 *Teachers' depression negatively impacts quality of care they provide:* Bridget K. Hamre and Robert C. Pianta, "Self-Reported Depression in Nonfamilial Caregivers: Prevalence and Associations with Caregiver Behavior in Child-Care Settings," *Early Childhood Research Quarterly* 19, no. 2 (2004): 297–318, doi:10.1016/j.ecresq.2004.04.006; C. Cybele Raver, Stephanie M. Jones, Christine P. Li-Grining, Molly Metzger, Kina M. Champion, and Latriese Sardin, "Improving Preschool Classroom Processes: Preliminary Findings from a Randomized Trial Implemented in Head Start Settings," *Early Childhood Research Quarterly* 23, no. 1 (2008): 10–26, doi:10.1016/j.ecresq.2007.09.001; Elles J. de Schipper, J. Marianne Riksen-Walraven, Sabine A. E. Geurts, and Carolina de Weerth, "Cortisol Levels of Caregivers in Child Care Centers as Related to the Quality of Their Caregiving," *Early Childhood Research Quarterly* 24, no. 1 (2009): 55–63, http://www.sciencedirect.com/science/article/pii/S088520060800077X; Lieny Jeon, Cynthia K. Buettner, and Anastasia R. Snyder, "Pathways from Teacher Depression and Child-Care Quality to Child Behavioral Problems," *Journal of Consulting and Clinical Psychology* 82, no. 2 (April 2014): 225–35, http://psycnet.apa.org/journals/ccp/82/2/225/; Marleen G. Groeneveld, Harriet J. Vermeer, Marinus H. van IJzendoorn, and Mariëlle Linting, "Caregivers' Cortisol Levels and Perceived Stress in Home-Based and Center-Based Childcare," *Early Childhood Research Quarterly* 27, no. 1 (2012): 166–75, http://www.sciencedirect.com/science/article/pii/S0885200611000378.

Chapter 6: Serious Play

103 *History of pre-K in DC:* Bernardine H. Watson, "A Case Study of the Pre-K for All DC Campaign," Foundation for Child Development, November 12, 2010, https://www.fcd-us.org/prek-for-all-dc-case-study.

105 *Learn* through *play:* Deena Skolnick Weisberg, Kathy Hirsh-Pasek, and Roberta Michnick Golinkoff, "Guided Play: Where Curricular Goals Meet a Playful Pedagogy," *Mind, Brain, and Education* 7, no. 2 (June 2013): 104–12, http://onlinelibrary.wiley.com/doi/10.1111/mbe.12015/full; Kathy Hirsh-Pasek, Roberta Michnick Golinkoff, Laura E. Berk, and Dorothy G. Singer, *A Mandate for Playful Learning in Preschool: Presenting the Evidence* (New York: Oxford University Press, 2008); Deena Skolnick Weisberg, Audrey K. Kittredge, Kathy Hirsh-Pasek, Roberta Michnick Golinkoff, and David Klahr, "Making Play Work for Education," *Phil Delta Kappan* 96, no. 8 (2015), http://pdk.sagepub.com/content/96/8/8.short; Cynthia L. Elias and Laura E. Berk, "Self-Regulation in Young Children: Is There a Role for Sociodramatic Play?" *Early Childhood Research Quarterly* 17, no. 2 (Summer 2002): 216–38, http://www.sciencedirect.com/science/article/pii/S0885200602001461; Rachel E. White, "The Power of Play: A Research Summary on Play and Learning," Minnesota Children's Museum (2012): 15–25, http://www.childrensmuseums.org/images

Notes

/MCMResearchSummary.pdf; Kenneth R. Ginsburg, "The Importance of Play in Promoting Healthy Child Development and Maintaining Strong Parent-Child Bond: Focus on Children in Poverty Abstract," *Pediatrics* 129, no. 1 (2007): 182–88, doi:10.1542/peds.2011-2953; Laura E. Berk and Adena B. Meyers, "The Role of Make-Believe Play in the Development of Executive Function: Status of Research and Future Directions," *American Journal of Play* 6, no. 1 (Fall 2013): 98–110, http://www.journalofplay.org/sites/www.journalofplay.org/files/pdf-articles/6-1-article-the-role-of-make-believe.pdf; Carol McDonald Connor, Frederick J. Morrison, and Lisa Slominski, "Preschool Instruction and Children's Emergent Literacy Growth," *Journal of Educational Psychology* 98, no. 4 (2006): 665–89, doi:10.1037/0022-0663.98.4.665; Deena Skolnick Weisberg, Hande Ilgaz, Kathy Hirsh-Pasek, Roberta Golinkoff, Ageliki Nicolopoulou, and David K. Dickinson, "Shovels and Swords: How Realistic and Fantastical Themes Affect Children's Word Learning," *Cognitive Development* 35 (July 2015): 1–14, doi:10.1016/j.cogdev.2014.11.001.

105 *Air traffic control for the brain:* "Building the Brain's 'Air Traffic Control System': How Early Experiences Shape the Development of Executive Function" (Working Paper 11), Center on the Developing Child at Harvard University, 2011, http://developingchild.harvard.edu/resources/building-the-brains-air-traffic-control-system-how-early-experiences-shape-the-development-of-executive-function.

105 *Importance of executive functioning for academic success:* Raver, Garner, and Smith-Donald, "The Roles of Emotion Regulation and Emotion Knowledge for Children's Academic Readiness"; Weiland, Barata, and Yoshikawa, "The Co-Occurring Development of Executive Function Skills and Receptive Vocabulary in Preschool-Aged Children"; Espy et al., "The Contribution of Executive Functions to Emergent Mathematic Skills in Preschool Children"; John R. Best and Patricia H. Miller, "A Developmental Perspective on Executive Function," *Child Development* 81, no. 6 (November 2010): 1641–60, doi:10.1111/j.1467-8624.2010.01499.x; Blair and Razza, "Relating Effortful Control, Executive Function, and False Belief Understanding to Emerging Math and Literacy Ability in Kindergarten"; Philip David Zelazo, Stephanie M. Carlson, and Amanda Kesek, "The Development of Executive Function in Childhood," in *Handbook of Developmental Cognitive Neuroscience*, 2nd edition, edited by Charles A. Nelson and Monica Luciana (Cambridge, MA: MIT Press, 2008): 553–74; McClelland et al., "Links Between Behavioral Regulation and Preschoolers' Literacy, Vocabulary, and Math Skills."

106 *Raver's interventions promote executive functioning:* Raver et al., "Improving Preschool Classroom Processes"; Raver et al., "Targeting Children's Behavior Problems in Preschool Classrooms"; Fuhua Zhai, C. Cybele Raver, and Stephanie M. Jones, "Academic Performance of Subsequent Schools and Impacts of Early Interventions: Evidence from a Randomized Controlled Trial in Head Start Settings," *Children and Youth Services Review* 34, no. 5 (May 2012): 946–54, http://www.sciencedirect.com/science/article/pii/S0190740912000497; Christine Li Grining, C. Cybele Raver, Kina Champion, Latriese Sardin, Molly Metzger, and Stephanic M. Jones, "Understanding and Improving Classroom Emotional Climate and Behavior Management in the 'Real World': The Role of Head Start Teachers' Psychosocial Stressors," *Early Education and Development* 21, no. 1 (2010): 65–94, http://www.tandfonline.com/doi/abs/10.1080/10409280902783509.

106 *Carlson study on promoting executive functioning:* Rachel E. White and Stephanie M. Carlson, "What Would Batman Do?: Self-Distancing Improves Executive Function in Young Children," *Developmental Science* 19, no. 3 (May 2016): 419–26, doi:10.1111/desc.12314.

107 *"Marshmallow studies":* Walter Mischel, *The Marshmallow Test: Mastering Self-Control* (New York: Random House, 2014).

108 *Guided play:* Weisberg, Hirsh-Pasek, and Golinkoff, "Guided Play"; Hirsh-Pasek, *A Mandate for Playful Learning in Preschool*; Katrina Ferrara, Kathy Hirsh-Pasek, Nora S. Newcombe, Roberta Michnick Golinkoff, and Wendy Shallcross Lam, "Block Talk: Spatial Language During Block Play," *Mind, Brain, and Education* 5, no. 3 (September 2011):143–51, http://onlinelibrary.wiley.com/doi/10.1111/j.1751-228X.2011.01122.x/full.

108 *Children learned less in literacy and math from free play:* Chien et al., "Children's Classroom Engagement and School Readiness Gains in Prekindergarten."

109 *Children learn more when their teachers talk less during play:* Dickinson and Tabors, "Fostering Language and Literacy in Classrooms and Homes."

116 *Tools of the Mind:* Elena Bodrova and Deborah J. Leong, *Tools of the Mind: The Vygotskian Approach to Early Childhood Education* (Englewood Cliffs, NJ: Prentice-Hall, 1996).

118 *Trauma, biology, and executive functioning:* Clancy Blair and C. Cybele Raver, "Child Development in the Context of Adversity: Experiential Canalization of Brain and Behavior," *American Psychologist* 67, no. 4 (May–June 2012): 309–18, https://steinhardt.nyu.edu/scmsAdmin/uploads/007/103/Blair%20%26%20Raver_2012.pdf; Clancy Blair and C. Cybele Raver, "Closing the Achievement Gap Through Modification of Neurocognitive and Neuroendocrine Function: Results from a Cluster Randomized Controlled Trial of an Innovative Approach to the Education of Children in Kindergarten," *PLoS ONE* 9, no. 11 (November 12, 2014): e112393, doi:10.1371/journal.pone.0112393; Jack P. Shonkoff, "Leveraging the Biology of Adversity to Address the Roots of Disparities in Health and Development," *Proceedings of the National Academy of Sciences of the United States of America* 109, suppl. 2 (2012): 17302–7, doi:10.1073/pnas.1121259109; Jack P. Shonkoff; Andrew S. Garner; Committee on Psychosocial Aspects of Child and Family Health; Committee on Early Childhood, Adoption, and Dependent Care; and Section on Developmental and Behavioral Pediatriacs, "The Lifelong Effects of Early Childhood Adversity and Toxic Stress," *Pediatrics* 129, no. 1 (2012): e232–46, doi:10.1542/peds.2011-2663; "From Best Practices to Breakthrough Impacts," Center on the Developing Child; National Scientific Council on the Developing Child, "Excessive Stress Disrupts the Architecture of the Developing Brain," Center on the Developing Child at Harvard University, 2014, http://developingchild.harvard.edu/wp-content/uploads/2005/05/Stress_Disrupts_Architecture_Developing_Brain-1.pdf; "Building the Brain's 'Air Traffic Control System,'" Center on the Developing Child.

120 *Vygotsky believed that children are not passive vessels:* Lev S. Vygotsky and Robert W. Rieber, *The Collected Works of L. S. Vygotsky, Volume 1: Problems of General Psychology, Including the Volume* Thinking and Speech (New York: Springer Science and Business Media, 1987).

124 *Day-Night Task:* Adele Diamond, Natasha Kirkham, and Dima Amso, "Conditions Under Which Young Children Can Hold Two Rules in Mind and Inhibit a Prepotent

Response," *Developmental Psychology* 38, no. 3 (May 2002): 352–62, doi:10.1037/0012-1649.38.3.352.

127-28 *Tools of the Mind evaluations:* W. Steven Barnett, Kwanghee Jung, Donald J. Yarosz, Jessica Thomas, Amy Hornbeck, Robert Stechuk, and Susan Burns, "Educational Effects of the Tools of the Mind Curriculum: A Randomized Trial," *Early Childhood Research Quarterly* 23, no. 3 (2008): 299–313, doi:10.1016/j.ecresq.2008.03.001; Sandra Jo Wilson and Dale C. Farran, "Experimental Evaluation of the Tools of the Mind Preschool Curriculum," Society for Research on Educational Effectiveness, 2012; Adele Diamond, W. Steven Barnett, Jessica Thomas, and Sarah Munro, "Preschool Program Improves Cognitive Control," *Science* 318, no. 5855 (November 30, 2007): 1387–88, doi:10.1126/science.1151148; Blair and Raver, "Closing the Achievement Gap Through Modification of Neurocognitive and Neuroendocrine Function."

Chapter 7: Ready to Read?

132 *Importance of knowing letters and letter sounds:* Shayne B. Piasta, "Moving to Assessment-Guided Differentiated Instruction to Support Young Children's Alphabet Knowledge," *The Reading Teacher* 68, no. 3 (November 2014): 202–11, http://onlinelibrary.wiley.com/doi/10.1002/trtr.1316/full.

134 *Children who know at least ten letters in pre-K are usually on course to reading well in second grade:* Shayne B. Piasta, Yaacov Petscher, and Laura M. Justice, "How Many Letters Should Preschoolers in Public Programs Know? The Diagnostic Efficiency of Various Preschool Letter-Naming Benchmarks for Predicting First-Grade Literacy Achievement," *Journal of Educational Psychology* 104, no. 4 (November 2012): 945–58, http://psycnet.apa.org/journals/edu/104/4/945.

134 *"Reading wars":* Diane Ravitch, "Why I Don't Care About the 'Reading Wars' Anymore," *Diane Ravitch's Blog*, August 5, 2014, https://dianeravitch.net/2014/08/05/why-i-dont-care-about-the-reading-wars-anymore; Maryanne Wolf, "How the Reading Brain Resolves the Reading Wars," *A Literate Nation*, Fall 2013, 2–5.

135 *Reading First corruption and poor results:* Beth C. Gamse, Robin Tepper Jacob, Megan Horst, Beth Boulay, and Fatih Unlu, "Reading First Impact Study: Final Report," National Center for Education Evaluation and Regional Assistance, November 2009, http://ies.ed.gov/ncee/pdf/20094038.pdf; Grunwald, "Billions for an Inside Game on Reading."

135 *"Balanced approach" to literacy:* Michael Pressley, Alysia Roehrig, Kristen Bogner, Lisa M. Raphael, and Sara Dolezal, "Balanced Literacy Instruction," *Focus on Exceptional Children* 34, no. 5 (January 2002): 1–14; Catherine E. Snow, M. Susan Burns, and Peg Griffin, *Preventing Reading Difficulties in Young Children* (Washington: National Academies Press, 1998); Susan B. Neuman, Carol Copple, and Sue Bredekamp, *Learning to Read and Write: Developmentally Appropriate Practices for Young Children* (Washington, DC: National Association for the Education of Young Children, 2001); Ravitch, "Why I Don't Care About the 'Reading Wars' Anymore."

135-36 *Finland's approach to educating young children:* Timothy D. Walker, "The Joyful, Illiterate Kindergartners of Finland," *The Atlantic*, October 1, 2015, http://www.theatlantic.com/education/archive/2015/10/the-joyful-illiterate-kindergartners-of-finland/408325; Claudio Sanchez, "What the U.S. Can Learn from Finland, Where School

Starts at Age 7," *Weekend Edition Sunday* on NPR, March 8, 2014, http://www.npr.org
/2014/03/08/287255411/what-the-u-s-can-learn-from-finland-where-school
-starts-at-age-7; Joseph Erbentraut, "Finnish Kids Don't Learn to Read in Kindergarten.
They Turn Out Great Anyway," *Huffington Post*, October 5, 2015, http://www.huffing
tonpost.com/entry/finland-schools-kindergarten-literacy_us_560ece14e4b0af
3706e0a60c.

136 *Percentage of children who can read in kindergarten:* Nadine Gaab, "Percentage of Children Who Can Read in Kindergarten," e-mail message to author, 2017; Nicholas Zill
and Jerry West, "Entering Kindergarten: A Portrait of American Children When They
Begin School: Findings from the Condition of Education 2000," National Center for
Education Statistics, March 2001, https://nces.ed.gov/pubs2001/2001035.pdf.

136 *"From learning to read to reading to learn":* Leila Fiester, "Early Warning! Why Reading by the End of Third Grade Matters," Annie E. Casey Foundation, 2010, http://
www.aecf.org/resources/early-warning-why-reading-by-the-end-of-third-grade
-matters.

137 *Children who use only phonics sometimes read so slowly:* Maryanne Wolf, *Proust and the
Squid: The Story and Science of the Reading Brain* (New York: Harper, 2007); Kathryn
H. Au, Jacquelin H. Carroll, and Judith A. Scheu, *Balanced Literacy Instruction: A
Teacher's Resource Book*, 2nd edition (Norwood, MA: Christopher-Gordon Publishers,
2001); Pressley et al., "Balanced Literacy Instruction."

137 *One hundred of the most frequently used words make up half of what students read:* Edward B. Fry and Jacqueline E. Kress, *The Reading Teacher's Book of Lists*, 4th edition
(New York: Prentice Hall, 2000).

138 *Harder for adults to remember a list of random words:* Marie Poirier and Jean Saint-
Aubin, "Memory for Related and Unrelated Words: Further Evidence on the Influence
of Semantic Factors in Immediate Serial Recall," *Quarterly Journal of Experimental
Psychology Section A* 48, no. 2 (May 1995): 384–404, doi:10.1080/14640749508401396.

138 *Readers understand words and sentences better when they are connected to some sort of
context:* Panayiota Kendeou and Paul van den Broek, "The Effects of Prior Knowledge
and Text Structure on Comprehension Processes During Reading of Scientific Texts,"
Memory and Cognition 35, no. 7 (2007): 1567–77; Panayiota Kendeou and Edward J.
O'Brien, "The Knowledge Revision Components (KReC) Framework: Processes and
Mechanisms," in *Processing Inaccurate Information: Theoretical and Applied Perspec-
tives from Cognitive Science and the Educational Sciences*, edited by David N. Rapp and
Jason L. G. Braasch (Cambridge, MA: MIT Press, 2014), 353–77.

138 *Background knowledge is one of the most important factors in reading comprehension:* Ibid.

139 *Multiple components of the reading process build simultaneously:* Susan B. Neuman and
Kathleen Roskos, "Nurturing Knowledge: Building a Foundation for School Success by
Linking Early Literacy to Math, Science, Art, and Social Studies," *Education Review*
(June 2015), doi:10.14507/ER.V0.847; David K. Dickinson and Susan B. Neuman,
Handbook of Early Literacy Research (New York: Guilford Press, 2007); Neuman, Copple,
and Bredekamp, *Learning to Read and Write*.

139 *Parts of the brain that play major roles in learning to read:* Stanislas Dehaene, *Reading
in the Brain: The New Science of How We Read* (New York: Viking, 2009); Nadine Gaab,
"The Typical and Atypical Reading Brain: How a Neurobiological Framework of

Reading Development Can Inform Educational Practice and Policy" (presentation to Landmark School Parents Organization in Beverly, Massachusetts, 2016); Wolf, "How the Reading Brain Resolves the Reading Wars"; Wolf, *Proust and the Squid.*

141 *Importance of vocabulary for learning to read:* Meredith L. Rowe, "A Longitudinal Investigation of the Role of Quantity and Quality of Child-Directed Speech Vocabulary Development," *Child Development* 83, no. 5 (September 2012): 1762–74, doi:10.1111 /j.1467-8624.2012.01805.x.

142 *Children learn more when given opportunity for questions, discussion, and interaction:* David S. Arnold and Grover J. Whitehurst, "Accelerating Language Development Through Picture Book Reading: A Summary of Dialogic Reading and Its Effect," in *Bridges to Literacy: Children, Families, and Schools,* edited by David K. Dickinson (Malden, MA: Blackwell Publishing, 1994), 103–28.

144 *Thirty-million-word gap:* Betty Hart and Todd R. Risley, *Meaningful Differences in the Everyday Experience of Young American Children* (Baltimore, MD: Paul H. Brookes Publishing, 1995).

144 *Quality of conversations and "wh" questions matter for children's language development:* Rowe, "A Longitudinal Investigation of the Role of Quantity and Quality of Child-Directed Speech Vocabulary Development"; Meredith L. Rowe, Kathryn A. Leech, and Natasha Cabrera, "Going Beyond Input Quantity: *Wh*-Questions Matter for Toddlers' Language and Cognitive Development," *Cognitive Science* 41, no. S1 (February 2017): 162–79, doi:10.1111/cogs.12349; Özlem Ece Demir, Meredith L. Rowe, Gabriella Heller, Susan Goldin-Meadow, and Susan C. Levine, "Vocabulary, Syntax, and Narrative Development in Typically Developing Children and Children with Early Unilateral Brain Injury: Early Parental Talk About the 'There-and-Then' Matters," *Developmental Psychology* 51, no. 2 (2015): 161–75, doi:10.1037/a0038476.

145 *Providence Talks:* "Providence Talks: Pilot Findings and Next Steps," Providence Talks, 2015, http://www.providencetalks.org/wp-content/uploads/2015/10/Providence-Talks -Pilot-Findings-Next-Steps.pdf.

145 *Hakim Rashid:* Hakim Rashid, "Significant—But Not Sufficient: Quality Early Childhood Education and the Development of Young African American Boys," in *Being Black Is Not a Risk Factor: A Strengths-Based Look at the State of the Black Child,* edited by National Black Child Development Institute (Washington, DC: NBCDI, 2013), 28–31, http://www .nbcdi.org/sites/default/files/resource-files/Being%20Black%20Is%20Not%20a%20Risk %20Factor_0.pdf.

145 *African American Vernacular English:* Holly K. Craig and Julie A. Washington, "The Complex Syntax Skills of Poor, Urban, African-American Preschoolers at School Entry," *Language, Speech, and Hearing Services in Schools* 25, no. 3 (July 1994): 181–90; Julie A. Washington and Holly K. Craig, "Dialectal Forms During Discourse of Poor, Urban, African American Preschoolers," *Journal of Speech, Language, and Hearing Research* 37, no. 4 (August 1994): 816–23.

146 *Language gap persists at kindergarten entry:* Rowe, "A Longitudinal Investigation of the Role of Quantity and Quality of Child-Directed Speech in Vocabulary Development"; Washington and Craig, "Dialectal Forms During Discourse of Poor, Urban, African American Preschoolers."

Chapter 8: Skills and Drills

151 *Tradition of oral storytelling:* Zaretta Hammond, "The Neuroscience of Call and Response," *Teaching Tolerance,* April 15, 2013, http://www.tolerance.org/blog/neurosci ence-call-and-response; Zaretta Hammond, *Culturally Responsive Teaching and the Brain: Promoting Authentic Engagement and Rigor Among Culturally and Linguisti cally Diverse Students* (Thousand Oaks, CA: Corwin Press, 2014).

156 *Roskos and Neuman guidebook:* Neuman and Roskos, "Nurturing Knowledge."

161 *"Benevolent pathology":* A. Wade Boykin, "On Enhancing Academic Outcomes for African American Children and Youth," in *Being Black Is Not a Risk Factor,* 14–17.

161 *"Learned how to fall asleep with my eyes open":* David Price, "Are Your Students Engaged? Don't Be So Sure," *MindShift,* January 21, 2014, https://ww2.kqed.org /mindshift/2014/01/21/are-your-students-engaged-dont-be-so-sure.

163 *Low-income children and children of color get more skill-and-drill:* Chien et al., "Children's Classroom Engagement and School Readiness Gains in Prekindergarten"; Valentino, "Will Public Pre-K Really Close Achievement Gaps?"

164 *Conformity in African American parenting style:* Mojdeh Bayat, *Addressing Challenging Behaviors and Mental Health Issues in Early Childhood* (New York: Routledge, 2015).

164 *Instructional approaches across ethnicity:* Valentino, "Will Public Pre-K Really Close Achievement Gaps?"

167 *Shame has a host of negative consequences:* Randall T. Salekin and Donald R. Lynam, editors, *Handbook of Child and Adolescent Psychopathy* (New York: Guilford Press, 2010).

171 *Time-outs:* Jessica T. Minahan and Nancy Rappaport, *The Behavior Code: A Practical Guide to Understanding and Teaching the Most Challenging Students* (Cambridge, MA: Harvard Education Press, 2012).

172 *Collaborative Problem Solving:* Alisha R. Pollastri, Lawrence D. Epstein, Georgina H. Heath, and J. Stuart Ablon, "The Collaborative Problem Solving Approach: Outcomes Across Settings," *Harvard Review of Psychiatry* 21, no. 4 (July 2013): 188–99, doi:10.1097/HRP.0b013e3182961017.

175 *"School-to-prison pipeline":* Johanna Wald and Daniel J. Losen, "Defining and Redirecting a School-to-Prison Pipeline," *New Directions for Youth Development* 2003, no. 99 (Fall 2003): 9–15, doi:10.1002/yd.51.

Chapter 9: Money Matters

178 *Most significant lawsuit since* Brown vs. Board of Education*:* "A Truce in New Jersey's School War," *New York Times,* February 9, 2002, http://www.nytimes.com/2002/02 /09/opinion/a-truce-in-new-jersey-s-school-war.html.

178 *Abbott program fifth-grade results:* Barnett et al., "Abbott Preschool Program Longitudinal Effects Study: Fifth Grade Follow-Up."

179 *Demographics of Elizabeth, New Jersey:* "QuickFacts: Elizabeth City, New Jersey," U.S. Census Bureau, n.d., http://www.census.gov/quickfacts/table/PST045215/3421000.

180 *Quality of Abbott program initially low:* W. Steven Barnett, Julie E. Tarr, Cindy Esposito Lamy, and Ellen C. Frede. "Fragile Lives, Shattered Dreams: A Report on Implementation of Preschool Education in New Jersey's *Abbott* Districts," Center for

Early Education Research, 2001, http://nieer-www1.rutgers.edu/resources/research /FragileLives.pdf.

181 *Steven Barnett court testimony:* Abbott v. Burke, 149 N.J. 145, 693 A.2d 417 (1997).

184 *Zuckerberg New Jersey education initiative failure:* Dale Russakoff, *The Prize: Who's in Charge of America's Schools?* (New York: Houghton Mifflin Harcourt, 2015).

184 *Abbott program quality improved:* "Fact Sheet: The Abbott Preschool Program Longitudinal Effects Study (APPLES)," National Institute for Early Education Research, August 2016, http://nieer.org/wp-content/uploads/2016/08/apples20fact20 sheet.pdf; Sara Mead, "Education Reform Starts Early: Lessons from New Jersey's PreK–3rd Reform Efforts," New America Foundation, December 2009, http://eric .ed.gov/?id=ED544682.

186 *Pyramid model for social and emotional needs:* Mary Louise Hemmeter and Lise Fox, "The *Teaching Pyramid*: A Model for the Implementation of Classroom Practices Within a Program-Wide Approach to Behavior Support," *NHSA Dialog* 12, no. 2 (2009): 133–47.

188 *Chris Christie proposes changes to education funding:* Adam Clark, "Christie: Give All School Districts Same Amount of Aid, Provide Some Towns Property Tax Relief," NJ.com, June 21, 2016, http://www.nj.com/education/2016/06/christie_nj _school_funding_announcement.html.

189 *Criticism of public funding for pre-K for middle-class families:* Fuller, "Expanding Preschool in New York City."

Chapter 10: Test Prep for Parents

194 *Many early childhood teachers feel unprepared to conduct the assessments:* Diane Schilder and Megan Carolan, "State of the States Policy Snapshot: State Early Childhood Assessment Policies," Center on Enhancing Early Learning Outcomes, March 2014, http://ceelo.org/wp-content/uploads/2014/03/CEELO_policy_snap shot_child_assessment_march_2014.pdf.

194 *History of the National Head Start Reporting System:* Cheri A. Vogel, Renée Nogales, Nikki Aikens, and Louisa Tarullo, "Implementation of the Head Start National Reporting System: Spring 2006," Mathematica Policy Research, February 2008, http:// www.mathematica-mpr.com/~/media/publications/PDFs/NRS_Headstart_2006 exsum.pdf.

194-95 *Criticism of National Head Start Reporting System:* Samuel J. Meisels and Sally Atkins-Burnett, "The Head Start National Reporting System: A Critique," *Young Children* 59, no. 1 (2004): 64–66.

195 *Backlash against NHSRS:* Valerie Strauss, "Preschoolers' Test May Be Suspended," *Washington Post*, March 18, 2007, http://www.washingtonpost.com/wp-dyn/content /article/2007/03/17/AR2007031700913.html.

195 *Kindergarten teacher resignation letter in Washington Post:* Valerie Strauss, "Kindergarten Teacher: My Job Is Now About Tests and Data—Not Children. I Quit," *Washington Post*, March 23, 2014, https://www.washingtonpost.com/news/answer -sheet/wp/2014/03/23/kindergarten-teacher-my-job-is-now-about-tests-and -data-not-children-i-quit.

197 *Pencil-and-paper tests unreliable for young children:* Karen M. La Paro and Robert C. Pianta, "Predicting Children's Competence in the Early School Years: A Meta-Analytic Review," *Review of Educational Research* 70, no. 4 (January 1, 2000): 443–84, doi:10.3102/00346543070004443.

199 *Early intervention most effective for addressing reading disorders:* Jeanne Wanzek and Sharon Vaughn, "Research-Based Implications from Extensive Early Reading Interventions," *School Psychology Review* 36, no. 4 (2007): 541–61; Joseph K. Torgesen, Richard K. Wagner, Carol A. Rashotte, Elaine Rose, Patricia Lindamood, Tim Conway, and Cyndi Garvan, "Preventing Reading Failure in Young Children with Phonological Processing Disabilities: Group and Individual Responses to Instruction," *Journal of Educational Psychology* 91, no. 4 (1999): 579–93, doi:10.1037/0022-0663.91.4.579; Joseph K. Torgesen, "Avoiding the Devastating Downward Spiral: The Evidence That Early Intervention Prevents Reading Failure," *American Educator* 28, no. 3 (2004): 6–19, http://www.aft.org/periodical/american-educator/fall-2004/avoiding-devastating-downward-spiral.

200 *ESEA requires non-academic assessment measures:* Evie Blad, "ESSA Law Broadens Definition of School Success," *Education Week*, January 5, 2016, http://www.edweek.org/ew/articles/2016/01/06/essa-law-broadens-definition-of-school-success.html.

200 *Social and emotional learning assessments for schools:* Clark McKown, "Challenges and Opportunities in the Direct Assessment of Children's Social and Emotional Comprehension," in *Handbook of Social and Emotional Learning*, edited by Joseph A. Durlak, Celene E. Domitrovich, Roger P. Weissberg, and Thomas P. Gullotta (New York: Guilford Press, 2015), 320–35; Susanne A. Denham, "Assessment of SEL in Educational Contexts," in *Handbook of Social and Emotional Learning*, edited by Durlak et al., 285–300.

203 *Study called into question reliability of QRIS:* Terri J. Sabol, Sandra L. Soliday Hong, Robert C. Pianta, and Margaret R. Burchinal, "Can Rating Pre-K Programs Predict Children's Learning?" *Science* 341, no. 6148 (2013): 845–46.

204 *Number of centers accredited by NAEYC:* "Benefits of Accreditation," National Association for the Education of Young Children, http://www.naeyc.org/academy/benefits.

Chapter 11: The Myth of the Silver Bullet

207 *Pre-K more cost-efficient than later remediation:* Heckman, "Skill Formation and the Economics of Investing in Disadvantaged Children."

207 *Early childhood brain development:* National Research Council/Institute of Medicine, *From Neurons to Neighborhoods*; "From Best Practices to Breakthrough Impacts," Center on the Developing Child; "Excessive Stress Disrupts the Architecture of the Developing Brain," Center on the Developing Child.

208 *Low-income children and cognitive stimulation at home:* David M. Blau, "The Effect of Income on Child Development," *Review of Economics and Statistics* 81, no. 2 (May 1999): 261–76, doi:10.1162/003465399558067; Lawrence P. Berger, Christina Paxson, and Jane Waldfogel, "Income and Child Development," *Children and Youth Services Review* 31, no. 9 (September 2009): 978–89; Elizabeth Votruba-Drzal, "Income Changes and Cognitive Stimulation in Young Children's Home Learning Environments," *Journal of Marriage and Family* 65, no. 2 (May 2003): 341–55, doi:10.1111/j.1741-3737.2003.00341.x.

208 *Believed that teachers should be responsible for education:* Nancy E. Hill and Kathryn Torres, "Negotiating the American Dream: The Paradox of Aspirations and Achievement

Among Latino Students and Engagement Between Their Families and Schools," *Journal of Social Issues* 66, no. 1 (March 2010): 95–112, doi:10.1111/j.1540-4560.2009.01635.x; Rosario Ceballo, Ruth Chao, Nancy E. Hill, Huynh-Nhu Le, Velma McBride Murry, and Ellen E. Pinderhughes, "Excavating Culture: Summary of Results," *Applied Developmental Science* 12, no. 4 (October 2008): 220–26.

209 *Home visits:* M. Angela Nievar, Laurie A. Van Egeren, and Sara Pollard, "A Meta-Analysis of Home Visiting Programs: Moderators of Improvements in Maternal Behavior," *Infant Mental Health Journal* 31, no. 5 (September 2010): 499–520, doi:10.1002 /imhj.20269; Monica A. Sweet and Mark I. Appelbaum, "Is Home Visiting an Effective Strategy? A Meta-Analytic Review of Home Visiting Programs for Families with Young Children," *Child Development* 75, no. 5 (September 2004): 1435–56, doi:10.1111 /j.1467-8624.2004.00750.x; Jill H. Filene, Jennifer W. Kaminski, Linda Anne Valle, and Patrice Cachat, "Components Associated with Home Visiting Program Outcomes: A Meta-Analysis," *Pediatrics* 132, Suppl. 2 (November 2013): S100–S109.

209 *Childcare workers paid less than pre-K teachers:* Kashen, Potter, and Page, "Quality Jobs, Quality Childcare"; Organisation for Economic Co-operation and Development, "How Do Early Childhood Education and Care (ECEC) Policies, Systems and Quality Vary Across OECD Countries?"; Whitebook, Phillips, and Howes, "Worthy Work, *Still* Unlivable Wages."

209 *"Women's work":* Beatty, *Preschool Education in America*; Whitebook, Phillips, and Howes, "Worthy Work, *Still* Unlivable Wages."

210 *"The new first grade":* Daphna Bassok, Scott Latham, and Anna Rorem, "Is Kindergarten the New First Grade?" *AERA Open* 1, no. 4 (2016): 1–31, doi:10.1177 /2332858415616358.

210 *Low kindergarten quality masks effects of pre-K:* Zhai, Raver, and Jones, "Academic Performance of Subsequent Schools and Impacts of Early Interventions."

210 *"Catch-up effect":* W. Steven Barnett, "Effectiveness of Early Educational Intervention," *Science* 333, no. 6045 (August 2011): 975–78, doi:10.1126/science.1204534; Maureen Kelleher, "Fading Out or Catching Up?" *Harvard Education Letter* 29, no. 6 (November 2013), http://hepg.org/hel-home/issues/29_6/helarticle/fading-out-or-catching-up.

211 *New principals not prepared to lead pre-K:* "New Principals: A Data Snapshot," *Education Week*, August 18, 2015, http://www.edweek.org/ew/section/multimedia/new -principals-a-data-snapshot.html.

224 *Obama on early childhood education benefits to society:* "President Barack Obama," *WTF with Marc Maron*.

Index

NIEER. *See* National Institute for Early
  Education Research
Nixon, Richard, 15
No Child Left Behind Act (2001), 135
North Carolina, 6
Number Pizzas (game), 80–81
number sense, 77
number talk, 79
nursery school. *See* pre-K programs
Nurtury (childcare provider), 92, 218

Obama, Barack, 7–8, 224
observation rooms, 185–86
Oklahoma, 16
one-on-one classroom aide, 39
open-ended questions, 69, 108, 115
Opening the World of Learning curriculum
  (OWL), 54, 93
"Open Shut Them" (song), 44
operant conditioning, 119–20, 165–66
"other regulation," 165
outcomes, predicting, 203
OWL. *See* Opening the World of Learning
  curriculum

Painting to Music (center activity), 59
parent-child interactions, 108, 113, 144
parents and parenting
  adult-centered, top-down approach to, 163
  child assessments and, 114–15, 200–202
  comparing pre-K programs, 8–9, 71, 92–93,
    97–98, 204–6
  comparing schools, 215–16
parent-teacher conferences, 113
Parklands. *See also* AppleTree Early Learning
  Public Charter Schools
  facilities of, 147
  student population of, 148
partnerships
  of Charlestown Nursery School, 102
  filming virtual tours, 205
  of public schools and community centers,
    13–15, 93
passive learning, 27
Perry Preschool Project (Ypsilanti, Michigan),
  5–6
Peter's Chair (Keats), 28
phonics approach, 135, 137
phonological awareness, 141
Piaget, Jean, 76–77

Pianta, Robert, 41–42
PIRT. *See* Preschool Intervention and Referral
  Teams
planning time, 85, 101, 126–27
play
  in DC Public Schools, 104–5
  dramatic, 45, 81–82, 106–7, 116
  free compared to guided, 108, 110
  learning through, 105
  parents supporting, 113
  pretend, 105–6
play planning (strategy), 111–12, 125
portfolios, 58–59
portraits, 45–46
positive reinforcement, 42, 69
Powell Bilingual Elementary School
  assessments at, 198
  bilingual lessons at, 111–14
  coaching at, 126–27
  guided play in, 104–5, 108–11
  planning time and teamwork at, 126
  Tools of the Mind at, 119
  virtual tours of, 205
power, 173
prefrontal cortex, 118
pre-K–3 approach, 212
Pre-K for All (New York City program), 202
pre-K programs (pre-kindergarten)
  achievement gaps and, 7, 134, 148, 161
  assessments of, 196–97, 201–3
  benefits of, 5–6
  certification of, 203–4
  cost-efficiency of, 8, 16, 186, 207
  cost of, 8–9, 11, 25, 187–89
  effectiveness of, 17
  environment in, 28
  expectations for, 211
  experiences in, 6–7
  financial sustainability in, 25, 187–89, 224
  funding for, 5, 15–16, 39, 177, 189–90, 224
  importance of, 225
  licensing of, 196, 202, 209
  in New Jersey, 6, 14, 177–92
  parents comparing, 8–9, 71, 92–93, 97–98,
    204–6
  private, 204
  quality of, 17, 52–55, 98–99, 163, 181
  rating systems for, 203
  safety and cleanliness in, 205
  as strategy to attract families, 103–4